RINGSIDE SEAT

Wisconsin Politics, the 1970s to Scott Walker

SENATOR TIM CULLEN

LITTLE CREEK PRESS®
A DIVISION OF KRISTIN MITCHELL DESIGN, INC.

Mineral Point, Wisconsin USA

TABLE OF CONTENTS

ACKNOWLEDGEMENTS

I wrote this entire book myself. There were no "ghost writers." I am solely responsible for its content. But that is different than saying I did it alone. So many wonderful people helped me. I can't thank them all enough, but let me try.

Thanks first to my wife, Barb, who supported me completely as I took most of 2015 to write (and rewrite, and rewrite!) this book.

To Bob Lange, my longtime friend and the late Les Aspin's first chief of staff (1971-1972). He helped, encouraged, and researched far too many hours and days to count. Who knows, I might have quit in the early months without his constant encouragement.

To my step-daughter, Erin Jacobson, who typed this book at least three times as I wrote it in longhand (I describe myself as a medium-fast hunt-and-peck typist!). She had to read my "questionable" handwriting, but also given her knowledge and interest in Wisconsin politics made many excellent suggestions on verbiage and content.

Now I must mention the many people in and around Wisconsin government and politics who were so generous with their time and their ideas and their input:

Thank you to Governor Tommy Thompson and Governor Tony Earl. They both gave me a lot of their time and candid input, not just about their governorships, but about their many other years in and around Wisconsin government. The people of Wisconsin should all know what high quality people we have in these two terrific public servants.

Thank you to Bill Kraus, the best walking historian on first hand knowledge of Wisconsin Politics since literally the 1950s. I mention him as one of the "wise men" of Wisconsin politics during the last half of the last century. His first hand knowledge of every Republican Governor since the 1950s was extremely helpful. He has the deepest knowledge of Governor Knowles and Governor Dreyfus. He now belongs to no political party and is Wisconsin Chairman of Common Cause. He was extremely generous with his time and knowledge.

Thanks to Tom Loftus, former Democratic Assembly Speaker (1983-1990), US Ambassador to Norway (1993-1997), member of the UW Board of Regents (2006- 2012), and a friend to this day. We have lunch many times each year. He was so helpful on the 1970s and 1980s, and on the many issues the Regents dealt with because of the Walker bombs dropped on the UW System.

Thank you to Matt Rothschild for providing me with data and for his willingness to read this document and make several suggestions on word choices and content. Matt is the Executive Director of the Wisconsin Democracy Campaign.

Retired State Senators Dale Schultz and Bob Jauch were both extremely helpful on details related to the mining chapter, gerrymandering, and the senators' time in Illinois.

I am very grateful to David Marinass, a truly accomplished author for meeting with me and sharing his views with me on my draft and the challenges of finding a publisher. His experience and willingness to share it with me was very helpful.

Many others helped so much, including retired state Representative Dave Travis, Jay Heck, Mike McCabe, and Jim Stoa. They were all helpful, but what was most gratifying was the willingness to talk with me, meet with me, and then do their best to answer my questions or steer me to the data I needed.

Last but certainly not least a very special thank you to two people: Doug Moe, a long time journalist and an author himself, for editing this book. His veteran advice to this rookie was terrific, from his help with the prologue and the flow of the book to suggestions on verbiage and more. And to Kristin Mitchell and Little Creek Press for all of the help in getting this book from my written document into a "book with a cover" and a variety of other services that I could not have done without.

It felt so good to me that this large group of quality people was so willing to help me. I'm a lucky person to have this large circle of people willing to help me out. A great big thank you to them all.

INTRODUCTION
WHY I WROTE THIS BOOK

People across Wisconsin and America ask, "What has happened to Wisconsin?" I believe this book provides an answer.

It is February, 2011 in Wisconsin. We have a new governor. The Green Bay Packers have just won the Super Bowl. We are a happy, united state when that happens!

However, our new Governor, Scott Walker, has a plan to drop a "bomb" (his word) on this unsuspecting, unprepared, Packer-happy state. He intended to angrily divide his citizens in order to further advance his political career. But most of Wisconsin doesn't know this reason. His plan comes in the form of legislation now known as "Act 10."

This book is about not just the Act 10 episode, but about my upbringing, how I came into public service, the two eras I served in the State Senate (1975-1987 and 2011-2015), the changes that occurred between those two time periods, and the observations I made from my ringside seat over 45 years of Wisconsin history.

I talk about the 12 governors that immediately preceded Walker (6 from each party), how they governed our state, and how Walker ignored the best judgment of all 12.

I talk about specific issues such as mining, gerrymandering, voter suppression, and how Walker tried to destroy the Wisconsin Idea (University Mission Statement).

I discuss the huge changes to Wisconsin politics between 1975 and 2010... and Walker had nothing to do with them.

If you were only alive for one era, it is almost impossible to recognize or fathom the other.

I discuss the many other "bombs" besides Act 10 that Walker dropped on Wisconsin with little or no warning.

This book is about my career, including 20 years in the private sector and my specific observations on the public and private sectors.

This book is also an effort to tell the true Wisconsin story, which is more important than any one person or any one governor. It is to lay out the case that the Walker direction for Wisconsin is wrong and out of touch with the long-held opinions of a significant majority of Wisconsin citizens and its former governors!

This book is part memoir, part an attempt to be a political-instruction manual, part a history of the last 60 years of Wisconsin politics, part a critique of modern-day politics, and part a critique of Walker.

What most people in America know about Scott Walker's record as Wisconsin governor is what Scott Walker has repeatedly told them. In many ways this book is what the late Paul Harvey famously referred to as, "the rest of the story."

I have not written this book to make friends. Nor have I written it to make enemies. I have tried as best I can to call it as I saw it.

This career I have been privileged to have had has been quite a ride. I hope you enjoy this view from my ringside seat.

— *Tim Cullen*

PROLOGUE

The most memorable day of my political life began with an emotional early morning telephone call that actually had nothing to do with a crisis in Wisconsin state government that had been building for days.

It was February 17, 2011. I was at my home in Janesville. The night before, there had been another telephone call, this one from Mark Miller, the leader of the state Senate Democrats in Wisconsin, a group I had rejoined—after an absence of 24 years—by winning an election, at age 66, the previous November.

Miller called to tell me our caucus—the 14 Democrats who made up the minority in the Senate—would be meeting at 8 a.m. the following morning in Madison. He didn't say why. It was an unusually early time to meet, and I told him I wouldn't be there. I knew it probably had something to do with the Senate's plans later that morning to take up new Republican Governor Scott Walker's Budget Repair Bill, also known as Act 10, which had little to do with the state budget but instead took away collective bargaining rights for public employees and abdicated legislative oversight of the state's health programs. It was a shocking and highly controversial power play by the new governor. In the days since its early February announcement, tens of thousands of protesters had descended upon the Capitol. The bill was destined in the coming months to pit neighbor against neighbor in Wisconsin, and turn politics in the state—which had a long history of mutual respect across the aisle—into an unbridled war.

It was also destined—almost certainly—to pass, because Walker had Republican majorities in both the Senate and the Assembly.

I knew Walker slightly. We'd had a brief chat the previous November, shortly after the election, in his transition office space across the street from the Capitol. It was a courtesy visit, a Democratic senator paying respects to the Republican governor-elect, and it was not particularly memorable. I'd hoped to have a chance to talk about the importance of working together through philosophical differences, but I never got the chance. After a few minutes, Walker received a phone call he said he had to take, and I left.

I had met him once before, under unlikely circumstances, in Mercy Hospital in Janesville. It was around 1994. Walker's father and my mother were both hospitalized at Mercy. I was born in Janesville; it had long been my family's home. His parents lived in Delavan, some 20 miles away. On that evening two decades ago, Walker and I happened to be visiting the hospital at the same time, saw each other, and said hello. We knew of each other, but hadn't met. He was a new Republican member of the state Assembly. I was seven years into an executive position with Blue Cross Blue Shield of Wisconsin, the job I took upon leaving state government. Walker and I had a pleasant conversation, mostly about things other than politics.

I doubt he knew much about my years in the Capitol. I was first elected to the state Senate in 1974, when I was 30. It was an historic election, in that the Democrats gained a majority in the Senate for the first time in 82 years. It was also groundbreaking because Kathryn Morrison, from the 17th District in southwestern Wisconsin, became in that election the first woman ever elected to the Senate.

My best friend and mentor in the Senate was Bill Bablitch, who became the Democratic majority leader soon after I was first elected. From 1976-1982, although I did not hold a leadership position in the Senate, Bill involved me in all the issues he was dealing with as majority leader. It provided me invaluable experience. More than that, I loved it.

In 1982, Bill Bablitch announced his intention to run for the Wisconsin Supreme Court. The election was the following spring. Bill stepped down as majority leader. I ran—the caucus votes by secret ballot—and won. The majority leader job—which I kept until I left the Senate to join new Governor Tommy Thompson's administration in 1987, as Secretary of Health and Social Services—was the one I most enjoyed over the course of my career. At least in part, I owed it to Bill Bablitch.

The phone call that I answered in Janesville on the morning of February 17, 2011—when I was back in the Senate, newly elected, after a quarter of a century away—was from Bill's younger brother, Steve Bablitch, calling to tell me that Bill had died the night before at his winter home in Hawaii. It was sad news, but not unexpected. Bill, who served with distinction two 10-year terms on the Wisconsin Supreme Court, had been battling cancer. The family, knowing the end was near, had been in touch, asking if I would serve as family spokesperson in Wisconsin once Bill passed away. Of course I said yes. I had been sent an advance obituary, a statement from Bill's wife, Ann, and names of those the family hoped might speak about Bill to the press. Upon his death, I would go to the Capitol, distribute the obituary, and help steer the press to those individuals.

I was preparing to drive to Madison and do just that, at about 8:30, when I received the second phone call of the morning. This one was from Mark Miller, who had called the previous evening to tell me about the early morning Democratic caucus. Now Mark was telling me that they had indeed caucused, and a decision had been made for all the Senate Democrats to leave immediately for the state of Illinois.

I was stunned. Miller had not broached that plan as even a possibility in his call the night before.

"We're going to do *what*?"

Now, I was as upset as anyone with what Governor Walker was trying to do. I had spent much of the past week attempting to figure out exactly what that was. In hindsight, I now believe he was beginning his run for president. At the time, it was only clear that Walker was using the budget and the "repair bill" as a tool to try to destroy the public employee unions in Wisconsin. And with Republicans in the majority in both the Assembly and Senate, he was trying to do it quickly, before—we Democrats felt—the public at large even understood what was really happening. The speed with which it was unfolding also hindered our mounting a strategy to try to stop him. I remembered a few weeks earlier, one of my Senate colleagues, Chris Larson, who had been on the Milwaukee County Board when Walker was county executive, saying we should watch out. Walker, Chris said, was more radical than he was letting on in the first January days of his administration. Within weeks of Larson's warning, Walker set off his Act 10 bomb.

The strategy my colleagues decided upon in my absence that Thursday morning was to leave the state. On the telephone from Madison, Mark Miller explained that if all the Senate Democrats left Wisconsin, there was no way the Senate could vote on the bill. They would lack a quorum—a majority of the senators. Because the bill would have a significant fiscal impact, the state constitution called for more than a simple majority: 20 out of the 33 senators needed to be present. Well, the math was easy: if the 14 Democrats weren't there, that left 19, insufficient for a quorum. They needed at least one Democrat.

The math may have been easy, but my situation wasn't.

I explained to Miller that Bill Bablitch had died overnight, and I had a responsibility to his family to come to Madison, and the Capitol, to carry out their wishes with the obituary.

"You better be careful," Miller said. He pointed out that I could get caught there, and forced to vote.

Miller was still worried when we hung up.

At that point, I called my friend Mike Ellis, a Republican senator of long standing, who had been in the Legislature in the 1980s, during my first service. Mike had also been a friend of Bill Bablitch. I told him that I was coming to the Capitol on a mission for Bill's family. Over the next couple of hours, Ellis showed real class in assisting me once I arrived at the Capitol. He knew, by then, of the Democrats' plan to leave the state, but he also knew that my presence that morning superseded politics. When I met with several members of the press outside the Senate Chamber, and shared the news about Bablitch, Ellis came out of his nearby office to say hello. There was going to be a call of the house—a motion compelling members of the Senate to attend a voting session—at 11 a.m.

Mike said, "Will you be out by 10:45?"

I told him I would. It wasn't even 10:30. But then I looked around, and the inside of the Capitol was like I had never seen it before. The building was packed. People knew the bill was going to be voted on that day, and protesters and police and the merely curious were shoulder to shoulder in the rotunda and the stairways. There wasn't an extra inch of space. It was difficult to move. I was more or less stuck on the second floor of the south wing, and beginning to wonder if I could get out by 11. Then a Senate Democratic staffer, who was by my side, started yelling: "There's a Democratic senator here who has to get out of the building!" It turned out word had spread about the quorum. It was partly why the place was buzzing. The crowd parted and I walked down the stairs and out the door with people cheering and calling encouragement. It was amazing.

When I got in the car to head for Illinois, my cell phone rang. It was Mike Ellis.

"Did you make it out?"

I told him I had. I appreciated that call very much. It was an honorable act. Later, Mike would be criticized by some Republicans who would say he instead should have tried to find some way to keep me in the building. But how Mike handled it was in keeping with the way the Senate had operated in the past, a show of mutual respect that had long defined relationships in the Capitol but now appeared to be quickly slipping away.

As if to echo the point, my phone rang again, and this time it was Mark Miller, encouraging me not to drive to Illinois via Interstate 90. My caucus was afraid there could be state police waiting at the border to prevent me from leaving Wisconsin. I couldn't imagine that. In any case, I had to stop at home and pack a bag. I know there were people in my caucus who were worried I wasn't on board with the plan. Remember, I was new, as strange as that seems given my experience. They needn't have worried. I had plenty of questions, but I was going to Illinois.

I took Highway 51 to South Beloit, and then drove to Rockford, where my Senate colleagues were gathering at the Clock Tower Inn, just off I-90. There were maybe half a dozen senators already there, including Fred Risser, Jim Holperin, and Bob Jauch. It turned out Jauch, too, had missed the early morning caucus.

I asked the others, "Tell me about the caucus. How did we get here?"

They couldn't add much to what Miller told me originally. Preventing a quorum was deemed the only way to allow time for the citizens of the state to truly understand what was happening with the bill.

Then I asked, "When you were in the caucus, did you talk about a strategy to get us back to Wisconsin?"

They said the topic never came up. I was astounded, but kept it to myself. I concede time was short, but making such a dramatic move with no thought of the end game seemed foolhardy. Others arrived, there was more conversation and a lot of people on cell phones talking to staff and family back in Wisconsin. Not surprisingly, before the end of the day, the press had learned where we were. It was announced we would head for Freeport, a city west of Rockford. It didn't make sense to me. We weren't on the run, at least not any longer. We were in Illinois. If reporters found us, we'd talk to them. No matter, they all headed for Freeport. I told Miller I was going home, and would talk to him in the morning. They stayed just one night in Freeport. Then it was back east, past Rockford, to Woodstock, Illinois, where Senator Kathleen Vinehout had a sister who lived in a big house she was willing to share. I joined everyone there, and it became our headquarters. The women actually stayed at the house, the men among the senators booked rooms at nearby motels. We caucused at the home at the end of the day.

There was still no real strategy, though in the first few days I don't think anybody thought we would be away for more than three weeks. It certainly wasn't on my radar. My view early on was that there was considerable upside to what we had done. We slowed down the bill and gave people a chance to know what was really going on. But the longer we stayed, I felt like sentiments in Wisconsin—apart from those with considerable skin in the game, like public employee union leaders—would turn against us. The Republicans were already saying, "They ran away to hide in Illinois, rather than do the job they are being paid to do." It's why I kept resisting when we switched locations. It made it look like we were on the lam. But when the press found out we were at Vinehout's sister's house in Woodstock, we moved to Gurnee.

I believe those public employee union leaders held considerable sway with a number of members of our caucus. Mark Miller never really entertained questions about when we would go back. He always put off any discussion about that.

I had one phone conversation with a labor leader—Marty Beil from AFSCME—while we were away.

I said, "What's the plan to get us back to Wisconsin?"

He said he was just going into a meeting with some other labor leaders and he would broach that point.

I said, "There's a shelf life to us being in Illinois, and it's running out. We need a plan to return."

Beil never got back to me. That was the one conversation I had with a labor leader.

I eventually learned—and this can't be anything but darkly humorous in retrospect—that we didn't actually have to go to Illinois to avoid a quorum. We thought the law was that if you were anywhere in Wisconsin, you could be compelled to return to the Capitol if there was a call of the house. That's not the case. I found that out during our time away on one of my trips back to Janesville. Both the Rock County sheriff and the Janesville chief of police told me that the only way they could detain any of us, and return us to the Capitol, was if we were arrested for a crime. Obviously it is not a crime to be in your house. After hearing that, I went back and forth fairly often. The sheriff told me that if I was in my house and any officers came to my door to arrest me, I should politely ask them to leave. If they would not, I could call the sheriff and he would send a deputy over to arrest the people at my door for trespassing. The reality was that the only thing we had to do was not be in the Capitol.

Yet we stayed in Illinois for 23 days. It may be that the seeds of this book were planted there. I know I wanted to try to understand how we possibly could have arrived at such a place. I don't mean Illinois. I mean how a new Republican governor could have managed in a few short weeks to turn our state's political history upside down. Wisconsin was never perfect, but I truly believe, as I will try to show in the pages to come, that we were different. With Act 10, and in the weeks and months that followed, Wisconsin became an angry, bitter state. In that spring and summer of 2011, there were golf foursomes that broke up and book clubs that didn't meet, because the friends could no longer get along.

I felt it personally. That summer, when I appeared in parades, I would get huge cheers from some, and one-finger salutes from others. That had never happened before, and I had been in something like 150 parades. That it even happened in Janesville told me something. In Janesville, my roots go deep.

CHAPTER 1

My Unplanned Route to Politics

MY EARLY YEARS

My family's time in Janesville dates to 1857, and I was born in the city on February 25, 1944, the son of William and Margaret Cullen. I have a brother, Tom, two years older. I owe a happy, loving childhood to my parents and brother. Tom always treated me kindly; I never experienced anything like the oft-heard stories of older brothers bullying, teasing, and hitting younger brothers. When we were very young, my mother was always there for us. Later, in our school years, she worked as a part-time bookkeeper for three different Janesville companies, but she still managed to be home for breakfast and to cook supper. She also read to Tom and me at night.

Our father never finished tenth grade. As the oldest boy in a family of four, he needed to get a job and help support the family. His father was a serious, hard-working man but as a janitor at a public grade school did not earn a large income (he also helped his brother's family financially). My dad drove a beer truck and then worked the last 27 years of his life as a UAW member at the Chevrolet Plant in Janesville. He also had a part-time job for many years as a bartender on the weekends.

My mother was a high school graduate and went to one year of bookkeeping school in Janesville. Our parents were determined that Tom and I would go to college. Tom's interests led him to an electrician apprenticeship, and he proceeded to have a great career as an electrician.

Our parents wanted us to get a Catholic school education even though it would cost them more for tuition. Our father's view of an issue that is still alive today impressed me then, and I still believe he was right over 60 years later. He explained his views on public vs. private religious schools. He told me in 1960 that he could have sent us to Roosevelt Elementary school about five blocks away for almost no cost, yet he chose to send us to St. Mary's. He believed that he, and not the taxpayers, should pay for his decision.

I enjoyed my years at St. Mary's—grades one through nine. I had nuns as teachers for all but two years when my teachers were Mrs. McNally and Mrs. Sullivan. (Like most grade school kids, I may never have known their first names.) They were all great and emphasized the fundamentals of math and English.

I ran for class president in third grade. My parents had taught me that you don't brag about yourself or push yourself out front. It lead me to think I shouldn't vote for myself in the class election, and I voted for my opponent, Carol Schultz. You can guess what happened. Carol won by one vote. It was the last election I ever voted for my opponent.

Our fourth grade class with Mrs. McNally was assigned a project where each of us wrote to a governor of a different state and asked for pictures, maps, and other types of information. By sheer coincidence there were 48 kids in our class and 48 states (yes, so long ago that Alaska and Hawaii were not yet states). I found this project so interesting that Mrs. McNally suggested I write a letter not just to the state I was assigned, but to the other 47 as well. I did and received responses from all 48 governors. I put all the information into two large scrapbooks.

So even when I was 8 and 9 years old, I was showing an interest in government and politics.

I loved sports: football, basketball, and baseball. At that time, we didn't have all the structure that kids have today from a young age: teams with uniforms, coaches, parents going to the games, out-of-town games, etc. It was just kids playing with other kids in our neighborhood, or me riding my bike about two miles from our home to play with Jim O'Connor, Larry Lovelace and their friends in that neighborhood. Jim, Larry, and I met in first grade and have enjoyed a lifelong friendship. Sports, playing war games in a nearby woods, and going sledding in the winter were our favorite things to do.

There was a city-wide sixth grade free throw tournament at the old high school gym. I entered the tournament, which took place on a Saturday that also happened to be St. Patrick's Day. I was—and still am—proud to be an Irish American. I showed it that day. With my mother's help, I dyed my white tee shirt and white canvas tennis shoes green and wore some green shorts I had. All decked out, I won the tournament—making 21 of 35 free throws—and got my name in the paper.

Starting in sixth grade, we did have basketball as a team sport with a coach and uniforms. Jim, Larry, and I played together all the way through Janesville High School, where all three of us were starters in our senior year. We had wonderful coaches, great team morale, loyal student and adult support... and a 6-14 record. We didn't like losing but the values of teamwork, practicing hard, and listening to our coaches served us all very well for the rest of our lives.

LEARNING ABOUT RACE AND CLASS

My parents never used the "N" word. When I was a child Janesville was almost entirely white, and the "N" word was commonly heard. In tenth grade I met Timmy Davis. He was the first black person I ever recall talking with or even meeting. Only two black families had children that attended Janesville High School: the Davises and the Scotts. I really enjoyed my friendship with Timmy and his sister Loretta. Looking back over 50 plus years, I wonder... was Timmy's constant humor and fun-loving personality a cover-up for how "different" he felt?

Of the 50 or so classmates I knew best, including the Scotts and the Davises, all had married parents. These homes may not have been "perfect," but most provided a base of stability. An outsider could usually determine a family's wealth and the roles played by Mom and Dad by looking at a home's garage size. I do not recall having any friends with a two-car garage.

When Dr. Martin Luther King, Jr. was assassinated on April 4, 1968, a group of about 12 Janesville citizens got together to put a statement in the Janesville Gazette expressing our sadness over this tragedy. We all chipped in and bought the space to put this statement in the paper and attached our names to the statement.

A couple of days after this was published, I ran into a guy who I had known for a long time. He was a few years older than me, but I think everyone in Janesville who knew him thought of him as a "good guy." We stopped on the street to chat briefly and he said to me (alluding to the item in the paper), "I never knew you were a n-lover." I was astonished, almost speechless. I made some attempt to mention that Dr. King was a peace-loving man. The conversation ended quickly.

I mention this as an example of many otherwise good people (he was hardworking, had served in the military, etc.) who had embedded in them these awful views of people they'd never met simply because their skin was a different color.

This incident taught me that racism runs deep in the North, and I realized that America had a long way to go on this issue. It also reminded me that our school books put emphasis on racism in the South, but really missed its presence across all of America.

I must point out that the Janesville of 2015 is much more racially diverse and the city is accepting of this change. Currently 26% of the students in the Janesville school district are students of color. Janesville now is part of the great melting pot that is America.

Growing up in an all-white community with some racism, I have often asked myself, "How did I become racially sensitive?" Credit goes first to my parents, then to Timmy and Loretta Davis. I was also influenced by my UW-Whitewater professors, specifically Professor Gaylon Greenhill, and a trip in 1964 through Alabama. During spring break in 1964 some friends from Whitewater and I drove to Florida. We went through Alabama and saw the chain gangs. The prisoners were all black and the guards watching them with rifles were all white. We stopped at a small gas station. The restrooms were at the back of the station labelled "men," "women," and "colored." I used the "men's" room, and then went into the "colored" restroom. The stark difference was disgusting to me. The "colored" one had no toilet tissue or towels and was filthy. The "men's" one was just the opposite. At 20, that made a huge impression on me.

Some other adults who really helped me were Mrs. McNally, my Aunt Grace Ford, Father Ty Cullen, Cecilia Howe, Don Ryan, Ken Cummins, Les Aspin, and Tom Hefty. I have also worked outside of Janesville most of my adult life, alongside many black people. My experiences proved to me that any "black" stereotypes—like most stereotypes—are bogus.

I mentioned earlier that my parents never used the "N" word, or any other ethnic slurs, even though racism was alive and well in Janesville. I believe they had a sense of fairness, and maybe they also truly understood Jesus. My dad never finished 10th grade, yet he was the smartest man I have ever known. My parents were Irish but never faced discrimination themselves. They heard stories, though, about discrimination against Irish immigrants from their parents and grandparents, and opposed it for anyone.

By the 1950s, class differences, more than nationality, mattered most in almost all-white Janesville. Status had mostly to do with the job your dad had. "Worker" or "boss" were the deciders. There is deservedly much discussion today about growing income inequality across America. In 1950s Janesville, "income inequality" was not as great as it is today, and therefore did not play as large of a role in Janesville society.

I look back at the homes of doctors, lawyers, bankers, and business leaders compared to the homes of factory or service workers. There was not usually a huge difference. Most of the more affluent people lived in nice yet modest homes on regular-sized lots with regular-sized lawns; same as the factory worker. Those houses are still there today, and the people who live in them are mostly middle-class. Growing up, there were no "rich home" areas in Janesville.

I frankly can't remember any of my classmates coming from "rich" families, and I can't recall many who were considered "poor." The majority of my classmates were just from nice, clean, regular homes.

I do remember that my dad did not like doing business with the bank, so he was overjoyed when the first credit union was opened in Janesville. Credit unions were owned and operated by people he felt were more like him. Despite this, and even though Janesville had a few "rich" families with large homes, I have concluded that income disparity was not widespread in my home town.

HIGH SCHOOL AND COLLEGE

I loved social studies in high school and I had several great teachers, including Miss Howe and Frank Douglas, who encouraged me. And I continued to do well in sports. In addition to basketball, I also played on the high school tennis team. I took up the sport in about eighth grade when I realized at 143 lbs. I had better find another non-contact sport.

I won two letters in each sport and they helped me with my self-confidence as I dealt with a pretty good dose of acne. I had what was called "cystic" acne, which meant I didn't just have ordinary pimples but rather cyst-like bumps that would sometimes break open unexpectedly. I would try to burst the ones on my face in the morning before school so that it wouldn't happen there. This largely worked, but there was still always a fear of one breaking open in class. Also, the ones I burst in the mornings at home didn't look that great the rest of the day. Still, a couple of girls actually said yes when I asked them out. All the pimples certainly affected me, but as I look back as a 71-year-old maybe they helped me to be more understanding of people and how we are affected by the problems that life throws at us.

My parents' hope and my plan for many years was to attend college at Whitewater State University (now UW-Whitewater), and study to become a high school social studies teacher. So I went off to Whitewater. It was 17 miles from Janesville, but I lived on campus all four years and came home nearly every weekend, which most students did at that time. I was the first person in my family to go to college.

The Chevrolet Plant had a tradition of giving summer jobs to the sons of workers. I don't recall anyone in 1962, including me, ever wondering or asking, "Why not the daughters?"

That job during all four summers allowed me to pay for my tuition, room and board, and books at Whitewater. My parents helped with an allowance, buying clothes, and of course I came home every Friday with a week's worth of dirty clothes that my mother always washed. They let me use the family car on weekend nights. My parents had already given me so much, including encouraging me to go to college and a wonderful value system that I have tried to live up to.

I loved my time at Whitewater. I majored in Political Science with a minor in History. I had many great professors, but my favorite was Dr. Greenhill. He taught several political science courses over the four years and I took four or five of them. He was a difference maker in my life. He cared about me, was interested in me. It has led to a friendship that endures today. He went on to be the Chancellor and was always supportive of me in all my campaigns.

I played on the tennis team and won a letter all four years. My tennis game consisted of a good first serve, decent forehand, and good hustle, but also a weak backhand and lousy second serve.

I made some wonderful friends and then in my junior year my boyhood friend Larry Lovelace transferred to Whitewater. We were roommates those last two years.

I had no idea at this time that I would or could be a candidate for public office. No one in my family ever had run for office and it wasn't something I ever remember thinking about.

"IT TAKES A VILLAGE"

Hillary Clinton famously said that it "takes a village to raise a child." I believe that this view is true for almost everyone. My careers after high school were influenced by some wonderful people who cared about me. I have mentioned many of those in people in this chapter, but I must emphasize my uncle, Father John T. Cullen, and Don Ryan of Janesville, whom I have known since 1962 (yes, he is the uncle of Congressman Paul Ryan). Again, these prominent people showed me they believed in me and encouraged me.

VIETNAM

I do not believe that a man from my generation can write about their life and not include the war in Vietnam. There were many important issues and causes in the 1960s, but that war has left a lasting impact, most certainly on those who served overseas, but also on those of us who did not go to Vietnam. My classmates and I were born at the end of World War II. I was just 6 when the Korean War began. We learned growing up that war was necessary. World War II may have been the most "just" war in history. We grew up in the Cold War. The last thing we grew up to be was "anti-war."

Then when we were still in our very early 20s, along came the Vietnam War. We were told that we had to fight that war or all of Southeast Asia would fall to the Communists, whom we had been assured were looking to conquer the world. Franklin D. Roosevelt, Dwight D. Eisenhower, and John F. Kennedy were all heroic figures. We had no reason not to trust our president. Then we spent our entire 20s with Lyndon Johnson and Richard Nixon! Is it understandable that my high school class of 1962 was confused, divided, and unsure about the Vietnam War? We got through it. Some fought in the war, some protested it, and some—like me— served in the Reserves or National Guard. We were all deeply influenced, and I might say scarred, in various ways by it.

I was opposed to the war, and much that has been disclosed since then has clearly shown that the kids of the 60s were right to have opposed it. Just listen to the tapes of Lyndon Johnson, or read the book by Defense Secretary Robert McNamara, who came to regret his role in this folly. I have no second thoughts on my opposition to it.

What gnaws at me to this day is that some 500,000 Americans served there, 58,000 died and among the 500,000 a year were some of my best friends to this day. I served my six years in the

Army Reserve, and was honorably discharged. I had this opportunity to serve my country, but to also know that this would mean I would likely avoid Vietnam. My good friends could have been killed and there was no chance that I would meet that fate. Now at age 71, I have concluded that there is no resolution to my feelings except to make sure my friends know how much I admire them. I often wonder how many others across America share my feeling.

AN UNPLANNED LIFE

Looking back on the opportunities and jobs I have had (and enjoyed), the best description of my career would be to call it "an unplanned life," a phrase I'm borrowing from a story the *Milwaukee Journal Sentinel* wrote about me when I retired from Blue Cross in 2007. They titled the article "An Unplanned Life."

My plan from roughly the fifth grade was to go to college at (then) Whitewater State University to study to become a high school social studies teacher. By the end of college I planned to go to graduate school with the goal of becoming a college professor in political science. I graduated in 1966, and then in 1967 spent one semester in grad school at Northern Illinois University, followed by six months in the Army. I subsequently gave up on spending another four years getting a PhD. I ran for Janesville City Council (losing by 58 votes), and then decided to go back to Whitewater to get my teaching certificate, and do a one-semester internship at Janesville Parker High School, in the fall of 1969.

I won election to the Janesville City Council in 1970 and then met soon-to-be-Congressman Les Aspin, which took me in another "unplanned" direction... politics. That relationship led to running for state Senate, and eventually I became Senate Majority Leader. I never thought of being in a governor's cabinet, but when newly elected Governor of Wisconsin Tommy Thompson asked me at the end of 1986 to be his Secretary of the Department of

Health and Social Services, I said yes.

I also never had any thought of being an executive with a Health Insurance Company. Blue Cross approached me in 1988 and asked me to join them as vice president of their newly opened office in Evansville, which was just 17 miles from my hometown. I worked for Blue Cross Blue Shield of Wisconsin and the two companies that acquired them (Wellpoint and then Anthem) for 20 years. It was a tremendous opportunity and I shall be forever grateful to the CEO, Tom Hefty, for hiring me and taking a chance on a Democratic politician who had never worked in that industry. Tom had a board of directors made up of many Republicans.

My retirement in 2007, at age 63, was to be final. I did win a seat on the Janesville School Board in 2007, but that was pure public service as there was no compensation. I had the time and the interest. I had no thoughts whatsoever of taking another paying job, and that included no thoughts of running for the state Legislature again. Our state Senator was Judy Robson. She was doing a good job, and I expected her to run again in 2010. Judy unexpectedly announced in January 2010 that she would not seek reelection. I had now been retired for three years and found I needed more to do. I decided to run again for the state Senate seat I had left 24 years earlier. Our home is just 37 miles from the Capitol and the district is compact so travel for the job would be easy and I could get home from Madison at night. And I was confident I could do the job of state senator again.

I did think about the old Irish saying, "You can't go home again." I believe this saying was intended to apply to many of life's situations, and I thought about it as cautionary advice for me if I went back to the state Senate. After winning the state Senate seat, finding myself in the middle of a tumultuous time in 2011, and being stuck in the minority for the next four years, I must acknowledge that I thought more than once that maybe I should have listened to the wisdom of that old saying.

I should add that at the end of the four year term, on balance I was glad I did run and am very grateful for the honor of serving.

I decided not to seek reelection in 2014. I had concluded that I could make a bigger difference in Rock County as a private citizen with the two foundations I started before I went back to the Senate and a third one that I started in the spring of 2015. All three focus on some combination of public education, diversity, and poverty. This work is meaningful and gives me a great deal of satisfaction.

I had sadly concluded that the Republicans (with the help of gerrymandering) would continue to have the majority in the state Legislature, would continue to be completely uninterested in bipartisanship, and I would be frustrated by going into the senate chamber day after day knowing I would be on the losing side of all of the big issues. You give your speech against the legislation, sit down to vote no, and lose. I felt it a better use of my time to retire, let another Democrat go there, and I could spend my time on the foundations.

It was a stark contrast to the mindset I had some 45 years earlier, when an unknown candidate for Congress asked me to support his campaign in my area of Wisconsin. That was a hopeful time. The candidate's name was Les Aspin.

CHAPTER 2

Knowing Les Aspin

The late Les Aspin had an enormously successful career in Washington. He represented the 1st Congressional District of Wisconsin (the Southeastern part of the state) for 22 years, including the last seven as chairman of the House Armed Service Committee. He then served as President Clinton's first Secretary of Defense. His life was cut way too short with his death in 1995.

In early 1970 he was a little known 31 year old trying to get elected to Congress for the first time. He came to my home to seek my support. He greatly impressed me and I supported him in the primary that he won in a recount after losing on primary night. He went on to defeat the Republican incumbent 60-40 in the general election. After his primary victory I spent most of my time helping Patrick J. Lucey get elected governor. His race was viewed as closer (and it was). Lucey won with about 53% of the vote.

WORKING FOR LES ASPIN

I had no thought or expectation that Aspin would ask me to work for him, but he did, contacting me before the end of 1970 and asking me to join his district staff. He had a special job in mind. He wanted me to be, as he called it, his ombudsman. It is a Swedish word meaning "people's representative." He wanted me to hold office hours in every—and I mean every—post office in the First Congressional District (Racine, Kenosha, Walworth, and Rock Counties), and help people with their problems. What an opportunity to be in politics and have your job be to simply help people! Les wanted me to resign from the City Council, and I did after a brief but exciting time when we had hired a new city manager and approved the site for the Janesville Mall that still draws people from miles around to Janesville.

The job of ombudsman worked out well. It introduced me to southeastern Wisconsin as a person who helps with problems and concerns rather than as a politician with partisan ties.

The ombudsman job involved me standing in post office lobbies (after press announcements of my schedule) talking with people and writing down the person's name, address, and their issue or problem.

I would travel and hold office hours three days a week and spend the other two days following up on the issues and problems people had brought to my attention.

I would go to the four largest cities (Racine, Kenosha, Beloit, and Janesville) every week, medium-sized cities once or twice a month, and the small post offices once a month. I would generally do four to six post offices per day or twelve to eighteen each week. There were about 60 post offices in the First Congressional District.

When I arrived at a post office, there would be anywhere from one or two people to a crowd of 30 people waiting for me. People came for a wide variety of reasons: to express their opinions on issues, for individual problems with the federal/state/local governments (I never said "that's a state or local issue so I can't help you"), or some issue that they wanted Les to get involved with on their behalf. Over the three and a half years I did that job, I would estimate that I talked with at least 10,000 people. The following are some of the most memorable issues in which we were involved:

1. The Commuter Train to Lake Geneva: For more years than I know, the commuter train to Chicago came out as far as Lake Geneva, Wisconsin. But in the early 1970s the federal Interstate Commerce Commission (ICC) was petitioned by the railroad to abandon the last leg of the service and have it stop at Richmond, Illinois, which was about twelve miles south of Lake Geneva. The main reason given was low ridership. The people of Lake Geneva said the problem was that the train was way too slow, thus the low ridership. The railroad tracks largely ran parallel to Highway 12. We hatched a plan to go to Richmond on our bicycles and race the train from Richmond to Lake Geneva to prove how slow the train was. With lots of media coverage, about 10 of us raced the train for about 12 miles to the Lake Geneva station... and we won. The ICC, however, was not moved enough and later approved the abandonment of the Richmond to Lake Geneva train. All of us involved felt disappointed with this decision, but we also felt great pride in showing that a train that is slower than a bike rider is too slow. Why should we be surprised when people didn't use it?

2. The trees on north 4th Street in Evansville: The Wisconsin Department of Transportation had a project to widen this street, which is also a county trunk highway, but this widening would eliminate all of the beautiful trees near the street. North 4th Street wasn't then and isn't now a busy street. Les

got involved and pushed and pushed the Wisconsin Department of Transportation to just redo the street rather than widen it. We finally won and the trees were saved. Forty some years later the trees are still beautiful and the street is plenty wide to handle the traffic.

3. The Milton Post Office: The Villages of Milton and Milton Junction were merged in 1967 to form the City of Milton. In 1971, however, there were still two post offices and two zip codes in a city of 3,000. The U.S. Postal Service announced that Milton needed to have one post office, one Post Master, and one zip code. This issue became a big deal. Which post office would survive? When I would hold office hours in each post office I would have many people urging Les to support their post office as the one site. This issue went undecided by the Postal Service for a couple of years and I talked with Milton citizens about it several times. Les would send letters to the Postmaster General encouraging a solution that would not unnecessarily divide this newly united city.

The solution is one you or I could have devised in about 15 minutes. Don't choose the site in the old Milton Village downtown or the site in the old Milton Junction downtown. Put it on a new site on the south side on the very street that was the dividing line for the former villages! That is what the Postal Service did. The people of Milton greatly appreciated Les' efforts and in his 1972 first reelection effort the people showed their appreciation as the campaign needed over 200 yard signs for a city of 3,000. By comparison, putting up 400 yard signs in Janesville, a city of 40,000 then, was generally considered sufficient.

If you're wondering what happened to the post office buildings that were closed, they were sold and are still occupied by local businesses today.

4. My most unusual post office conversation: I was holding office hours in the Burlington Post Office within earshot of people doing their business, when a man came in to talk with me about his issue. It was one I wasn't ready for.

He spoke with a somewhat loud voice and started telling me about his problem. I will tell this as delicately as possible: It was a sexual dysfunction issue. He took a piece of paper and pen and drew me a picture of his body parts and where a doctor had done a medical procedure that he was sure caused his problem. He also told me, and not in a whisper, that his wife was not happy! I will always wonder what the people in earshot must have thought: "What type of program is the Congressman running?"

The man told me—he was not from Burlington—that he could not get a doctor in his community to confirm to him that his problem was caused by the procedure that his doctor had performed on him. He asked me if I would find a doctor over in Janesville (40 miles away) who would see him. I said I would try, and in fact I did find a doctor. I know the appointment was made, but I never heard from him again so I do not know the end of this episode. I do hope that he found comfort. As for me, I was certainly unprepared for someone to come to the post office with this issue, but I was able to do the thing he asked me to do!

RUNNING FOR THE STATE SENATE

I had done the ombudsman job since February of 1971. After three years, I loved the job and didn't have any plans other than to keep working for Les.

The 15th district state Senate seat was within Les' congressional district. The seven-year incumbent, Republican State Senator James Swan, was running for reelection in 1974. The Democratic candidate was going to be Kay Gruetzner, a Beloit City Council-woman. She was an excellent candidate and I planned to support her. However, sometime around April of 1974 she announced that she would not be a candidate. This caused me to consider for the first time whether I should run for the state Senate.

I decided to do it, knowing that this was somewhat late to get into a race to challenge an incumbent. I was driving with Les to the First District Democratic Convention, sometime in May, when I took the opportunity to tell Les what I intended to do. He was quiet for a few seconds, then said, "Tim, do you realize what the 15th District Senate Seat is?" I said, "No." He said, "The 15th District is the 1st Congressional District minus the Democrats!" He was, of course, basically correct. The district had been reapportioned after the 1970 census to benefit Swan. They had taken away all but one ward in Janesville, my home town. It did have the Democratic city of Beloit, but then had all of Republican Walworth County except for the Democratic-voting campus of Whitewater. It also included the Republican-voting western part of Racine County. Les was sure right. The experts said it was a 58% Republican district based on past election results.

I had a few things going for me, however. It was the year of Watergate, 1974, when the Republican President Nixon would resign. My reputation as the ombudsman was clearly a positive. I had also watched and learned from Les about how to run a campaign. I left Les' staff when I became an official candidate in late June. The bottom line is that I worked hard, Les helped, and we had a great campaign of volunteers all across the district. President Nixon resigned on August 9th, and it was pretty clearly going to be a Democratic year. It was a perfect storm if ever there was one.

Election night came all too quickly and the first returns were from Beloit, where we had to do extremely well to have a chance. Beloit came through beyond my hopes, as we carried the city with 72% of the vote. Now could we hang on? We did, and ended up winning with about 54% of the vote. I had carried the one ward in Janesville (which was the most Republican ward in the city) by one vote. And I did vote for myself; the lesson I learned in third grade paid off.

My relationship with Les continued for the next 21 years until his death in 1995. We cooperated on issues. We became friends beyond the boss/staff relationship. He would call me relatively frequently just to talk about "what's going on." I enjoyed this a lot.

Les faced his toughest reelection in a long time in 1992. He was concerned. I had come to believe that if I went out and knocked on doors for three hours or so in a ward that was about 50-50 in term of whether it voted Democrat or Republican, I could use my political instincts to determine how a candidate (in this case Les) was doing. I was working for Blue Cross at the time. I offered to go out to a ward in Janesville. The response was terrific, and I came back and told Les he was going to be fine. Les was pleased, as I believe he trusted my judgment. He won comfortably, but not by the margins he had been used to.

LES' CAREER

Les' career deserves more mention. He was appointed to the Armed Services Committee in 1971 in his first term. He had a PhD from The Massachusetts Institute of Technology. He worked in the Defense Department during the Vietnam War and was one of the bright young people who were referred to as "McNamara's Whiz Kids." This experience helped Les get the committee appointment. He grew to be recognized as the defense expert in the House Democratic Caucus. Les leaped over four more senior democrats in 1985 to get elected chairman of the committee. He had a very distinguished career as chairman, sometimes working with President Ronald Reagan, which irritated people in his own party. Because Les knew what he was doing, I don't believe this party opposition ever worried him too much. Les was chairman from 1985 until he became Secretary of Defense in the first term of President Clinton. During Les' time as chairman, Clinton, then the governor of Arkansas, would meet with Les to learn about defense issues.

Les became Secretary of Defense in January 1993 with every expectation that he would be a long-serving and successful secretary. One could say very easily that his life's work from the McNamara days in the 1960's through his chairmanship had been preparation to be our country's Secretary of Defense.

He only lasted one year as secretary. Why he was ousted should be examined in depth, but needless to say for all of us who knew him and believed in him, we feel to this day that he got a raw deal from the Clinton Administration. This early departure shocked people who knew how talented and qualified Les was.

AN END ALL TOO SOON

The last time we saw each other was in April 1995, and Les was holding a listening session at Marquette University in Milwaukee. He was working on a project for the Defense Department. I met him at Marquette and he wanted to have an early dinner before he caught a later plane back to Washington. It was a wonderful time together in the Marquette student cafeteria. Little did we know that this would be our last time together.

I particularly remember a couple of specific things he said. The most remarkable thing he told me was that President-Elect Clinton never personally offered him the Secretary of Defense job; Transition Director Warren Christopher did! Les had traveled to Little Rock twice to meet with the President-Elect about the cabinet job. But the President-Elect did not make the job offer. I found this astonishing: that the Chairman of the House Armed Services Committee would resign that job and not insist that Clinton himself ask, therefore having a personal obligation to make the relationship work. Clinton, by not having to personally offer the job, had a lesser level of obligation to Les. Only one year later we would find out how this ended in disaster for my friend. Les was arguably one of the brightest and most qualified people to ever hold the Secretary of Defense position. President Clinton replaced Les in early 1994.

I spent time after that evening trying to understand how this could have happened. My conclusion is that Les knew he could do that job. His career had been one of uninterrupted success, and he was perfectly qualified for it. After all, while Clinton was Governor of Arkansas he seldom went to Washington without meeting with Les to get a "tutorial" on defense issues from the best instructor around. This multi-year relationship may have overly reassured Les that working with the President would be no problem.

I think just as highly of Les as I ever have. He is the brightest public servant that I've ever known.

We also talked about what future political plans he had. I suggested he run for governor in 1998. Tommy Thompson would be completing his third four-year term and not likely to run again. (Wrong.) He was already the longest-serving governor in Wisconsin history. Les had gubernatorial ambitions during the 1970's as he hoped to succeed his friend and mentor Patrick J. Lucey, who was governor of Wisconsin from 1971 to 1977. However, Lucey resigned in 1977 to become Ambassador to Mexico. The governorship and likely 1978 Democratic nomination went to Lt. Governor Martin Schreiber. So 1982 would have been Les' next possible chance. By then, however, he was gaining seniority on the House Armed Services Committee—and by 1985 he would be its chairman.

The U.S. Senate would have been of great interest, but Wisconsin already had two well-entrenched Democratic Senators in Bill Proxmire and Gaylord Nelson. Nelson would be upset in the 1980 election, but it would be 1986 before Les could run, and by then he was the chairman and no longer interested. Proxmire served until 1988.

Les said he was not interested in running for governor in 1998 and said I should. That was kind of him, but it was not in the cards. Les said what he intended to do was run in 1996 for his old Congressional seat. A Republican had won it in 1994. I was shocked again, but there was something I didn't know. I thought, "Why would he want to be a powerless freshman again?" But committee seniority stays with you. His 22 years of seniority on the Armed Services Committee would apply if he returned. Now it made sense to me. I would have loved to have helped him in that race.

He passed away one month later, in May of 1995, of heart-related issues.

AMONG MANY THINGS I LEARNED FROM LES:

1. People would tell me how upset they were about something Aspin said or did, then they would walk over to Aspin and tell him what a great job he was doing. I learned that if you are the person in power you can discount about 80% of the flowery things people say to you.

2. I rented him a campaign office for $30 per month. Les was so happy with this good deal, but it was rented in August when it was hot. We found out in late September there was no heat! There were senior citizens with coats and gloves on stuffing and sealing envelopes in October. Asking about the heat is a good idea before you rent space.

3. Volunteers lie. At 9:00 p.m. Friday night 40 promise to go door to door Saturday morning, but you should discount half of those people. It is highly likely 20 will show up. Actually "lie" is too strong of a word. They just don't want to say no.

4. Les believed deeply in volunteer door to door campaigning, but I don't think he actually knocked on one door himself.

5. Details matter. He wanted details on local projects and local issues. That way he was able to know that staff was actually on top of the matter and not just appeasing him. I adopted this method for the rest of my life.

6. Long hours are normal.

7. Doing what you believe and voting the way you believe are more important than party loyalty.

8. Public service is an end in itself. You do not try to enrich yourself while in public office.

9. Listening to people is better than talking.

Clearly, the things I learned from Les Aspin would serve me well as I headed to the state Senate.

CHAPTER 3

Being in the State Senate

I was sworn in as a state Senator in January 1975. I was 30 years old.

I mentioned in this book's prologue that the 1974 election was historic for a couple of reasons. The Democrats took control of the Senate for the first time in a very long time; but maybe even of greater note was Katie Morrison being elected the first female Wisconsin state senator—ever.

That's right. Wisconsin became a state in 1848, but had never elected a woman to the state senate until 1974. It had taken 126 years! Katie was the perfect "first." She was smart, pleasant, hard-working, and serious about the issues. It was impossible not to like Katie. She served on the Joint Finance Committee, the most important committee in the Legislature. She had won in a Republican-leaning district in southwestern Wisconsin, but sadly she lost her reelection bid in 1978—a Republican year.

I have to add one anecdote about Katie. There had never been a woman in the state Senate when our current Capitol was built in 1918, and I guess the architects assumed there never would be.

Therefore there was only a men's restroom near the Senate chamber. Well, we fixed that little oversight in a hurry. We took some space from an office and reduced the size of the men's room to build a women's restroom just as close to the chamber as the men's room. Katie never complained about this. We simply did it as fast as possible. I am also certain that women staffers and senate pages appreciated Katie's arrival!

Katie went on to a great career. She had been an economics professor at UW-Platteville before her election. She became the Chief Financial Officer for the National March of Dimes and then went on to do the same job at the Coalition of Public Hospitals in New York City. Katie's life was cut all too short in 2014 after a long battle with cancer. We all loved Katie.

I enjoyed my first three terms in the Senate and had the chance to work on important legislation. It was a pleasure to work with three Democratic Governors—Patrick J. Lucey, Martin Schreiber, and Anthony Earl—and Republican Governor Lee Sherman Dreyfus. Working with people in the other party was expected and accepted. How different from today.

I became chairman of the Senate Democratic Campaign Committee for the 1980 election. I had been reelected to another four-year term in 1978 so I was not up for election in 1980. I spent a lot of time when we were out of session recruiting candidates where we did not have one. I also traveled to many districts to campaign for our candidates. Back then this largely consisted of knocking on doors with the candidate, stopping in at stores in the downtowns of the smaller towns, stopping at every radio station to talk up the candidate, and of course visiting all the editorial boards of every daily and weekly paper that would talk with us.

I also had an idea to get more publicity for the local candidate. We had several senators who were pretty good slow-pitch softball players, so we created the "Senate Democrats" slow-pitch team. I had tee shirts made with our team name on the front and the number on the back was each senator's district number. Then we would travel to a district, spread out and campaign during the day, and then find a local team to play in the evening. We had a lot of fun, raised some campaign money, and got a fair amount of local publicity for the candidates. We usually lost the game but it was pretty good politics to have the local team beat "those politicians from Madison."

We kept our majority in a tough year for Democrats. Longtime Wisconsin Democrat U.S. Senator Gaylord Nelson was defeated and Ronald Reagan was elected president over incumbent Jimmy Carter.

The best spokesperson for Democrats in 1980 (and many other years) was Bill Proxmire, the highly popular United States Senator from Wisconsin. I asked him if he would cut a TV spot supporting Senate Democrats that we would run in several television markets in Wisconsin. We did all this in the last week before the election. I tell this because it is illustrative of how technology has changed in 35 years.

Senator Proxmire cut the ad in Washington. It was then flown to Madison where we made copies for each TV station. On the Friday afternoon before the election, senators fanned out to drive to each TV station with the copy and a check to buy the TV time. The whole process took over two days. Today it would be done in a few hours at most.

All of the efforts I made in the 1980 elections helped me further build relationships with my colleagues, which helped when I ran to succeed Bill Bablitch as majority leader in 1982.

The other key job in the state Senate was the co-chair of the Joint Finance Committee. Jerry Kleczka had that position. Jerry and I got along very well and I went to him to seek his support. Jerry gave it and I was on my way.

The assistant majority leader, Jim Flynn, was seeking the position, too, but Jim was also running for lieutenant governor and that probably hurt his case. I won on a secret ballot of our caucus by a vote of 15-3. I'm sure you are saying, "If it was secret, how do you know it was 15-3?" Well, it is amazing how poorly secrets are kept. I was even able to find out who the three were who voted for Jim. A firm caucus rule is that whoever wins in the caucus gets everyone's vote on the floor.

I was voted into the job on the floor of the state Senate in May 1982. For the next four and a half years I had my favorite job of my whole life... and the salary was $22,000 a year!

SENATE MAJORITY LEADER

During my time as Senate majority leader someone anonymously called me "the prince of darkness." I don't know who called me that but I never considered it a compliment. Some friends have tried to put a positive note on it by saying it meant that when there was a seemingly intractable problem or issue, almost out of the night I could figure out a compromise. Kind, but I don't think that was the intention.

I generally did the job without wanting to know who was bad-mouthing me. Every time you make a decision, someone or some group is happy and another is unhappy. I had a terrific chief of staff named Jennifer Donnelly. She was better at keeping track of my opponents, and I told her to not tell me except in emergency situations. I couldn't try to lead a Senate with as few as possible personal problems between members if I was going to waste my energy on these matters myself.

I worked hard as majority leader to have the support of all the members of my caucus. I did it by keeping in touch with each member, and by working hard to let them know they had a big role in the business of the senate—either on the Joint Finance Committee or chairing a committee that would have one or more important issues referred to their committee.

I also did "little" things to help them. The 1980s were of course the "pre-GPS" world, and state highway maps were a great advantage to incumbents. They would hand them out to constituents, and, better yet, they could put a sticker on the maps with their name prominently displayed. Handing out these taxpayer-paid maps was great politics: Everybody wanted one, but there was a problem. The press would keep track of how many maps each senator was asking the Department of Transportation (DOT) for and the news stories were never friendly. So I would ask the DOT for thousands and thousands of them (way more than I needed), take the heat for the "bad" story in the paper, then give most of them to my members. They liked not having to read their names in the story, and they had plenty of maps.

I also worked hard to treat the minority leader and the minority party with respect. Two ways I did this were: one, even though I had the power to adjourn the Senate whenever I wanted to, I never adjourned without the agreement of the minority leader, and two, I never imposed any time limits on debate without the agreement of the minority leader. I love the institution that is the State Senate, and at its core, the ability of a senator to speak should not be limited by the power of the majority. It never happened on my watch.

WORKING WITH GOVERNOR EARL AND SPEAKER LOFTUS

A major reason I truly enjoyed being majority leader was the close, outstanding relationship between Governor Tony Earl, Assembly Speaker Tom Loftus, and me.

We genuinely liked each other, trusted each other, and our lines of communication were always open. This all means so much because there are traditional challenges that make a good relationship between the individuals holding these positions very difficult.

There is the usual (and intended by our constitution) tension between the governor and the Legislature. The constitution establishes co-equal branches, but there is a never-ending struggle to have the upper hand.

The Assembly and State Senate are always experiencing either a little or a lot of tension. It is never a lovefest.

Special Interest groups of all persuasions are looking to get some advantage if turmoil exists between houses of the legislature or between the Governor and one or both houses.

There are always future elections and these three leaders are often considered likely candidates perhaps destined to run against one another. These political rivalries can make working together more difficult. The key to Governor Earl, Tom, and I working well together was we did not let these possible future races interfere with performing the jobs we held.

These challenges exist whether the three leaders are in the same political party or not. These are built-in institutional challenges. The three of us just refused to let them get in our way.

One tradition that I enjoyed was when as Senate Majority Leader I would go over to address the Assembly Democratic Caucus (always after Tom and I agreed that I should do it). The caucus always boos the majority leader. It is pretty good natured and I loved the booing and verbal cheap shots.

Governor Earl, Tom, and I still keep up a wonderful friendship and have lunch with each other several times a year including just recently, in 2015. I will always be grateful to both of them for making my job more pleasant.

The very next part of this chapter is about the importance of trust in legislative relationships. Trusting each other was the number one reason the three of us were able to work together so well.

HAVE A DRINK AFTER WORK?

A common comment on what is wrong with relationships among legislators today is that they don't get together for a drink at the end of the day the way they did in the "good old days." The standard line goes like this, "They would argue and debate all day but go out for a drink" and that is what kept disagreements from getting personal and allowed legislators from different parties to start out the next day with a good personal relationship.

The President Reagan/Speaker Tip O'Neill story about having a drink, which led to them working together, is a favorite. But I believe the big reason they worked together is that they had to. Reagan was a Republican and the House was controlled by the Democrats. Nothing could happen unless they worked things out.

I'm not against having a drink. I'm not at all against having one with a Republican legislator. But I believe this scenario is as much myth as it is valid. I believe the key to legislators and governors not letting political differences prevent cooperation on issues is more about something else: trust.

I worked well with many Republicans in the 70's and 80's and never had a drink with most of them. But we trusted each other because we built that trust (it's not built in a day). It's built by working together over time, and the key factor is showing every time that you keep your word. When talking with a legislator from either party about the items at issue and how you will vote or what you need changed are often not written down. "Yes, I will vote for that amendment (a bill) as is or with this change" are serious things to say. Keeping your word: That is how you build trust. And not keeping your word—even once—destroys trust. I've heard it said that "when you break your word, trust and credibility in you gallop away and only return in a very slow walk." I don't know who said this but it is absolutely true in legislative relationships (and others, too). Working out a compromise verbally requires

Senator Tim Cullen

that your word be good all the time.

Here's an example. I've had a wonderful relationship with Tommy Thompson. I was Senate Majority Leader for four and a half years—1982 to 1986– while he was Assembly Minority Leader. In 1987/88 (when he was governor) I served in his cabinet as Secretary of the Department of Health and Social Services. We had (and have) a great friendship and tremendous trust in each other to this day. Because we always kept our word.

We never had a drink together.

THE MISUSE OF WORDS IN POLITICS

I have found a major disconnect between the dictionary definitions of certain words and what they mean in political usage and discussion. I will focus on two words: "friend" and "complex."

The common dictionary definition of friend "is a person who you like and enjoy being with; a person who helps or supports someone or something." Politicians are always referring to another politician as "my friend" or "my good friend." I tell my "real" friends my deepest secrets, weaknesses, mistakes, etc., because I fully trust them to keep it all in confidence. Does anyone really think that an elected official would share all their weaknesses and mistakes with another elected official?

After watching politics and/or being in it for 45 years, it is extremely unlikely that one ever makes a true, close friend among other politicians. My one exception in 40 years is Bill Bablitch, the late State Senator and Supreme Court Justice. We used to joke that with all we knew about each other's faults, if we ever ran against each other and both told all, neither of us would get any votes and "none of the above" would get 100%.

A much more serious misuse of a word in politics is the word "complex" (from this point on you can substitute the word "complicated" in all my mentions of the word "complex"). The dictionary definition of complex is "having parts that connect or go together in complicated ways; not easy to understand or explain; not simple." I have heard, hundreds of times over the last 45 years, candidates and elected officials describe an issue as "complex" or "very complex." This almost always is intended to leave the impression with the public that the solution is factually or substantially very difficult to figure out or put together. Now, let me readily admit, that some problems are actually "complex."

I am talking about the number of times the word is used when the answer to an issue is pretty obvious. When politicians use the word "complex" they really mean it is politically complex, not substantively complex. The solution might be unpopular and might cost them donations and votes in their next election. So calling it "complex" is an explanation for taking no action on an issue—the familiar "kick the can down the road" route. My humble advice? Be alert to the use of this word when you hear it.

EVERY ANSWER OTHER THAN "YES" IS "NO"

One of Bill Bablitch's favorite sayings was, "Every answer other than 'yes' is 'no!'" I have found it to be so true in legislative politics and governing.

A core example of this statement is when a legislator asks another legislator, "Can you vote for this bill?" A one word "yes" answer is the only one that matters. However, legislators are also politicians. So they have devised an unlimited number of answers that sound like yes but are not "yes" and therefore are actually either "maybe" or "no." Here are just a few examples that sound great but are not "yes."

"I really like the concept behind the bill." That's not a yes.

"I like the bill a lot but I want to look at the amendments." That's not a yes.

"I voted for it in committee." That's not a yes.

"I intend to vote for it but I need to talk to my staff." That's not a yes.

"That shouldn't be a problem." That is not a yes.

"We ought to be able to work that out." That is not a yes.

"Not a bad idea." That is not a yes.

Legislators who take these answers as yes are very poor vote counters. Why do legislators not just say "no," or, "I haven't decided?" I believe it is related to the basic personality trait that attracts many people to politics: The desire to please, hence the preference to not offend. So they believe giving these answers makes that conversation end more pleasantly than a blunt "no." And, no, all legislators do not operate this way.

HOW WISCONSIN POLITICS WORKED IN THE 1970S AND 1980S VS 2010S

The following is the best example I know of to explain the difference in how Wisconsin government operated in the early 1980's and how it works under Governor Walker.

1983 was early in Governor Earl's term and early in my first full year as the majority leader. The state's unemployment compensation fund was $750 million in debt to the federal government and going further in debt at the rate of one million dollars a day. The federal government loans this money to states, but we have to pay it back.

Since the 1960s, Wisconsin has had an organization called the Unemployment Compensation Advisory Council (UCAC), created by Republican Governor Warren Knowles. Knowles understood that this program—a lifeline to unemployed workers in the form of a weekly check—should not be placed at the whim of whichever political party had power in Madison. Let me explain that. The program is funded with taxes on employers. The amount of these taxes and the level of weekly benefits to the unemployed are ultimately set by the Legislature. Governor Knowles did not want to see a program where the level of taxation on businesses or the level of benefit checks change depending on who is in power. So he structured the UCAC to consist of an equal number of members from business and labor. Business wants taxes controlled (or lowered) and labor wants benefits maintained (or increased). Hence with equal membership, a consistent, reasonable agreement on changes was guaranteed.

The UCAC, in 1983, could not agree on the change necessary to pay back the $750 million (and rising at $1 million per day) that was owed to the federal government, so it was going to have to be solved by the Governor and Legislature. Governor Earl had the good judgment to construct a route to a solution and retain the balance built into the UCAC structure by Governor Knowles. His solution—even though Democrats controlled all of state government—was to ask the four legislative leaders to serve on a committee to work out a solution. This meant two Democrats, Speaker Tom Loftus and me, plus two Republicans, Assembly Minority Leader Tommy Thompson (later four-term Governor of Wisconsin) and Senate Minority Leader Susan Engeleiter, would be equal at the table. Hence he structured a committee that would force a compromise solution keeping intact the spirit of the UCAC. What a great way to proceed, and Governor Earl has received little credit for this leadership.

The four of us met only in public meetings and reached a compromise that spread the pain. We raised taxes on businesses and froze benefits for unemployed workers for, I believe, five years (they had been increasing annually in an era of real inflation for many years). Governor Earl's idea for sharing power equally with the minority party was terrific, yet seemed not so surprising then as it does as we look back on it thirty plus years later.

We needed to get the compromise passed by the Legislature and we did, but not before a public hearing in front of the Joint

Finance Committee.

I recall it like it was yesterday, as the president of the State AFL-CIO strongly criticized Speaker Loftus, me, and my fellow Democrats for making the deal that he opposed. But we knew we did the right thing in the long run. All four of the legislative leaders on the committee supported the agreement and voted for it. The spirit of the UCAC structure was retained and lasted for thirty more years, until Governor Walker and his approach to an almost identical problem in 2013.

The same unemployment compensation fund was in debt to the federal government by $1.5 billion in 2013 and the Republicans let the UCAC recommend changes to the Legislature as had been the hoped for course of action since the 1960s, and they did reach a compromise. Except unlike the Governor Earl approach, Governor Walker and the Republican Legislature just ignored the compromise recommendations and passed a Republican pro-business solution.

My deep belief is that like many things in life, once you break something it is almost or totally impossible to put it back together. Well, Governor Walker destroyed the UCAC structure put in place by a governor of his own party nearly 50 years ago. What a sad comparison of the way government in Wisconsin used to work and the way it performs today.

CLIFFORD "TINY" KRUEGER FAREWELL SPEECH

I loved the Majority Leader job, but I also came to feel that you can stay too long in the job. Also, many of the senators who elected me in 1982 were gone by 1986. They included Senators Bablitch, Kleczka, Maurer, Offner, Flynn, Moody, and Berger. There was someone else who was gone: Republican Senator Clifford "Tiny" Krueger. Tiny wasn't tiny. He had actually been the "fat man" in the circus back in the early 1940s when somehow people thought that was entertaining. Tiny was the greatest state senator I ever served with: honorable, straight-shooting, full of integrity, and dedicated to what was best for Wisconsin. Except for a brief interlude, he served in the State Senate from 1947 until his retirement in 1983. Tiny had been a Progressive before going with Robert LaFollette, Jr., to join the Republican Party in 1946. He represented a huge area of Northeastern Wisconsin. His farewell speech in the State Senate will live forever. It should be required reading for all state senators and suggested reading for everyone else.

Here is the speech:

January 3, 1983

The thought of reflecting on 34 years of service presents a temptation to talk about how things have changed. It is more appropriate, however, to talk about things that endure—for those are more important.

The oath you took today is the same one I took so many years ago in 1947. Today, as it did then, that oath confers two very important obligations. There is the obligation to provide vigorous leadership in solving the state's problems. There is an equal obligation, one often overlooked, to be sensitive and compassionate toward those who lack the power, or the means, to compete in the society you govern.

In our state motto, Wisconsin's founders gave us a command to go forward. Through our political traditions, our progressive ancestors gave us a mandate to care for those who cannot walk at our pace. While here, I have always listened to both those voices from the past. I ask you to always do the same.

I began my political career the same week Robert La Follette, Jr., ended his. I did so determined to continue the tradition of the Progressive Party whose banner we both carried. I was also committed to the dream of the man who began that tradition, Robert

La Follette, Sr. His was the dream that one day every human being would have a life of dignity and honor.

I still believe in that dream. Today, I ask you to make it your own. That is not easy. In 1947 Wisconsin, like the rest of the country, was prosperous, growing and confident. Today, many do not share that confidence. In 1947, the Progressive dream was an opportunity. Today, many consider it a burden, a luxury which today's economy cannot afford. I and my friends had to convince our generation that the Progressive dream was possible.

Today, you must convince yours that it is not a mistake. You must also remind those who want to delay the dream that human dignity is not a privilege dependent upon prosperity. It is a right upon which prosperity itself depends.

Please remember something else: Be proud of what you are. Elected office is a noble calling. There is nothing lazy, immoral or selfish about being a career politician. The giants of our republic were political animals. They spent their lives at politics because being good at it demands a great deal.

Career politicians—the Adamses, the Jeffersons, the Clays, the Websters, the Lincolns and the La Follettes of our system—have kept us together in times of crisis. They put party interests aside when the going got tough. I leave here confident you will do the same.

Finally, you must keep the Legislature accessible to all people. Legislative service must remain a career that people of modest financial means can afford. Political life imposes too many burdens on families as it is. It should not impose financial hardship as well.

Legislative pay raises are never popular. Even in prosperous times some people will criticize them because they set a bad example. Legislative salary increases always carry a political cost, but the effect of eliminating the common man or woman from legislative service is infinitely greater.

Now I must go. I have enjoyed my life here. For that, I thank all of you, the senators who have served with me, the legislative staff, the media and the employees of our state agencies. No one goes it alone in life. I have walked this far because you have walked with me. Life here will go on. I believe in the saying, "You change the spokes but the wheel keeps turning."

I want to conclude by paraphrasing St. Paul: "I have fought the good fight. I have run the race. I have kept the faith" with you, my colleagues, with my constituents and with my God.

Thank you and goodbye.

I agree entirely with Tiny's speech. I can only wish that I had his eloquence in saying it! I find it informative to compare the words (backed up by his votes) of Senator Krueger to the words and actions of Governor Walker. Could two people be in the same political party and be so far apart? I do believe that Republican Governors Warren Knowles (1965-1971), Lee Sherman Dreyfus (1979-1983), and Tommy Thompson (1987- 2001) would all have been pretty comfortable giving Tiny's speech. It is inconceivable to me that Walker could give it with a straight face.

It's hard, if not impossible, to conceive of Scott Walker ever reaching across the aisle and asking a top Democrat to join his cabinet, but at another time, and with a much different newly elected Republican governor, that's just what happened.

CHAPTER 4

A Democrat in a Republican Governor's Cabinet

I went from being Senate Democratic Majority Leader to Secretary of the Department of Health and Social Services in a Republican governor's cabinet. How did it happen?

I loved being majority leader, but the Senate was changing. At least half of the caucus was new since I was elected the leader. My job as leader was secure, but it was decision time in my life. The political pundits presumed that Assembly Speaker Tom Loftus and I would both seek the 1990 Democratic gubernatorial nomination to run against newly elected Republican Governor Tommy Thompson. Loftus and I had a great relationship after working together the previous four years. That relationship is still there today, as we have lunch together several times a year. I did not look forward to that battle with a good man.

I also thought, more so than many other Democrats, that Thompson would be very difficult to beat in 1990.

Jim Klauser, Thompson's top advisor, approached me shortly

after the 1986 election to measure any interest I had in joining Governor Thompson's cabinet. I was not initially too interested, but did ask, "Which cabinet job?" Apparently there were several possibilities. The only cabinet position that truly interested me was Health and Social Services. This was the largest state agency, with 11,000 employees, and, at that time, Corrections was included. I would have the opportunity to lead the prison system, oversee the Medicaid program, develop regulations for nursing homes and mental health programs to protect some of our most vulnerable citizens, plus much more. It was a great opportunity.

The Governor-Elect wanted me for this job. We spent a couple of evenings at Jim Klauser's home working out our relationship. We trusted each other and also trusted Klauser. It felt right to me. In a May 2015 interview, Tommy Thompson talked about bringing me into his cabinet and working together:

> I said, "Jim, why don't you see if there's any Democratic legislators that we might be able to encourage to come into the cabinet." I was going to have a really tough time because the Democrats controlled both houses of the legislature, and having a partisan cabinet would have been the worst thing for me to try to get any kind of legislation passed. I needed some strong Democrats in the cabinet.
>
> Jim started looking and said, "Would you ever consider putting Tim Cullen in the cabinet?"... I have a good relationship with him and I'm going to see whether or not he would be at all interested."... Jim called back and said, "Tim said he is not totally opposed to it. He said he would at least think about it." Jim then called me and said, "Tim is at least asking questions about which cabinet position he could have." And I said, "He can have anything he wants, whatever he wants, just see if you can put the deal together."
>
> And so we announced it (Tim's acceptance of the Secretary of DHSS appointment) and I was absolutely shocked by the positive

vibes that I got. It seemed that by appointing Tim Cullen—being a strong Democrat and more likely my opponent in four years—it was going to be a way to show the people of the state of Wisconsin that the state was going to be governed, and governed correctly, and was going to be run, as Tim Cullen always says, center/center right.

Tim wanted some assurance that if he took it he was not going to get fired, and that he was going to have a lot of input into policy. I said, "First, you're not going to get fired, and secondly, I want you very much involved. You're going to have as much input as you want and hopefully more than you want, and I want you to be an equal partner."

I always respected Tim, but did not know him that well. Klauser knew him better than I did. We served in different houses and different political parties but I have always had a great deal of respect. Maybe it was because of his Irish heritage; the fact that he was always nice and friendly when I met him and talked to him. Plus I worked as a minority leader and he was a majority leader and we didn't work that closely together, but we had a working relationship and I found him to be honest and straightforward.

He knew that I wanted welfare reform, and he also wanted to make sure that if we did welfare reform we wouldn't hurt people. First, one of his conditions, was not that I just put him on just to get rid of a Democrat, and secondly, that he was going to have a very active interest in running his department. He didn't need to ask- I wanted both of those things. And third, he said he wanted to be very much involved in setting up and formulating the welfare reform. I loved it because he had great ideas and he helped me a great deal.

Tim Cullen didn't always agree with me... but he was always honest, always straightforward, always approachable, and he always gave me his best. And more than likely I would say 75%/85% of his advice I took, especially in welfare reform. He was very close to Jim Klauser and they spent a lot more time, probably, discussing things than I did. But when Klauser would come over I could always tell when he had spoken to Tim and they were both in agreement.

It's nice to be able, in this very partisan environment that we live in in this country and this state today, to have a loyal friend on the opposite side that can always give me his best advice, and you can trust him, you know? In politics trust is so godly important. And I always knew that the conversations that Tim and would have either alone, or with Klauser, or with other cabinet members, I could trust; and he wouldn't run off to the press, and you wouldn't read about that conversation or [it] wouldn't have been leaked. I trusted Tim immensely, and he always repaid that trust with loyalty. What I like about it was he gave me his best advice on everything that he was involved in.

ANNOUNCING THE APPOINTMENT AND SOME CONSEQUENCES

The best way to tell how politics has changed in the past 25 years is that Governor-Elect Thompson would pursue a Democrat for his cabinet and that I would trust him enough to say, "Yes." I agree with Thompson that that could not occur today.

The Department had eight top administrators that would be my direct reports. We agreed ahead of me saying "yes" that he would name four and I would name four, and that we both could veto any of the other's choices. Well, not to my surprise, we were both okay with all of the other one's choices. We both wanted the best people to lead the Department and help our relationship be a success.

The Governor-Elect never raised the subject of the 1990 race and certainly never asked anything about my intentions. I decided myself to tell him I could not take this job and plan a campaign against him four years later. I had completely ruled out running against him in 1990 and told him so after I took the job.

We surprised the state in December 1986 by announcing that I would become Thompson's Secretary of Health and Social Services. It was received favorably—a clear sign that this new governor wanted to be governor of all the people. I must also say that many Democrats were disappointed (to say the least), and some have not forgotten to this day. I have just always thought they did not know all my reasons, they didn't know the real Tommy Thompson, and they didn't consider the important problems I could and did work on at Health and Social Services.

My state Senate seat was won by a Republican, a really good person named Tim Weeden. This loss of a Democratic Senate seat added to the strong belief that my appointment was all part of the Republican plot that I had allowed to happen. A word about the state Senate seat: I had won re-election in November of 1986 with 63% of the vote. That election year resulted in a Democratic majority in the State Senate of 20-13. This is historically very large. I felt that if I could get 63%, then a good Democratic candidate ought to be able to win my seat. Even with this loss of a seat, however, the Democrats still had a 19-14 majority, which is the same majority the Republicans have today in 2015.

WELFARE REFORM

My time as secretary was truly rewarding. The governor was committed to welfare reform. I helped him develop it, and I found his goal was to help people on welfare get off welfare and on to a better life. Even though benefits were cut 5% (Klauser and I, for different reasons, both opposed this but lost this one to Thompson), the governor poured all of the savings—plus additional money—into day care, transportation, and other assistance programs for people getting off welfare. His welfare reform program actually cost more than the system he replaced.

DIVISION OF CORRECTIONS

The governor also approved of my idea for an early release program in the Division of Corrections. As secretary, I had the paroling authority for the state. I delegated some of this authority to the State Parole Board. This authority allowed me to release any prisoner who had served at least 25% or his or her sentence. I could exercise this authority irrespective of any decisions of the parole board.

The staff in Corrections made recommendations, and then Steve Bablitch—Bill's younger brother—the 32-year-old head of the Division, made a final recommendation in advance of my making each decision. Steve had been the number two person in the Dane County District Attorney's office for several years and was my choice to head the Division of Corrections. He did a great job and a few years later the Division of Corrections was transferred to a new Department of Corrections and Governor Thompson named Steve the first secretary. By the way, Steve was also a Democrat.

I released 300 prisoners in the early release program. I read the report on every one of them, often at home in the evening or on weekends. This was probably the most serious responsibility of my entire career. On my signature alone, I was letting a convicted criminal back into society before the sentence was up. If someone committed a violent crime while on early release, there would be only one person responsible for the fact that he or she was not still behind bars—me. To my knowledge, none of the 300 did that. We had screened the prisoners well. No rapists or murderers were eligible for consideration. We had run this program to try to better manage the prison population because the prison system was overcrowded.

Governor Thompson knew about the program and approved of me running it, but we both clearly understood that if a tragic crime occurred, that person was free because of my signature. That was okay with me. I was proud of the governor for approving of the program.

I decided to try out another idea in Corrections with the governor and Bablitch. The three of us were riding in the back seat of the Governor's vehicle on our way to visit the Waupun prison. I asked the two of them about instituting a conjugal visit program in our prisons. They both looked at me with the same look. They didn't need to say a word, but the governor did. He said, "No." The topic was dropped. I'm no genius, but I was smart enough to not suggest that idea again. I was ready with my argument for it, but I never got to my "talking points."

REGULATION OF NURSING HOMES

I also spent a lot of my time overseeing nursing home regulations. I visited over 25 nursing homes across the state. I watched for little things that needed improvement as well as the big problems the Department regulators would find. The regulators did a great job of protecting these very vulnerable citizens. I worked hard to support their findings.

A "little thing" example: I was visiting a nursing home and noticed that the dining room tables were so low that the residents in wheelchairs could not properly pull up to them—the chairs' arms would not fit under the table. Try eating like that when you are possibly frail and shaky. I ordered higher tables.

AN UNEXPECTED OPPORTUNITY

In the spring of 1988 I had been Secretary for about 16 months and I loved the job. Out of the blue, I was approached by Blue Cross Blue Shield of Wisconsin about joining their company as the vice president of their newly-opened Evansville office (about 17 miles from my home). It was decision time. My wife, Barb, and I were about to have our first child. I knew I couldn't be secretary forever, and maybe I needed to get a job with a more predictable future. But I loved my job, so (as incredible as it seems to me now) I asked the CEO of Blue Cross Blue Shield, Tom Hefty, if the job could be held open for another year.

In retrospect, this was a very naive request, and he said they couldn't hold the job. I accepted the offer, announced the change in June, and stayed on as secretary until August. I stayed with Blue Cross for 20 years.

The governor and I had a wonderful conversation about this move. I urged him to replace me with Patricia Goodrich, the current Deputy Secretary of DHSS and a former Republican legislator. She was a first-class administrator and a first-class person. I made this suggestion to the governor in private probably because I worried that this suggestion from a Democrat might make it more difficult for the governor to do it. The governor appointed her and she did a good job as secretary.

Our son, Timmy, was born in April, and I now had a job with a future to support my family, which also included four step-children—Mark, Michele, Erin, and Loren. Our daughter, Katharine, would arrive a few years later.

I was destined to remain outside of state government for nearly a quarter of a century, but I trust no one will be surprised to learn I was watching what was happening in the Capitol in those years—and have some thoughts on it.

CHAPTER 5

Political and Campaign Changes Between 1975 and 2010

The astonishing changes in politics, media coverage, campaigns, campaign money, lobbying, special interest groups, political parties, legislative backgrounds, legislative leader selection, and gubernatorial power that took place across the past four decades had one thing in common: They all contributed to the growing partisan divide of 2000-2010.

Let's start with the teachers' lobbying group, the Wisconsin Education Association Council (WEAC) and the business interests' lobbying group, Wisconsin Manufacturing and Commerce (WMC). The political importance of WEAC and WMC in Wisconsin between 1975 and 2010 was enormous, and each played a major role in the dramatic changes in Wisconsin politics during that time.

These two organizations in 1975 were far less partisan than they had become by 2010. WEAC certainly always tilted Democratic, but they would work with and endorse Republicans who supported their issues most of the time. Republican State Senators that WEAC endorsed in the 1970s and 1980s included Clifford "Tiny" Krueger, Walter John Chilsen, Dan Theno, and Brian Rude. By 2010 they were endorsing no Republican state senators. WEAC had become very substantial supporters of Democratic candidates across the board. They were "all in" with the Democrats, which worked really well for them when the Democrats were in power.

WMC in the 1970s and 1980s certainly tilted towards the Republicans, and while I do not recall their outright endorsements of any Democrats, they would work with Democrats and "stay out" of races involving Democrats they were reasonably happy with. "Staying out" meant little or no resources spent on behalf of the Republican candidate. At that time there were not a large number of independent expenditure groups and the U.S. Supreme Court had not yet allowed groups and individuals to give large sums and hide them from the public (and from candidates they oppose). So WMC "staying out" of a race was a big deal and of great benefit to the Democratic candidate.

By 2010 WMC strongly supported Republicans, didn't "stay out" of any races as a favor to Democrats, and their political arm, their Mobilization Fund, was spending millions every election cycle on television ads and other campaign help to only Republicans. They were now "all in" with the Republicans.

What happened? Put simply, they both rolled the dice. An organization "all in" with one party better hope and pray that that party is in power—or at least has part of the power (at a minimum one house of the Legislature or the governorship). However, they will likely lose big time if the party they oppose achieves total control of state government.

In 2009-2010 WEAC was the better "gambler" as the Democrats controlled all of state government. Since 2010 WMC has been the much better "gambler." With total Republican control, the WMC agenda has been almost totally adopted: tax cuts, a lax mining law, altering the unemployment compensation program, passing so-called tort reform, an end to most collective bargaining rights, followed by the passage of "right to work." Do I have to tell you what has happened to WEAC? Can you say, "Act 10?" Its power has vanished along with much of its membership. And the policy results have been nasty: Wisconsin has seen state cuts to public K-12 education and the statewide expansion of the private school voucher program, which is already taking millions of dollars that would otherwise go to public education.

When the Democrats regain power (and everything in the political history of Wisconsin says this will happen) times will get better for WEAC, but they will still have a problem. Their diminishing membership (read dues money and therefore dollars for political activity) means it is less likely to be as key a player in those future Democrat victories. This makes it less likely that those Democrats will owe them as much in the future as they did in the past. Maybe all of this is why so many of our parents urge us to be wary of gambling.

WMC might want to worry about the future under Democrats. My own feeling is that these developments mirror (or maybe contributed to) the partisan divide which began in the late 1990s and got worse as 2010 approached.

I also must ask the big picture question: Is Wisconsin better off when the key business lobby and the key public education lobby are each locked into one political party without any longer considering the need and importance of the other party? Are kids and economic development best served this way? I do not believe they are. Put another way, did they have to "roll the dice?"

THE LOBBYING BUSINESS CHANGES

Another clear sign of the growing partisan divide involved the lobbying business itself. During the 1970s and 1980s and most of the 1990s, one lobbyist could represent his or her clients with both the Democrats and the Republicans. By 2002 that had changed. Republican legislators wanted to deal with lobbyists who had a Republican background and Democrats wanted to deal with Democratic lobbyists. This became a growth industry: Clients needed two lobbyists instead of one.

Part of my job at Blue Cross was to hire and direct our lobbyist, although I did not lobby myself. The company always had one lobbyist, going back at least to the 1960's. In 2003 I realized that I needed a lobbyist with a Democratic background to deal with the Democratic Governor's Office and one with a Republican background to deal with the Republican-controlled Assembly. And that I did.

MEDIA COVERAGE OF STATE GOVERNMENT

The onset of the Internet is not a partisan change, but affected coverage of state government. The Internet has created significant financial challenges for newspapers. During the 1970s, there were 20 or more reporters whose full time job was to cover state government: the governor and Legislature in particular. The impact of the Internet on newspapers' bottom line led to a dramatic cutback by 2010. During the 1970s several state newspapers had a full-time reporter covering state government: La Crosse, Appleton, Green Bay, Janesville, and Racine to name a few. And then there were two Madison and two Milwaukee papers each with full time reporters, sometimes as many as three for each paper. Today's reporters do a good job but with far fewer sets of eyes on state government there is simply less coverage and investigative journalism. Also, today there is no state paper that does home delivery statewide. I can't quantify the impact of this on Wisconsin politics, but I don't believe it has helped.

BUSINESS AND LABOR IN THE 1970s AND AT THE END OF 2010

The definition of what is the "business community" and what is "labor," as it relates to who spoke for them to the governor and Legislature, changed dramatically between the 1970s and 2010.

The "business community" consisted of multiple entities in the 1970s, with varying degrees of power and influence. There was, of course, the Wisconsin Manufacturing Association, the chamber of commerce (within communities and the state-wide organization), the realtors, road builders, bankers, utilities, restaurants, etc. By 2010 they all still existed, but in terms of political power in the Capitol, WMC (the Wisconsin Manufacturing Association had merged in the late 1970s with the Chamber of Commerce to form WMC) was the dominant force for all of them. WMC had become by far the most important voice for business interests in the Capitol. Only the roadbuilders still had a significant separate presence. All of the others still existed but now money, "the mother's milk of politics," or more accurately, "the crack cocaine of politics," flowed largely through WMC and their Mobilization Fund.

There was also a change in the power structure of WMC. Gone were the days of policy dominance at WMC by major Wisconsin CEOs serving on their board. Many of the CEOs are gone and power has shifted significantly to WMC staff, most of whom had past political and job connections with the Republicans in the Legislature and governor's office.

Organized labor in the 1970s was led by powerful and influential leaders. WEAC had Morris Andrews, the AFL-CIO had Johnny Schmitt, the UAW had Ray Majerus. There were other unions that held influence with certain legislators or in certain areas of the state, but most of these operated under the umbrella of the AFL-CIO. They were collectively highly influential with Democrats and in some cases with Republicans.

What had happened by 2010? While consolidation had occurred on the "business" side, "labor" influence in the Capitol centered on WEAC and AFSCME, with WEAC being number one. And these two were tightly associated with just Democrats.

Globalization had reduced private sector union jobs in Wisconsin and hence influence in the legislature.

It was hard to tell whether WMC and WEAC were subsidiaries of the Republican and Democrat parties or was it the other way around? They both had bet all their "chips" on only one party.

This conclusion about the bets WMC and WEAC made make it very easy to understand the Walker agenda in 2011, highlighted of course by Act 10, which crushed public sector unions. WEACs and AFSCME's "horse" had not won and what a price they paid!

Governor Walker understood all of this and found a way to decimate WEAC and AFSCME; just eliminate all or most of their collective bargaining rights and take away the ability to have their union dues automatically deducted from members' paychecks. It is hard to get exact numbers, but current estimates are that membership in AFSCME has shrunk by 60% and WEAC by a huge percentage as well.

The governor used the law to destroy a political opponent and did it in legislation that was explained to the public as necessary to balance the budget: by having public employees pay more for the costs of their health insurance and pensions. As Mr. Dooley said, "Politics ain't beanbag."

I believe an unanswerable question is whether WMC and WEAC had a real choice to remain somewhat bipartisan. Did the political winds of the 1990s and 2000s that swept across Wisconsin and the nation—bringing increased partisanship, huge chunks of campaign money from the left or the right, the "are you with me 100% of the time" politics, plus more efforts at gerrymandering creating safe Democratic and Republican seats—require them to pick a side?

The other question is whether these groups helped lead the parade to blatant partisanship or were they just following the crowd?

LOCAL CONTROL

Wisconsin legislators and the two major political parties have all claimed to be the supreme champion of "local control," seemingly forever.

Local control means the state government should not dictate to local governments what actions the local government (town, village, city, county, or school board) must take. But if it does, the state must allocate the tax money to pay the cost of whatever action the state has ordered the local government to do.

The Republicans were more vocal as the party of local control in the 1970s era.

The Republicans of the 2011-2014 era had stopped being the party of local control and the Democrats took up that cause. In the forty years between 1975 and today the parties' positions on this issue have completely flipped. Why?

My conclusion is that many Republican legislators in the 1970s had served in local government before being elected to the Legislature (many would continue to serve on a town or county board after being elected to the Legislature). This made them very sensitive to "local control" issues. Also, Republicans tended to represent more rural, small-town areas that had a lot more local governments, especially townships. Democratic legislators by the 1970s tended to have less local government experience and usually represented larger communities that had their own corp of lobbyists to look out for the community's interests.

What I observed that changed Republican support for local control by 2011 was the rise of outside groups wanting things that went against local control. Republicans now care more about the support of these special-interest groups (and their campaign contributions) than their local government's support. Hence we see Republicans telling local government employees where they have to live, telling all local employees except fire and police that they have to abide by the Act 10 provisions, and trying (unsuccessfully so far) to tell local government how they can or cannot regulate frac sand mining in their township! And since there are few if any voids in politics, the Democrats became the champions of local control. This was a 180 degree change between the 1970s and today.

CAMPAIGN MONEY

There has always been money in politics. Contributions are essential to meeting the cost of campaigns. Skeptics and the public in general have forever pondered over its degree of influence on public officials.

The two key differences regarding campaign money between the 1970s and 2010 is the enormous increase in the volume of dollars spent on political campaigns and the ability to hide sources and amounts of money from disclosure to the public. Take gubernatorial campaigns: Until 1990 the two major party candidates for governor never spent more than $3 million combined. That number jumped to $8 million in 1990 and has dramatically escalated (way beyond inflation) since then. Now we have $80 million campaigns, with independent expenditures, often by groups which are now not required to disclose all the contributors or what they spend (we can get some estimates from television buys, as the stations must disclose that). We only have estimates of how much is being spent. The sad truth, of course, is that the candidates know who spends on their behalf. It is just the voters who do not.

The following is a chart that shows the dramatic increase in spending in Wisconsin's gubernatorial races (the outside spending estimates are not available before 2000):

	Outside Money	Candidate Committee	Total Spent
2002	$3.9 million	$19.2 million	$23.1 million
2006	$12.5 million	$19.8 million	$32.3 million
2010	$12.1 million	$25.2 million	$37.3 million
2012	$36.5 million	$44.4 million	$80.9 million
2014	$28.1 million	$53.7 million	$81.8 million

The Government Accountability Board (GAB) provided the candidate committee numbers and the Wisconsin Democracy Campaign provided the known estimates of outside group spending.

State Senate races in the 1970s and early 80s were generally $50,000-$200,000 campaigns. There was no such thing as a $500,000 campaign. Since 2011 we have seen $5-$10 million dollar state senate campaigns.

Groups not "connected" to the candidate's own campaign can now take unlimited amounts of donations from people from anywhere and spend as much as they want in Wisconsin and not disclose anything. This, to say the least, is not healthy for our democracy.

Like the slippery slope on the use of staff for campaign purposes, it may have been kind of a ratcheting thing. Up until 1990, no candidate for governor of Wisconsin in either party ever spent more than a million and a half dollars on their campaign.

Tommy Thompson and Jim Klauser saw a tough race coming in 1990. People thought Tommy might be a one-termer; Tommy's team thought that they would have to raise a lot more money to win in 1990. Bottom line is that Governor Thompson, who, like everybody else, spent less than $1.5 million in 1986, spent $5 million in 1990. Also, it would be fair to point out that Tom Loftus, who was the Democratic candidate and lost, raised closed to $3 million, which was still an unheard of number, twice as much as anyone before.

The governor won. Scott Jensen was working for the governor around that time. He was chief of staff, a young guy. He saw all this fundraising, saw how it took place, saw where the money was, and so on. He ran for the Assembly and was elected Assembly Speaker, then brought that knowledge to the Legislature and started raising a ton of money for Assembly people, and took over the majority.

Senator Chuck Chvala was sitting over in the Senate trying to hang on to a Democratic majority—or get it back—and all of a sudden he had to try to figure out how to match that fundraising. It's not quite so easy for a Democrat because most of the money belongs to Republicans. Chvala's sin was that in order to get the money he needed to get to keep up with the Republicans, he apparently held up, or pushed legislation, depending on if people were "helping out." He got himself in trouble. The thing about Chvala was that it was never anything to line his own pocket; it was about trying to keep the Democrats in power.

So I think each side saw the other raising a lot of money and thought, "We better raise a lot more." We're seeing it right now with the Democrats in Washington. They railed about Romney's Super Pac in 2012, and now they have Super Pacs. That's usually what happens. Everybody defends themselves saying, "Well I'm not going to unilaterally disarm, but if we get in power we'll get rid of this. But for the meantime..." In fact some Democrat said, as it relates to Super Pacs and this excessive fundraising, "As soon as we get control of the Supreme Court, Presidency, both Houses of Congress, and a veto-proof US Senate, we're gonna get rid of it!"

Yeah, right!

Speaker Jensen was also charged along with Chvala. The press called it the "Caucus Scandal of 2002." Both were indicted and Chvala served some time in jail. Jensen delayed his trial for eight years and ended up not going to jail, but he was banned from ever seeking public office again.

CHANGES IN ELECTION OF LEGISLATIVE LEADERS

Sometime in the 1990s legislative leaders started getting elected by narrow margins. It was suddenly not unusual for the majority leader or minority leader in both parties in the state Senate to be chosen 9-8 or 10-8 for the majority or in the minority 8-6 or 9-7.

I can't say that I can point to any specific damage to the general public because of this change, but it overall is not in the public interest. The leader is under pressure to reward the ones "on his/her side" with committee assignments, etc., and they always worry that just one or two senators could change allegiance and throw out the leader. I have found that any "fragility" or perceived weakness in legislative leaders works to the benefit of special interests, and not the public interest.

WISCONSIN'S POWERFUL GOVERNOR STRUCTURE

No book about Wisconsin politics can ignore the fact that the Office of Governor contains more levers of power than any other state's governor. This is true for several reasons. Number one is the partial veto power.

According to a January 2004 report from the Wisconsin Legislative Fiscal Bureau entitled "The Partial Veto in Wisconsin," "Students of government consider the partial veto power as exercised by Wisconsin governors to be the most extensive in the nation." It was created by constitutional amendment in 1930.

The governor may veto individual words, letters, and digits, and may also reduce appropriations by striking digits as long as what remains is a complete workable law. The governor may strike a number in an appropriation bill and write in a smaller one.

Wisconsin governors of both parties have, particularly since 1970, increased, expanded, and stretched their veto authority.

The language in the constitution that gives the governor this broad authority is found in Section 10. "Appropriation bills may be approved in whole or in part." "In part"—these two plain, little, one syllable words—are the tools modern Wisconsin governors have used to accumulate maximum power.

The Legislature's reluctance to provide the two thirds vote in both houses that would override a veto has greatly empowered our governors. No gubernatorial veto has been overridden since 1987. Vetoes are overwhelmingly upheld for partisan reasons: To support their party's governor (and avoid his wrath). Many legislators in both parties have upheld "their governor's" veto when they did not agree with the veto.

A great example is Governor Jim Doyle's so-called "Frankenstein" veto (Appendix B).

This is an enormous power. For a Legislature to override his veto it must do so by a two-thirds vote of both houses. This means if the governor can find either 34 out of 99 state representatives or 12 out of 33 State Senators to support him, his veto stands. A political scientist would describe the Wisconsin government structure as a "strong governor, weak Legislature" model.

This line-item veto power gives the governor a lot of additional power over the legislators as they realize that in order to not have the governor veto the language they have inserted into the budget (or any bill that has a fiscal effect), they need to get him to largely agree to their language in the first place.

The difference between before the 1970s and 2010 is the increasingly bold and sometimes frequent use of the veto power by each succeeding governor regardless of party. Its use was expanded by Governor Lucey, and everyone after him has found a new and exotic way to expand the power. This was indeed a dramatic "bipartisan" expansion of executive power in Wisconsin. It is not an exaggeration to say that because of this power, the governor of Wisconsin is not only the chief executive but as a practical matter is "Legislator in Chief" too.

The biennial budget contains arguably at least 95% of all of the taxing and spending decisions for the following two years. The governor presents this document to the Legislature, therefore he gets first crack at it as he proposes the tax and spending initiatives. Therefore if, for example, legislators want to spend more in a certain area, they must either cut spending in another area (make some group happier but another group unhappy), or raise taxes to fund one so as to not cut the other. They generally don't like doing that. So over hundreds if not thousands of issues in this $70 billion document, governors get most of what they want. The Legislature usually ends up tweaking the governor's budget, but not substantially changing it. Also, this is the only bill that must pass, and it must be (at least arguably) balanced at the end of the two-year period.

Over the last forty years, Wisconsin governors have expanded their power by putting policy items in the budget Why do this? Because it is the easiest way to get these items passed (remember the budget bill is the only bill that must pass), but it also makes those items subject to the partial veto (because the budget bill has fiscal items in it).

The budget bill can be 2,000 pages long, and the governor can make line-item vetoes throughout or insert policy items. The general public can't possibly keep up with all of these decisions, but each special interest knows exactly what the governor did, so there is plenty of room for influence peddling, and the rewarding of friends and punishing of enemies. This is the enormous power that Governor Walker inherited.

BIG CHANGES IN HOW AND WHY LEGISLATIVE CANDIDATES RUN AND WIN

During the late 1970s and 1980s legislative leaders (surely on the Democratic side but I think also on the Republican side) stayed away from primaries like they were the plague. The reason then was pretty simple. If the legislative leader is involved in supporting a losing candidate in the primary, then when the winner comes to the Legislature that person not only owes nothing to their leaders but—depending on their personality—can be a real irritant. It was also true that legislative leaders did not have much to offer a primary candidate compared to today in terms of money, staff, etc., which would have increased the likelihood that their preferred candidate would win.

This changed dramatically by the 2000s. Legislative leaders started working more closely with groups that supported their party's candidates. This allowed them to pick a primary candidate and steer support to that candidate. This reduced the likelihood that their candidate would lose.

In the primaries and for sure in the general election, the state Legislature started to see what I call "the centralization of legislative campaigns" by legislative leaders. Leadership began to identify people to send to districts to run or help run campaigns and would raise the funds to pay them. Under this centralization, legislative leaders now (with party staff help) would develop the campaign theme for the candidates, provide draft press releases, direct polling efforts, etc. Most of all, legislative leaders urge friendly interest groups to give their money where the leaders decide it is needed the most. Little of this was going on in the 1970s.

The results are obvious. Legislators who get elected through this system are greatly indebted to leadership on their first day in office. Not just because of what leaders have done for them, but also for what the leader can do or refuse to do at re-election time.

The state Legislature of the 1960s and before could be broadly described as part-time, male, middle aged or older, white, having local government experience, and were often employed as farmers or lawyers. This began to change in the 1970s most obviously to include younger people, women (a trickle at first), people without local government experience, teachers, and people who looked at the Legislature as a career and therefore a stepping stone to higher office. At first, not a lot of legislative staff people were running; nor were people who were staff to organizations that worked around the legislature. By 2010, however, there was a large number of legislators who had previously worked in or around the Capitol before going back home to run for the Legislature.

CAREER LEGISLATIVE STAFF

It used to be that the people who helped you win came with you to Madison as your staff. What's now happened at the Capitol is largely a permanent staff. When I returned in 2010, there was an expectation that I would hire my predecessor's staff. They were staffers who had been there for years, so why wouldn't I want them? The assumption was they were entitled to a job with the next senator. Before, you knew you only had a job as long as your original boss was there.

In the past, the legislator made the decisions; now staffers have much more influence. I had an interviewee in 2010 who had worked for a Democratic representative in the Assembly. That representative had two staffers. The ex-staffer I was interviewing said what they did in their office when it came to key decisions was vote between the three of them. I was astounded. The elected official could lose 2-1.

STATE SENATE—"PROMOTIONS" SHUT OTHERS OUT

Something else had happened to the state Senate. In 1978 only 11 out of the 33 state senators had previously served in the state Assembly. By 2012 it was 25 out of 33. I find this to be a disturbing change. However, I can say that several people from the Assembly have done a good job as a state Senator.

Can it be that out of 100,000 adults in a state Senate district, the only people capable and qualified to be the next state senator are one of the three people who represent one-third of that Senate district in the Assembly? Really! It seems that we are creating a brand new political class. How unqualified must the other 99,997 adults be? My concern is that state representatives, far more than anyone will admit, want to be state senators for two reasons that are not in the public interest: They want a four year term so they don't have to run every two years, and they want the title "Senator."

Their ability to move from the state Assembly to the state Senate has far more to do with contacts the state representatives make in Madison than with any issues in the State Senate district. They learn who the interest groups are and which ones can help in their campaigns. They can curry favor with (and get to know well) the legislative leaders who have so much power in primaries and the general election. They have paid staff who can take time off plus weekends to work on campaigns. And those staffers know other staffers to recruit to help.

They of course have one advantage that they earned. They were elected by one-third of the State Senate district to represent them in the State Assembly. This brings a "name recognition" advantage. They also have a campaign organization in one-third of the district, although this has diminished in importance compared to the Madison connections—money, staff, endorsements, leadership and friendships.

GLOBALIZATION AND INDUSTRY CONSOLIDATION: IMPACTS ON WI GOVERNMENT AND POLITICS

This change has received little attention as it relates to state politics, but I believe it has made a significant impact. Much has been written on the globalization of our economy since about the 1970s and its impact on jobs in Wisconsin. The impacts have been enormous: some good, like exports, and bringing our world community closer together. Other impacts, however, have been damaging: mainly the loss of manufacturing jobs by the thousands in a heavily dependent manufacturing-job state like Wisconsin. Other books and authors can and have focused on the broader impacts of these changes. I want to focus here on several impacts globalization and industry consolidation have had on Wisconsin politics between the 1970s and 2010.

First, globalization and industry consolidation took many corporate headquarters and thus their CEOs out of Wisconsin. This had a political impact in at least one specific way. Going back to Republican Governor Warren Knowles (1965 to 1971)—and probably further—there had been, for lack of a better term, an "environmental wing" of the Republican Party. The large number of CEOs then in Wisconsin included many hunters and fishermen who enjoyed Wisconsin's pristine North Woods and lakes. This included Governor Knowles himself. They wanted a clean environment, they believed there was a significant role for the Department of Natural Resources (DNR) to play in protecting that environment, and they were politically influential with the Republican Party. Republican governors (Knowles, Dreyfus, Thompson, McCallum) and Republican candidates for governor listened to them. They were influential within the state chamber of commerce. These CEOs also made political contributions. When the CEOs left Wisconsin, so did the Republican "environment wing."

Hence, Walker and the Republican Legislature could jam through a bill to greatly diminish environmental protection in our mining laws in 2013 and not worry about much grief from within the Republican Party. Again, an issue that had not been partisan in any big or automatic way, is now sadly partisan. Those long-gone CEOs might well have stopped or modified that bill.

Second, globalization and industry consolidation cost Wisconsin tens of thousands of manufacturing jobs in the 1970s and later. Many of these were union jobs. With their demise went some Democratic voters and untold amounts of union dues and political support for largely Democratic candidates. This was a major factor in reducing private-sector union influence in the Legislature.

Third, prior to the full damage of globalization and industry consolidation, there existed a roughly equal balance of power between business and labor. For example, from the 1960s until Scott Walker, councils made up of an equal number of members from business and labor would mutually agree on the laws that would govern our unemployment compensation and worker compensation programs. For over forty years the legislature respected this compromise process and would pass their agreements without change. With Walker in 2011 the Legislature and governor would start ignoring the compromise process and pass legislation affecting these two programs that pleased only Republicans and the right wing. He destroyed a 40-year process of successful compromise on taxes, benefits, and eligibility in these programs that had served Wisconsin very well.

Fourth, although not directly partisan, globalization put a significant dent in the great private sector middle class that Wisconsin had enjoyed.

TO SUMMARIZE

The changes described in this chapter impacted the unannounced move to the political right by new governor Scott Walker. These changes all created a much more politically divided Wisconsin.

Walker could count on 100% support from WMC. They were all in with the Republicans. Since WEAC was all in with the Democrats, he would have no need to try to work with them or expect their support or even their neutrality.

The legislative leadership broadly expanded their involvement with and control of candidates, which meant Walker would have a more conservative Republican Legislature to help him and a more liberal Democratic minority to oppose his proposals.

Almost all the changes created an environment that made it easy for the governor to throw out the "containment" policy of his 12 predecessors. Walker was free to govern in a way that pleased only the right wing of his party and have institutional and legislative support. The general public was unprepared for this dramatic change, and I believe it took several years for them to completely digest the changes and make conclusions about what Walker did. It does seem, based on recent push-back by his own party's legislative majority, and the latest Marquette University poll, that they are concluding that they do not approve of the unexpected changes dropped as "bombs." The September 2015 Marquette poll had Scott Walker's support level at 37%, which is his lowest approval rate ever as governor.

In the six decades prior to 2010, it often didn't matter all that much whether a Republican or Democrat was in the governor's chair. The next chapter will show you why.

CHAPTER 6

60 Years of a "Containment Policy" and "Citizen Participation"

What is the "containment policy" as it relates to Wisconsin governors? It is a consistent way of governing by 12 consecutive Wisconsin governors—6 Republican and 6 Democrat—who led Wisconsin between 1950 and 2010 by never governing too far to the left or too far to the right. All of them, to a significant degree, followed the containment strategy... until Walker. Democratic governors kept the far left under control, and Republican governors kept the far right under control. Republicans governed center right and Democrats governed center left. I firmly believe this is what a strong majority of Wisconsin citizens approved of... and came to expect.

The governing approach of his 12 predecessors gave Walker enormous "inherited prestige." The people had an expectation, having observed the previous 12 governors, that he would operate somewhere near the middle. Walker threw all that out the window. It developed he had no intention of continuing the tradition. It didn't fit his political plans.

List of Wisconsin Governors Between 1950 and 2010

1951-1957	Walter J. Kohler, Jr. (R)
1957-1959	Vernon Thompson (R)
1959-1963	Gaylord Nelson (D)
1963-1965	John Reynolds (D)
1965-1971	Warren P. Knowles (R)
1971-1977	Patrick J. Lucey (D)
1977-1979	Martin J. Schreiber (D)
1979-1983	Lee Sherman Dreyfus (R)
1983-1987	Anthony Earl (D)
1987-2001	Tommy G. Thompson (R)
2001-2003	Scott McCallum (R)
2003- 2011	James Doyle, Jr. (D)

I credit Bill Kraus—a Dreyfus aide and savvy political observer—with the word "containment." I had reached this conclusion of how Wisconsin governors governed but it is Kraus' perfect word that describes it. He was also able to confirm for me that two governors he knew and I didn't—Walter Kohler and Vernon Thompson—also followed this policy.

Wisconsin state government for at least 60 years before Scott Walker became governor was a "participatory" government. Governors went out of their way to involve citizen groups in studying proposed changes to state government. A key element of this "participatory" approach to governing was to not spring "surprises" on the people of Wisconsin. I believe this had become a "given" in the expectations of most citizens for how their governor would do his job. They often used "blue ribbon commissions" or other panels that were composed of citizens from all points of view on the topic being studied.

Scott Walker stopped "participatory" government and replaced it with "imposed" government. He announced broad changes to state government (often with no warning). He referred to it as "dropping the bomb." No citizen groups representing a wide range of views on a topic have ever been appointed during his nearly five years as governor to study his major initiatives. Walker has not appointed a single Blue Ribbon Commission. During the previous 45 years, eight Wisconsin governors of both parties appointed numerous blue ribbon commissions and other study committees that represented a wide range of views on the topic being studied:

Governors' Commissions
Knowles: 33 over 6 years
Lucey: 40 over 6 ½ years
Schreiber: 4 over 1 ½ years
Dreyfus: 35 over 4 years
Earl: 22 over 4 years
Thompson: 87 over 14 years
McCallum: 11 over 2 years
Doyle: 23 over 8 years
Walker: 13 over 5 years

The numbers tell some of the story about the "participatory" style of government of these eight governors who preceded Walker and his "imposed" style of governing.

Walker's eight predecessors (I could not find this information for the governors before Knowles) appointed 265 of these commissions and Walker 13.

The real point, however, is made by broad substantive changes that came from these commissions, task forces, etc. of the previous eight governors. Their broad, big initiatives to make major change came only after the citizen commissions with a broad range of viewpoints first studied the possible changes and the public and media were aware of their ongoing work.

Walker's 13 commissions have nothing to do with the "bold

bombs" he dropped on the people of Wisconsin... just read their titles.

I must acknowledge one exception. Governor Lucey did not appoint a commission to study the proposed merger of the University of Wisconsin campuses. He did, however, talk about it in his campaign for governor so it was hardly a "bomb" when he proposed it in his 1971 budget (all of these governor-appointed groups are listed in Appendix A).

The Walker way is not the Wisconsin way and it will be reversed—the sooner the better.

I remember all of the Wisconsin gubernatorial elections since 1964 (Wisconsin governors had two year terms until 1970). What is very clear to me is that the people of Wisconsin were never terribly upset regardless of whether a Democrat or a Republican was elected. Of course, strong partisans were disappointed if their candidates lost. But why were so many not upset? Because as Democrat or Republican governors came and went, people saw that the basic values of a strong majority of Wisconsinites were not disrupted or attacked. Governors did propose changes of course, but never as a surprise. The changes were discussed during the campaign and came usually after appointment of some type of commission or blue ribbon study group. Significant change would come after much public debate and public input.

The following is a list of what I refer to as basic values of a consensus of Wisconsin citizens since at least 1950:

- Strong support for public education
- Strong support for clean air and water standards
- No direct attacks on public or private unions
- Opposition to the property tax
- Support for the University of Wisconsin
- Strong support for unemployment compensation and worker compensation programs

- A strong Medicaid program
- Strong citizen input before changes are made
- Governors frequently appointing cabinet members from the other political party
- Support for the Wisconsin Public Broadcasting System
- Support for at least some gubernatorial pardons for Wisconsin citizens convicted of crimes after paying their debt to society
- Support for expanding voter rights and opportunities
- Support for state parks
- Suspicion of the need for tax increases
- Support for state land purchases (named the Knowles-Nelson Fund for former Republican and Democratic governors)
- Clean and open government that cannot be bribed

I believe an important thing to mention about these 12 governors is that none of them left office wildly unpopular—seldom personally unpopular at all. The people of Wisconsin had a generally high personal view of them. What other state in America can say this? Also important is the fact that none of the 12 were ever accused of any even remotely serious ethical violation or scandal. What a contrast with neighboring Illinois!

CONTAINMENT AND THE WISE MEN

How did containment happen? Sixty straight years, six Republicans and six Democrats?

First, all these governors had a good understanding of the people of Wisconsin and what policies and values were shared by a strong majority of the people.

Second, none were running for president where an appeal had to be made to a primary voter base consisting of voters with significantly different views than a strong majority of Wisconsinites.

Third, and I believe this is enormously important to continuing this governing style, was a small group of men who I would describe as the "Wise Men." Of deep concern is the fact that as governor, it is not publically clear who Scott Walker's key advisors are on policy or politics. This is unusual for Wisconsin governors. The role of Walker's cabinet members as advisors is not clear. They appear to be people who simply carry out orders rather than develop the policy direction.

So, who were these "wise men?"

Ody Fish was a key Republican leader and "wise man" from about 1963 until the end of the century. He was the President and CEO of a Wisconsin company name Pal-O-Pac. At different times he was the state Republican Party Chairman and served on the UW Board of Regents. His strength was to lead the Republican Party structure and be a common sense advisor to Republican candidates for statewide office. They all listened to him.

John MacIver was a senior partner in the Milwaukee law firm of Michael, Best, and Frederich. He was a major advisor in Wisconsin to Republican candidates for president from Richard Nixon to the Bushes. He was also a "wise man" and advisor to Republican gubernatorial candidates during most of the last half of the last century. He clearly wanted Republicans to be in power but he wanted them to govern Wisconsin wisely. One of his most admirable (to me) strategies was to first figure out what was the best policy for Wisconsin and then make the politics of that policy work for Republicans. What a refreshing approach to government and politics. I got to know John pretty well as Blue Cross was one of his legal clients.

Bill Kraus started helping Republican candidates in 1952 with Mel Laird's first run for Congress. Laird would later be President Nixon's first Secretary of Defense (1969-1973). Kraus later ran

Warren Knowles' winning gubernatorial campaigns in 1966 and 1968, then ran Lee Sherman Dreyfus' successful campaign in 1978. He served as Dreyfus' top staff person in the governor's office from 1979-1983. Kraus' day job was as a Vice President at Sentry Insurance, which included being in charge of all of Sentry's domestic insurance operations and the company's budget. He later joined the Equitable Insurance Company in New York City as Vice President of Communications.

The Democrats had one giant "wise man"—Governor Patrick J. Lucey. From the mid-1950s until 1980 he was clearly the wise man for the Democrats. He governed under the containment policy and advised other Democrats as well. He ran for vice president in 1980 as an Independent on the ticket with Republican John Anderson. This hurt him with several Democrats in Wisconsin (but not with me). So after 1980 Democratic governors and candidates still sought his advice, but it was not in as public a way.

I cannot think of another Democratic wise man nor have others I have spoken with been able to name one. Governor Lucey lived to age 96 (he passed away in 2014) and every Democratic Governor and candidate confided in him up to and including Governor Jim Doyle (2003-2011). Lucey was the "wise man" for the entire 60 years.

What was the great role these "wise men" played that helped lead to this 60 years of containment? They all had great stature and credibility in their party. A governor or governor wanna-be wanted to listen to them. The candidate sought them out, not the other way around. They were all partisans but they all had in common a desire to make government work in Wisconsin. They all agreed on a common list of Wisconsin values that led them to strongly urge their party's governors to govern somewhere near the middle. None of the Republican "Wise Men" ever sought political office, but they provided a continuity of advice and cared that the Republican Party not be taken over by the far right members of the party.

What happened to 60 years of containment when Scott Walker took office in 2011? The answer partly is the philosophical make-up of the 2011 and 2013 Legislatures that benefited from the 2011 gerrymandering. They were further to the right than any Republican majority in those previous 60 years. Governor Walker didn't need to work too hard to take this Legislature to the far right, much further than any of the six previous Republican governors. For most of the previous years the Legislature included more conservative Democrats and more moderate Republicans.

It is clear to me now that Governor Walker was running for president from day one of his governorship. He clearly would know that the Republican nomination would be won in primaries where the voters are to the right of general Election Day Republicans and clearly to the right of a significant majority of voters in Wisconsin.

The containment policy of his twelve immediate predecessors did not fit with Walker's national political ambitions. Hence, he dumped it.

WISCONSIN—A PURPLE STATE

Scott Walker says he "has been re-elected in a 'blue state' that hasn't voted Republican for president since 1984." While it is true that Wisconsin has voted Democrat in the presidential elections, it is also true that Wisconsin is far more "blue" in those presidential election years than in the off years when Governors and other officials are elected. Now, how incredible or unheard of is it for a Republican gubernatorial candidate to get 52% of the vote three times in the "blue state" of Wisconsin? Ever heard of Governor Tommy Thompson? He was elected to four consecutive four-year terms between 1986 and 1998 with the following percentages: 53% in 1986, 58% in 1990, 67% in 1994, and 60% in 1998. All of those elections occurred during the time when Wisconsin was voting Democratic in presidential election years. How did Thompson do it? In the interest of full disclosure I like Tommy Thompson, and we are actually friends to this day. I served as a Democrat in his cabinet, and I think that is a clue to how he did it. Thompson wanted to be governor of all the people, not just those who agreed with him 99% of the time. His intentions as governor were to unite the state, not divide it intentionally. He was willing to listen to and work with anyone who would help him achieve that. People liked that, and it is what the people of Wisconsin had been used to for a long time.

TOMMY THOMPSON ON "CONTAINMENT"

I interviewed former Governor Thompson on May 20, 2015. I asked him about his approach to governing and what he thought a governor needed to do to successfully govern Wisconsin. I also asked for his thoughts regarding the overall "containment" view of the governing strategy of the twelve governors that immediately preceded Walker. Thompson's response was as follows:

"I agree with your basic premise. I was there for Warren Knowles and Pat Lucey and for Lee Sherman Dreyfus, and Tony Earl. I also think not only did we sort of operate center right/center left depending, but also the legislators- there was a lot more autonomy from the Legislature than what there is today. I think your theory is correct, but I think you have to add that.

In the 70s under Lucey, Republicans controlled the Senate and Democrats controlled the House and the legislative leaders, Walter John Chilsen in the Senate and Ray Johnson from Eau Claire, were stronger, and the legislature was much more independent. There were much more liberal, moderate, and conservative Democrats and much more liberal, moderate, and conservative Republicans in the 60s, 70s, 80s, and 90s. The governors would try and make sure there was containment, as Bill Kraus would say, much more center-right and center-left, but also the Legislature was much more independent and stood up much stronger. There was much more co-equal branches of government than it's morphed into now.

There's a stronger governorship, and I probably had something to do with that because of my use of the veto- and then I think Jim Doyle expanded on that and Walker has too- but Walker also has more Republicans that are more on the conservative philosophical side leading him and helping him be more conservative, whereas when I was governor and when Pat Lucey was, there were a lot more moderates and Democrats at that time- the Burt Grovers and the Tim Cullens- that would also be strong leaders and moderates, and in my case I had the Mary Panzers and a lot of strong leaders on the Republican side that were also moderate.

So it was much easier and it was the right thing to do because I believe very strongly—and I think to be a successful governor you also had to realize—that the state of Wisconsin is not a conservative state or not a liberal state. We are a state that goes back and forth. I felt the political winds strongly and I realized that if you're way out here on one side that you're just not going to be able to do a decent job in Wisconsin because Wisconsin is so diverse and has such a strong political history of really governing from the middle.

I wanted to be successful, and to be successful I think that you had to bring in Democrats, Independents, and Republicans. I think that was the same thing that Tony Earl, Pat Lucey—Pat Lucey did it very well because he had a lot of Republicans supporting him. I also think that Warren Knowles and myself, and I think less under Jim Doyle and less under Walker, because the members of the political party on the Democrat side are much more liberal and the members of the political party on the Republican side are much more conservative and I think that has a tugging impact on the governor.

And in Walker's case it's a tugging that he is helping to lead and *therefore it's much more of conservative administration, whereas in my case Democrats controlled both houses so even if I wanted to be- which I didn't, I wanted to be center right- it would have been impossible. And I wanted to be successful and to be successful you have to be able to govern from the middle out."*

THROWING "CONTAINMENT" OUT THE WINDOW

Maybe the most uniting event that can occur in Wisconsin happened on February 6, 2011, when the Green Bay Packers won the Super Bowl. We don't have Republican Packer fans or Democrat Packer fans, we are just plain Packer fans. If a governor wanted a united state, this Super Bowl win was a gift any other new Wisconsin governor would die for and would use to his political advantage to broaden his base. We learned one week after that victory that this governor, unlike his twelve predecessors, had no intention of using this Packer victory to unite the state. He had a secret, dramatic plan to abolish "containment," introduce legislation that is now known as "Act 10," and deliberately divide our state in an angry way (that still exists today). He then continued to push through the legislature a right wing agenda without any interest whatsoever in compromise. Compromise would hurt the national image he was building.

I was appalled that a Wisconsin governor would divide his state in two for no urgent reason other than his own political career. I could never conceive of that happening. It could not happen in the Wisconsin I knew.

By "angrily dividing" Wisconsin I mean that roughly 40% believe that Governor Walker is out to destroy the Wisconsin they love and another roughly 40% absolutely love him. (Though polls in summer 2015 indicated that Walker was losing support, particularly among the 20% in the middle.) Both sides don't just disagree with each other, they angrily disagree and believe the other side is borderline evil. I am talking about feelings that have consistently existed from February 2011 to today. How can I say this? When you are a state senator during this time you can't only talk to people who agree with you. I have heard the strong feelings in person, in emails, in parades, in letters to the editor, etc. from people on both sides. I have never heard or felt this deep division in my lifetime.

In Walker's own words, he was "dropping the bomb." "Bombs" have dramatic and destructive results. So did Act 10.

One highly important issue came to the fore just as I was returning to the Senate in 2011—mining in northern Wisconsin.

CHAPTER 7

Mining and Political Pollution Come to Wisconsin

When I came back to the state Senate in 2011, I had no idea that one of the biggest issues I would work on would be mining. There are no mines in the Rock County area that I was elected to represent. It was never an issue in the campaign. However, 2011 saw the public arrival in Wisconsin of a West Virginia coal company owned by Florida billionaire Chris Kline. He purchased mineral rights and created a new company named Gogebic Taconite, and gave $10,000 to Walker's gubernatorial campaign. Gogebic Taconite also contributed over $100,000 to the WMC Mobilization campaign to run ads against Democratic Senator Bob Jauch, who represents the area. This is the campaign spending in 2010 we know about.

The company announced that it intended to build a large open pit iron ore mine in the Penokee Hills of Southern Ashland and Iron Counties (at the top of Wisconsin near Lake Superior). This was 350 miles from my home. The company said 700 jobs would be created at the mine, along with another 2,000 in the area of the mine. Wisconsin was desperate to create more jobs in the state, but numbers on prospective jobs were always provided only by the company; no independent source ever verified them.

For months company spokespeople stressed that Gogebic Taconite had no interest in changing Wisconsin regulatory procedures, however in April of 2011, it suddenly announced that the Legislature needed to change the existing laws that regulated mining from an environmental standpoint and change the regulatory process for receiving a permit to construct the mine (a permit to mine needs state and federal approval before it can be issued).

Company officials didn't just request legislative changes, they demanded them and in fact wrote the bill, and pressed action within two months even though the Legislature was embroiled in controversial budget debates. This out of state mining company quickly became a political force as it closed its Wisconsin office for the first of three times when they did not get their way quickly enough in July 2011.

At the beginning of the mining issue in 2011, I knew very little about mining or the issue at hand because I had been gone from the Legislature for 24 years. My first instinct (coming from an economically devastated Rock County) was to feel that if mining could occur in an environmentally safe way, and if the company could get a permit approved by the state and federal government, then go ahead and create the jobs. I had never been in the Penokee Hills. I had never talked to the people of Ashland and Iron Counties, including anyone from the Bad River Band of the Lake Superior Chippewa whose reservation the waters of the Penokees pass through.

The proposed mine would have potentially stretched across 22 miles of the Penokees. The project initially would have chopped off the top of the Penokee Hills and dug a 1,000 foot deep hole, one-half to one-mile wide and four miles long. The dominant concern was the impact such a mine would have on the water of the Penokees. Opponents wanted to protect the water, and the mining company wanted the laws changed so they could dump the mining waste in the water, just a few miles from Lake Superior. Surrounding all the politics, the campaign money, the rhetoric... the central issue was always the water.

This issue spilled over into Wisconsin politics and other legislation in ways that could not be foreseen in 2011—at least not foreseen by the general public and Democratic legislators. I believe this mining legislation was the second most significant legislation (only after Act 10) of Walker's first term.

It clearly impacted environmental laws, but the mining company's impact stretched far beyond mining. The episode displayed the role of campaign money—including mostly secret money—and its resulting severe damage to Wisconsin's environmental laws;the impact of the mining industry's money on the partisan makeup of the state Senate following the 2012 election; and the Republicans', including Governor Walker's, complete disinterest in the impact this mine would have on the Penokees and the people who live there.

The following is an outline of the major issues and the politics that ensued. This mining bill legislation needs a discussion of the several pieces of the issue:

1. The central role water played in this entire issue.

2. Gogebic Taconite, the mining company, and what they wanted from Governor Walker and the Legislature.

3. Understanding of the proposed site of the mine in the Penokee Hills of northern Wisconsin, and the plans for the mine.

4. The legislation itself, written by the mining company, for the mining company, and how it dramatically changed

Wisconsin environmental law regarding iron ore mining across the state, not just the Penokees site.

5. The first mining bill that failed in 2012 by one vote in the state Senate and its role in the political recall elections and general elections of 2012.

6. Gogebic Taconite's partially known, partially still unknown role in Wisconsin elections which resulted in them investing in the legislative makeup they needed (they helped buy the Legislature they needed... they already had Governor Walker).

7. Understanding the Penokees and the people who live there.

8. The 2013 mining bill's passage and how it happened.

9. Environmental concerns become greater to the people of Wisconsin.

10. Gogebic Taconite announces in 2015 that they have stopped the process of seeking a permit to build the mine because the area contains "significantly more wetlands than they had thought."

11. The sad trail that Gogebic Taconite leaves on Wisconsin. They soiled our politics, they soiled our environmental laws, and they made the lives of the people living in and near the Penokees miserable for four years.

Let's begin with the things that are known about the mining bill and the issue:

- The mining company, not legislators, wrote the original bill that was defeated by one vote in 2012. After the defeat of the bill, there were various attempts and public comments by legislators to try to modify the bill so it could pass. This effort went almost nowhere.

The following statement from Republican Assembly Speaker Jeff Fitzgerald, reported in the *Wisconsin State Journal* on March 7, 2012, leaves little doubt why compromise ended, and should also erase any doubt about who was in charge of the contents of this proposed law that would apply to all of Wisconsin. Fitzgerald said, "Assembly Republicans are done compromising because Gogebic Taconite won't accept any more concessions." Most if not all the legislators knew that this legislation was written by Gogebic and controlled by them, but I was astounded that an Assembly Speaker would so arrogantly say it in public!

This prompted company officials to withdraw from Wisconsin for the second time because they didn't get their way.

With only modest tweaks the bill became law when Republicans regained control of the state Senate in 2013 (millions of dollars had been poured into a close Senate race in eastern Wisconsin). Governor Walker and Republican lawmakers made adoption of the mining bill a top priority.

- The bill drastically changed Wisconsin environmental law relating to protecting our waters from mining waste and attacked the Wisconsin Public Trust Doctrine included in our constitution that says that the waters of the state belong to the public.

- There is an enormous amount of water in the Penokee Hills. The rivers, streams, lakes, and wetlands of the Penokees and the headwaters of the Bad River watershed contain 40% of all Lake Superior wetlands. DNR data indicates the Penokees get more precipitation than anywhere else in Wisconsin. Also, because of an east-west continental divide a few miles south of the Penokees, all of the water from the Penokees flows north through the Bad River Reservation into the largest freshwater body in the world... Lake Superior

The mining industry's estimate is that when you dig for iron ore, about 25% might be the iron ore you want, and 75% is waste that needs to be dumped somewhere. With a mine this size we are talking about millions of tons of waste that has to be put somewhere.

The mining company legislation provided them with the solution it needed. How could a company profitably dispose of millions of tons of waste? It changed our laws so the company could dump its waste in the water! The bill they wrote and the law the Legislature passed and Walker signed did just that in the following ways:

- The Republicans and the mining company said that it should be OK to let the mining company fill with waste the "small, minor" rivers and streams if they are shorter than two miles. The simple reality is that water merges with other water.

  It is not isolated, unconnected water—and the total length of all these "small, minor" rivers and streams laid out end to end totals 108 miles! So it would be dumping its waste into 108 miles of rivers and streams. One hundred eight miles is close to the distance between Camp Randall Stadium in Madison and Lambeau Field in Green Bay!

- The supporters also said there were these "puddles" that it should be OK to dump the waste in. It turned out that their definition of a "puddle" was up to two acres. That is almost the size of two football fields. So much for that real puddle we step around on the sidewalk (and little kids love to step in).

- They did a complete 180 degree change in Wisconsin wetlands law. Existing law, adopted with strong bipartisan support, stated it "was presumed unnecessary" to dump mining waste in the wetlands. The mining-company-written-law now says that it is "presumed necessary" to dump mining waste in wetlands. Amazing how deleting two letters can change so much.

TAXES

Mining companies, be it for oil, natural gas, iron ore, gold, copper, silver, are extracting from the earth natural resources that are irreplaceable. Therefore, states with extensive mining or drilling activity (Texas, Alaska, North Dakota, Minnesota to mention a few) all charge these companies a severance tax or extraction tax to assure costs of extraction are paid by the producers rather than the taxpayers. They don't give it away. But if you want to see a state that intends to virtually give it away, come to Wisconsin and read our new iron-ore mining law that Governor Walker signed in 2013.

The bipartisan legislation authored by Senators Jauch and Schultz, and included in the Republican legislation in 2012, required an "up front $5 million" in payments from Gogebic Taconite which would be distributed to local governments to offset their costs. In 2013 the mining company insisted that this advance payment language be taken out of the law.

The law also contains a taxing mechanism known as a "net proceeds tax." This is a tax on profit after the mining company deducts its expenses to operate its Wisconsin mine. The number one way most of us wanted to disperse the taxes an iron-ore mining company would pay was to return it to the near-by communities to cover additional costs they would incur. These costs would likely include legal help to protect their interests vis-a-vis the mining company, road repair costs, and other costs the local governments would incur because of the mine.

Gogebic Taconite (and therefore Walker and the Republicans) wanted to pay a "net proceeds tax." This tax could vary widely, and was not a predictable source of revenue for the local citizens and local governments. The mining company got their way.

An alternative form of taxation, which is used in neighboring Minnesota, is a tonnage tax. A tonnage tax is an alternative method of calculating corporation taxes by reference to the net tonnage of iron-ore extracted. A mine extracts an irreplaceable natural resource from our earth. They should pay for this with certainty. A tonnage tax does that. The legislation developed in the mining committee I chaired in 2012 had a tonnage tax slightly lower than Minnesota's, where mining has thrived for generations. It was rejected by the Republicans 17-16.

The bottom line is that Wisconsin (under this law written by the mining company) will virtually give this irreplaceable natural resource away. Why? Gogebic Taconite has stated many times that this will be a $1.5 billion project. With a net proceeds tax this amount can be tax deducted first before they start paying their net proceeds. I once said publicly (with some hesitancy) that if this governor and the Republicans who voted for this were to operate a house of ill repute, they would go broke because they wouldn't charge anyone.

JOBS, JOBS, JOBS!

The Governor and Republican legislators from day one blasted one message regarding this mine: jobs, jobs, jobs. Wisconsin was trying to recover from the deep national recession, and this jobs, jobs, jobs message was a powerful political message that resonated throughout 2011 and 2012. The mining company's claim that the mine would employ 700 people at good wages and would create additional thousands of jobs in the area moved public opinion.

However, "the rest of the story," as Paul Harvey used to say, would only become widely known later, near the end of 2012 and 2013.

The mining company gave the impression in 2011 that these 700 jobs would be created at the start of the mine. Only much later would the mining company acknowledge that these 700 jobs would be added over the thirty-five year life of the mine. For people desperate for jobs, this was news. Also, the mine was at least five years away from initial construction.

Iron ore mining today is not hundreds of workers with pick axes. Giant mining machines do the work that literally hundreds of workers used to do. I visited the Caterpillar plant near Milwaukee to see one of these machines. They are huge! At least sixty feet wide and two to three stories high, the scoop is so large that it can scoop up 120 tons of earth at once. There would be one and maybe two of these in this proposed mine. Therefore, a highly paid operator (likely not from the area of the mine), some engineers, electricians, and other professionals (not all from the area) would be needed to operate and do maintenance on this machine.

The company heavily oversold the jobs impact. The governor participated in this. Through testimony in front of the Senate Mining Committee and through public comments made by the chairman of the Wisconsin Mining Committee and representatives from the Army Corp of Engineers, we knew the permitting process to get this mine up and running would take seven to ten years—if not longer—depending on lawsuits. Yet the "political messaging" of the company and Walker said that if the Legislature would pass the mining bill quickly, jobs would be just around the corner; not only in the Penokees, but in the Milwaukee area at companies that manufacture mining equipment.

MEETING THE PEOPLE OF THE PENOKEES

The vast majority of the Legislature knew little or nothing about the proposed mining site. This changed when Senator Jauch, who represented the area, invited legislators to come to the Ashland area and the Penokees, to see the area and talk to the people, local elected officials, and the tribe. I took him up on it, along with Senator Dale Schultz and a few others. I visited the area three times for two or three days each time. I will remember these visits until the day I die.

Some highlights:

1. Going to the Penokees, twice in winter and once in the summer, and seeing their beauty, meeting in the homes of the residents who lived there, sitting at their kitchen tables, and hearing their deep concerns, their feelings of desperation and helplessness because members of the majority party (other than Schultz) would go to Iron County and Hurley but not come to the Penokees to talk to the people who would be directly affected (their fresh water, their livelihoods, their multi-generational way of life). The waters of the Penokees flow north to Lake Superior entirely through Ashland County, not Iron County.

2. Meeting with local elected officials such as Joe Barabe, the mayor of Mellen, a community that sits right next to the Penokees and within a few miles of where the mine would be dug, Ashland County Board Chairman Pete Russo, and many others. The mayors of four area cities, Mellen, Ashland, Washburn, and Bayfield, all publicly opposed the mine. Their basic message was that they need jobs badly, but the trade-off of a mine with some jobs and its damage to their land, water, and the destruction of the beautiful Penokees was not a good deal.

3. Standing in and near the Penokees and comprehending what a four-mile-long, 1,000-foot-deep, half-mile-wide open-pit mine would actually look like and mean.

4. Seeing and visually understanding how much water is in the Penokees and that it all flows north into Lake Superior through the Bad River Reservation.

5. Learning that there is just too much water in the Penokees to mine there. Also, too much beauty to be destroyed and real people's lives disrupted forever.

I met so many remarkable people in and around the Penokees. They deeply moved and impressed me as honorable and committed. Following is a brief list of several of the folks I met (and I realize I will be leaving out some wonderful people who deserve recognition):

"Grandma" O'Dovero (aka Monica Vitek) and her family for five generations have lived and worked on their farm within sight of the Penokee Hills. I sat at her kitchen table several times and learned about their love of the Penokees and their deep fear that a 1,000-foot-deep mine would pollute their well water. Their tight-knit family was reassuring to me far beyond the mining issue.

Joe Rose is a Bad River Elder and a retired professor of Native American Studies at Northland College in Ashland. He is also now an elected member of the Ashland County Board. Professor Rose is an enormously impressive man with an encyclopedic mind when it comes to Native American history, including the history of tribal treaties with the United States government in the 1800s. I have listened to him for many hours over the past three years and could listen for many more. I was especially moved by the basic yet profound wisdom in his words, "The wetlands speak for themselves, and on this mining issue they spoke," and, "We must treat Mother Earth with the same kindness and care that we treat our own mothers."

Mellen Mayor Joe Barabe, at the start of the mining issue in 2010-2011, was accepting of a mine because his community desperately needed more jobs. Mellen is the small city in Ashland County closest to the Penokees. The more Mayor Barabe learned about the mine's impact on his community, the more his views changed to opposition. He was a wonderful man to meet, who fought this fight while also courageously battling cancer... what an inspiration!

Bad River Tribal Chairman Mike Wiggins was a key figure in the fight to stop the mine. He spoke calmly and clearly at locations across the state. He would say that you could tell if it rained a lot in the Penokees because two days later the water would reach Lake Superior and change its color along the shoreline. These environmental changes and relationships have been understood by the Bad River Band and others for hundreds of years, long before outside "experts" came along with their studies that determined the same thing.

Ashland County Board Chairman Pete Russo became a strong opponent of the mine. He was an example of so many who initially was open to the mine with its massively oversold jobs promise, but ended up opposing it because of the environmental damage it would cause.

John and Connie Franke have a home in the Penokees. I had the chance to visit with them in their home and they showed me the beauty and tranquility that would be destroyed by the mine.

VISITING THE SOURCE OF THE BAD RIVER

The Penokees are at 1,800 feet above sea level. The water then flows down 1,200 feet to enter Lake Superior, which is at 600 feet above sea level. The Bad River is the main waterway that ultimately carries the water from the Penokees north to Lake Superior. It flows entirely within Ashland County and passes through the Bad River Reservation.

The river's source is Lake Caroline high in the Penokees. A group of us traveled up to this site. It was beautiful. The Bad River starts out as just a 2 to 3 foot wide stream coming out of the lake. I actually bent down and drank some of this fresh water. This was and will always be a meaningful moment for me. This little stream gathers size and strength as it flows down the hills as the Tyler Forks River, other small rivers, streams, and wetlands join it on its way to Lake Superior. This gave me a complete visual understanding of what is a known fact: that water bodies join each other. This is why the law that was passed and signed by Governor Walker was so awful: the language that allowed the mining company to dump their waste into just "small" rivers and streams and other "puddles." There are many ways for a legislator to get educated on any issue and for me, drinking from the Bad River on a very cold day in February in the pristine hills of the Penokees was one.

LEARNING FROM THE BAD RIVER ELDERS AND THE PEOPLE OF ASHLAND COUNTY

In February 2013, the new Republican majority was hell-bent on passing their version of the mining bill. They never held a public hearing in Ashland County in all of the three years this issue was in front of the Legislature. That did not prevent some of us in the Senate from traveling north in February to hold an all-day "listening session" in the city of Ashland on a Saturday. That nine-hour session was a chance for the people to speak without the two-minute time limits that the Republicans imposed on their hearings in Madison.

Senator Jauch had another good idea on how to help educate the senators who had traveled there. The Bad River Band reservation is just a few miles east of Ashland, and Senator Jauch and Chairman Mike Wiggins discussed having us go to the reservation, meet at their Round House, and listen to the tribal elders talk about the mine's impact on their world.

So on the Friday night before the listening session, we (five senators) spent over three hours sitting in the Round House listening to the elders talk about how the Penokees and the Bad River affected their lives today and for the past seven generations. They talked about "Mother Earth" and that we should love and respect her. It was a very moving evening for all of us. As an aside, it was also a historic meeting of sorts because we had five state senators listening, not talking, for three hours! Possibly a national record! All of us drove away from that meeting with a better understanding of the tribe's deep concern. Another education session in Ashland County that I will never forget.

2012

2012 was the key year in the four-year saga of the "mining issue."

The first attempt to pass the legislation that the mining company wrote failed to pass the state Senate in the spring of 2012. Republican Senator Dale Schultz showed political courage in voting with the sixteen Democrats to kill the company-written bill 17-16.

Through the results of the state Senate recall elections, the Democrats regained the majority in the State Senate in July and would retain it until January 2013. The November 2012 legislative elections would restore the Republican majority (with the help of mining company money and the new gerrymandered legislative maps).

The six months of Democratic majority control of the state Senate provided the opportunity to create a State Senate Special Committee on mining (which I had the privilege of chairing). We held lengthy public hearings with people from all points of view invited, experts on mining, state and federal officials involved in the regulation of mining, organizations in favor of the mine, and those with serious reservations or who opposed it. Our committee drafted a bill that would eventually be rejected by the state Senate 17-16 in early 2013. Our bill was not what the mining company had invested millions of dollars to get out of the Wisconsin Legislature.

Governor Walker needed an accommodating Republican majority in the State Senate to push through his right-wing agenda, including the bill the mining company wrote. His major problem was that one Republican Senator, Dale Schultz, would not go along with his entire agenda. Therefore, what Walker needed was a large enough Republican majority in the state senate so that they did not need Schultz's vote. The "water cooler" chatter in the Capitol called this "Schultz-proofing" the state Senate in the 2012 elections. Since 17 (out of 33) gave the Republicans the majority, they needed 18 in order not to need Schultz. The 2012 state Senate elections all came down to the 18th District (the Oshkosh-Fond du Lac area south of Green Bay). Incumbent Democrat Jessica King (who got to the state Senate by winning a recall election in 2011) needed to win to keep the Republican majority at only 17-16. If she won, Schultz would have been in the cat-bird's seat. He would be the key vote on all of Walker's agenda, mining, public education, unemployment compensation, etc. This one out of all 33 state Senate seats, out of all 99 Assembly seats would decide the major issues of the 2013-2014 Legislature.

Jessica King narrowly lost the election and Walker and his Republican allies had their 18-15 "Schultz proof" state Senate. This resulted in an environmentally destructive mining bill and more of Walker's right-wing agenda. Why did Senator King lose?

Senator King was outspent by about $5 million to $1 million when you included money spent by third-party groups. A WMC spokesperson, James Buchen, publically acknowledged (I personally heard him say it) that they dumped $2 million into the 18th District in the last 60 days. We may never know how much of that came from Gogebic Taconite. Previously undisclosed emails (released by a third party John Doe investigation) stated that Gogebic Taconite had spent at least $700,000 in the earlier recall elections, and they spent $120,000 against Senator Jauch in 2010. It is hard to imagine with the high stakes involved that the company didn't spend another million or more to defeat King.

I knew the election results meant that the Republicans, free from the need for Schultz's vote, would jam through, 17-16, a very environmentally destructive mining bill in 2013. And they did. And they acted on even more legislation that I firmly believe is bad for Wisconsin. They passed a tax cut based on a projected revenue surplus—18 months in the future—which put the state back into a deficit, which they then used to justify cuts to public education and many other programs that have made Wisconsin a great place to live.

So here is the connection of the dots: A West Virginia coal company announces plans to dig a huge open pit mine near Lake Superior... which leads to Republican's need to win (buy?) one state Senate seat near Green Bay... which leads to Republicans in Madison being able to give a mining company legislation that the mining company itself wrote... And it gives Walker the majority he needs for other large legislative proposals.

THE MINING COMPANY STOPS THE COMMITTEE EFFORTS

While I chaired the Senate Mining Committee we heard public testimony from George Meyer, a former DNR Secretary and now the executive director of the Wisconsin Wildlife Federation, and Tim Sullivan, the chairman of the Wisconsin Mining Association. I talked with them about whether they could get together and agree on what changes needed to be made to our mining laws. They did talk and they were making progress and they were trying. I felt if we could get those two to agree on a bill, it would have broad support. Then a letter emerged signed by James Buchen, lead lobbyist for WMC (Appendix C). Guess what? The Mining Association backed off from negotiations.

James Buchen was clearly a powerful voice on behalf of Gogebic Taconite. Kennan Wood was the lobbyist for the Mining Association. A question I have—and only Mr. Buchen can answer—is whether at the time he sent this letter suggesting discussion of the issue be put on hold until the upcoming elections, did he know about the $2 million that the WMC Mobilization Fund would spend to help elect a Republican in the 18th State Senate seat that November? We do not know how much of the $2 million was mining company money. If it looks and quacks like a duck, it's a duck. If it is ever disclosed, I'd wager a lot that most of the money came from the mining company.

GOGEBIC TACONITE'S LASTING IMPRESSION

The mining company announced early in 2015 that it was suspending operations in Wisconsin. Beside the politically cute excuse of blaming the federal government (read Obama), they announced with presumably a straight face, that they had discovered—after further exploration of the Penokee Hills—that there was more water there than they thought! This statement by the mining company made me think that it was paraphrasing the famous line from the great 1943 movie Casablanca, "I'm shocked, shocked, there is water in the Penokees." DNR staff, people who live in or near the Penokees, and thousands if not tens of thousands of others could have told them that. Had they listened at hearings I chaired in 2012 they could have learned that. I did. The Committee did. The media did. The public did.

I am extremely pleased this company will not be mining in the Penokees, but what a path of destruction it left in its wake. The legislation is still a statewide law. Any future efforts at iron ore mining in Wisconsin will be done under this law unless a future Legislature changes it.

Wisconsin mining law before 2013 did not place any time limits on when the DNR had to either approve or reject an application. The mining permit application process needs to work as a partnership between the state and federal government as they both have to approve the permit for it to be issued.

Throughout the four-year discussion, the Army Corps of Engineers, DNR staff, and even Wisconsin Mining Association Chair stressed the need for collaboration between the Federal, Tribal, and State officials. During committee hearings we learned that it would take the federal government at least five years to approve a permit, so our proposal included time lines but also "off ramps" allowing flexibility for regulators and the mining company. The Wisconsin Mining Association testified that it is in the mining industry's best interest to have the state and federal governments' approval processes stay parallel.

In addition to all the environmental and tax changes, the new mining law also directed the DNR to make a decision on a permit application in 420 days with one possible 60 day delay... 480 days maximum while knowing the federal process was estimated by the federal government to take five years or more.

The Republicans rammed through their bill (no surprise it passed on a 17-16 vote with Dale Schultz voting "no" along with all Democrats. The "Schultz-proof" plan worked.

Gogebic Taconite's decision to cease efforts to build an open-pit iron-ore mine means that it will not be polluting the waters of the Penokees and the Bad River Watershed, but it is leaving a trail of pollution nevertheless. It polluted our political campaigns with huge donations that they tried to keep secret. Of course, "keeping it secret" only from the voters and Democratic legislators. I have no doubt that Wisconsin Manufacturing and Commerce, through its political arm called the "Mobilization Fund," knows the exact dollar amount the company spent in 2012 to buy the state Senate majority it needed to pass the mining bill that the company wrote. I realize "buy" is a strong word, but as the old saying goes, "if the shoe fits...."

The end result, at least for some time and hopefully forever, is that there will be no mine in the Penokees. This was the most rewarding, substantive result of my four year term. We lost the battle (the legislation), but won the war (no mine). We moved public opinion as the public changed from majority support of the "jobs, jobs, jobs" argument to—at a minimum—support for mining but not at the expense of the environment. I believe mining company executives read the poll results and it was a factor in their throwing in the towel. It would likely have taken them 8-to-10 years to get a permit if they did at all, and a future Legislature may well have reacted to public opinion and restored the protection for the water in the Penokees.

My final words... goodbye Gogebic Taconite, and I urge other states to read the Wisconsin story if these folks come to your state.

TWO YET UNANSWERED QUESTIONS

First, why did the mining company write a bill (which became law in 2013) that literally wrote Wisconsin regulators out of the iron ore mining permitting process? Gogebic Taconite knew that a mining permit needs the approval of both the federal and the state government. A state law that clearly would not meet federal clean water standards with a timeframe so short that the federal government would not be able to work with Wisconsin would result in the federal government making the ultimate decision to approve or not approve a permit to mine. Did they have a long view that a future Congress controlled by Republicans with a Republican president would essentially make the Wisconsin law the federal law as well? This would require the federal government to throw out the Federal Clean Air and Clean Water Acts.

Second, did Gogebic Taconite come to Wisconsin to change the law so they could build the mine, or was there some other purpose that involved another company buying the rights after the law changed? Did they come to Wisconsin for some other reasons?

As a friend of mine loved to say, "There are no mysteries, just unanswered questions."

As of the writing of this book, this second question became more interesting. On August 3, 2015, it was reported in the Milwaukee Journal-Sentinel that officials of La Pointe Iron Company, one of the owners of the property in the Penokees that Gogebic Taconite tried to mine, have met with local officials to discuss resurrecting this mine project. People will need to stay tuned as one reality exists: The iron-ore is still there and iron-ore mining is still a very profitable industry.

This news story is just another reminder that citizens, organizations, and the Bad River Tribe will need to stay aware and vigilant in their involvement. I find no comfort in the low price of iron-ore in 2015. A mine would take 7-10 years to receive a permit so current prices do not matter. Gogebic Taconite's option for the mineral rights in the Penokees expired in September, 2015. It can be expected that La Pointe and another owner of the land, RGGS Land and Minerals, Ltd. of Houston will continue to market the mineral rights to the land.

CHAPTER 8

The "State" of Pre-Walker Wisconsin

Scott Walker became governor in January 2011, and was soon demanding initiatives like the Penokee Hills mine to turn the state's economy around. The real question is, just how bad off was Wisconsin before he took office? What made him believe his "unintimidated boldness" was needed?

First, let's look at the economy. Wisconsin was suffering, like all 50 states, from the greatest recession since the Great Depression. Wisconsin was hit harder than many states because the recession hit manufacturing harder than most sectors of the economy, and Wisconsin is heavily dependent on manufacturing jobs. No remotely reasonable person could say this recession was caused by state government.

A chart (Appendix D) from the Federal Government's Bureau of Labor Statistics (BLS) compares job creation in Wisconsin between 2001 and 2014 to other Midwestern states. Governor Doyle's last year as Governor was 2010. Governor Walker is governor for

2011 through 2015. These are the federal government's quarterly statistics, which are widely acknowledged as highly reliable. Clearly Wisconsin was doing relatively well before Walker took office and has done just awful ever since.

Walker may have done things he considered "bold" to help the Wisconsin economy but the numbers show he wasn't effective. His "boldest" action, arguably, was simply a campaign promise to create 250,000 jobs during his first term. He fell over 100,000 short. "Bold" turned out to be baloney.

I have listened to eight Wisconsin governors of both parties all talk about the jobs they will get created in Wisconsin during their terms. Yet any objective person knows that Wisconsin governors are somewhat limited in their control over job creation. They can primarily help or hurt on the margins. The only significant thing they can do that would have an impact within a year or two would be public spending on job creation. This was out of the question in Walker's case. A governor can also hurt job creation, and Walker has yet to accept any responsibility for this awful record. Through Act 10 he reduced the take home pay of 200,000 state and local employees. That does not improve the economy but did help his political career.

Next let's look at the state budget. We do a two-year budget in Wisconsin and the biennial budget that Walker inherited in its last six months was estimated to be $137 million in deficit out of a $60 billion budget. It was two tenths of one percent off. In fact, our non-partisan budget agency, the Legislative Fiscal Bureau, stated that a "budget repair bill" for this small percentage number was not even necessary.

However the next biennial budget, which would be Walker's first (July 1, 2011 to June 30, 2013), was estimated to have a $2.4 billion deficit. Walker has, on too many occasions to count, stated this deficit was $3.6 billion. He has said it so often that the media treats it as a fact. What causes the difference? The $3.6 billion number adds in $1.2 billion in state agency requests for additional new spending in that next biennium. Only politicians and others who are loose with the truth would label unapproved future spending requests as part of a deficit. Past governors of both parties have dealt with those requests by using Nancy Reagan's most famous advice... "just say no!" Governor Walker did, too.

Governor Walker now faces another deficit for his next budget (2015-2017). This deficit was to be expected for several reasons. The slower Wisconsin recovery from the recession compared to most other states resulted in less income and sales tax collection.

Walker, however, did make some specific "bold" moves that did help create this projected deficit. He reduced the take-home pay of 200,000 middle class Wisconsin families of public employees through Act 10. This pleased his right wing base. He also cut taxes by about $1 billion in the spring of 2014 based on estimates of a surplus that was supposed to materialize at least 15 months later. It didn't. Bold is not always smart.

The state of Wisconsin's environment and environmental laws preWalker should also be examined. Our environmental laws have overall always enjoyed broad public support as we love our outdoor activities, vacations, and understand the importance of a huge tourism industry. These laws enjoyed even broader public support when there was an "environmental wing" of the Republican Party. There has been, and probably always will be, friction between the desires of private development and the public's expectation that our government will protect our natural resources. This would be true in any state. The bottom line is there was no need for dramatic changes.

What was the nature of the relationship between businesses and labor in 2010? These relations were pretty much "settled" and calm in the private sector. Public sector labor relations were much better than they were in the early 1970s, but I believe that public sector union power—and its relationship with Democratic elected officials—had created the need for some modest tweaks. But the "unintimidated" and "bold" declaration by Walker that related to changing public employee union laws was never mentioned—nor even hinted at—by Walker during his campaign for governor in 2010. Apparently those two words were added to his vocabulary after the election. The bottom line was that "dropping the bomb" (Act 10) was not needed.

Public education—the University system and pre K-12—were overall in good shape in 2010. The flagship campus, UW-Madison, is most important. A degree from UW-Madison really means something, and its research engine brings enormous revenue, start-up business ideas, and major economic gain to Wisconsin. UW-Milwaukee and other UW campuses also contribute in these areas.

The flagship Madison campus and all the other state university campuses had the common name "UW Madison," "UW Whitewater," "UW Green Bay," "UW Platteville," etc. It was one system, one Board of Regents, etc. The political struggle in 1971 was just that... a struggle. There was a major concern that giving all the campuses similar names would diminish the Madison campus.

However, the experience of the 40 years between 1971 and 2010 had proven that this fear was unfounded. The issue was a settled one. There was no public demand to undo this merger. No major commission or study group had been appointed to study the need for a dramatic reversal of the 1971 decision.

WHAT WAS WRONG IN WISCONSIN?

Our pre-K through 12th grade public education system faces two significant challenges: More kids are coming from dysfunctional homes, and poverty is impacting how children learn (this cannot be an excuse, but it is a reality). Neither of these challenges is easily tackled not only in Wisconsin but across the nation. They require enormous, steady attention. A huge priority must be made of meeting this challenge by parents, politicians, educators, and taxpayers in general. What these problems didn't need were Walker's "bold" approach of destroying the teacher's unions or blaming the "failing" schools. If you really want to be bold, Governor, say what you mean by the term "failing schools"... are you blaming the walls and floors or are you saying teachers today are lousy?

Is it wise or sensible to take hundreds of millions of dollars of tax money away from public schools and use those tax dollars to finance a private education system? Taxpayers will tell any politician willing to listen that they are stretched enough paying for one education system.

The city of Milwaukee certainly needs help economically and with its public education system. Their needs and problems have been growing for decades for a variety of reasons, which have led to high unemployment and poverty. It is very difficult for a state to be successful when its largest city is lagging behind.

What Milwaukee needed from Governor Walker was his full attention and state assistance. What it got was vilification by the governor in his 2012 recall election because his opponent was the mayor of Milwaukee, and this vilification—which only hurt Milwaukee—helped him win the election.

So what else needed tweaking in Wisconsin in 2010? A growing imbalance existed between what private sector employees paid for their health insurance and their pensions and what public employees paid. This assumes that the private sector employees had any health insurance through their job or any decent coverage and any type of retirement fixed benefit pensions (there is a national movement toward the elimination of this and toward the 401 k type program), a 401k type program, or nothing at all. This was fixable in 2011 without largely destroying public employee unions and therefore collective bargaining. But fixing this problem would not have fit the national political ambition of the governor. When faced with the choice between was what was good for Wisconsin or what was good for his political ambition, Wisconsin always finished second. What a lousy silver medal we have to show for it.

In 2010, Wisconsin also needed laws to help jump start and supplement venture capital investment. Wisconsin ranked 50th, dead last, in the number of business start-ups. Venture capital helps people with a business idea or those who have already developed a start up company. These businesses could create an untold number of jobs. People have the ideas, they have the drive, but they lack the capital to start or grow. We passed a bill providing a meager $25 million (the actual need was for $100 to $200 million), but the payoff for that investment in jobs would be 5 or 10 years away. Guess what? This time frame didn't match Walker's personal political time frame, so he was satisfied with just $25 million.

The major reason for this public investment in Wisconsin venture capital is that absent it, the Wisconsin startups will go elsewhere for this money and most of it is outside Wisconsin and often on the East or West Coast.

This creates two succeeding problems. The investors often want the ideas and startup companies they are investing in to locate near them, i.e. not in Wisconsin. Then if they want to acquire a promising company they largely prefer that company locate near them. Hence, jobs created from the great ideas of Wisconsin's citizens and from Wisconsin innovators end up being created outside of Wisconsin—a sad result that a major public commitment of money in Wisconsin could help avoid. Also a major public commitment of money tends to attract to Wisconsin more private venture capital money.

Walker pushed through legislation to replace the Department of Commerce with a quasi-private organization called the Wisconsin Economic Development Corporation (WEDC) in 2011. He created a board to oversee this new entity and declared himself the chairman. This would be the lead agency responsible for economic development in Wisconsin.

Economic development programs needed more urgency, and to be non-political on grants, loans, and tax credits. This is the opposite of how Walker and his lieutenants operated the Wisconsin Economic Development Corporation (WEDC).

Senior citizens programs in Wisconsin in 2010 were doing great. Look at Medicaid, Senior Care, Family Care, nursing home regulation and enforcement, and others: Bold action was not needed. What did Walker do within one month of taking office? He pushed through a special session bill labeled as "tort reform" and reduced legal protections for people who are injured or die for unclear reasons in nursing homes and hospitals.

The long fight in Wisconsin against poverty has been ongoing and has never been enough. The Walker approach is to blame the people in poverty. He implies that alcohol and drug abuse are major causes of poverty and would drug test anyone who moves and is poor or gets some form of public assistance. He knocked people making more than $11,800 a year off of Medicaid. Walker by his own policies and frequent statements defines poverty as only individuals who earn less than $11,800 per year.

MY CONCLUSION ON THE STATE OF PRE-WALKER WISCONSIN

Wisconsin was suffering from the Great Recession. The people were frustrated. Wisconsin was being governed by the Democrats. There had been a Democratic governor for eight years. Anyone who has watched elections over time knows that the party in power during difficult times will likely be thrown out at the next election. "It's time for a change" is one of the oldest and most effective election slogans of all time.

Did this situation call for a clandestine series of "bombs" by Governor Walker? Did the electorate choose him with 52% of the vote to lead a huge swing of state government to the right? I believe the clear answer to both of these questions is "NO."

Did we need some tweaks... some changes that a broad coalition could support? Yes, of course we did. What we did not need was the wholesale destruction and divisiveness that Walker ushered in.

CHAPTER 9

Wisconsin's "Unintimidated" Governor

I think it's important to point out that Scott Walker's take on events is often at some distance from what actually transpired. Yet that seldom stops him from weighing in.

"I WON 3 ELECTIONS IN 4 YEARS"

"I have won three elections in four years." Governor Walker has said this so many times that the media now reports it without putting quotes around it. Only one problem... it's not true. Governor Walker has won three elections in five, that's five, years. Let's do the math: 2010 (won first gubernatorial election), 2011, 2012 (won recall election), 2013, 2014 (won second gubernatorial election). The nuns at St. Mary's grade school in Janesville taught me that adds up to five years! Is this inaccuracy by one year earth-shattering? No. Does it hurt the economy? No. But what is he up to? It's one of two things. Either he and/or his staff can't count to five, or he is deliberately misstating the facts.

Okay, so that's three times in five years. How unheard of is that in Wisconsin? Before 1970 when Wisconsin switched from two to four year terms for governor, any governor who wanted to seek a third two year term had to run three times in five years. And that is what happened with Republican Governor Walter Kohler, Jr. in 1950, 1952, and 1954 and Republican Governor Warren Knowles in 1964, 1966, and 1968. Both won three times in five years.

"I INHERITED A $3.6 BILLION BUDGET DEFICIT"

Governor Walker also continues to say almost everywhere he goes that he inherited a $3.6 billion budget deficit and he eliminated it. Only one problem again: It's not true. He inherited a $2.4 billion deficit. A sizable number and a serious challenge, but it is not the same as $3.6 billion. Why the discrepancy? That added (difference of) $1.2 billion was an amount the state agencies asked for in future spending for the next biennium. That is not a deficit. It is just a matter of saying yes or no to the request. He said no, but continues to include that extra $1.2 billion when he talks about his inherited deficit.

The point in both the three in four years claim and the $3.6 billion inherited deficit claim is that they are just plain not true. Further, the truth in both cases is somewhat impressive. Why does he feel the need to misstate the facts? I have no idea, but maybe someone will eventually ask the governor.

WALKER AND PUBLIC SPEECHES

The late Governor Patrick Lucey used to say that you could learn a lot about a governor by reading his speeches. He said he believed this because governors would be forced to follow (or live with) the public words they spoke and the positions on issues and their views on issues expressed in those speeches.

I find it informative that Governor Walker has given very few major speeches on broad topics or to explain his vision for Wisconsin. I am not talking about brief comments at ribbon cutting ceremonies or bill signings or campaign type speeches in favor of jobs.

I am talking about speeches in Wisconsin on broad topics that would indicate his planned vision for Wisconsin. Commencement speeches are often such an opportunity. I am not aware of Walker giving a commencement speech at a public institution of higher education in Wisconsin in five years. Also, governors have no problem in finding a forum if they wish to make an important policy speech aimed at all of the people of Wisconsin.

This is another piece of a larger picture of the most private, secretive governorship in at least sixty-five years.

WISCONSIN'S MEDICAID PROGRAM AND SCOTT WALKER'S DEFINITION OF POVERTY

Governor Walker's definition of what constitutes living in poverty and his refusal to accept federal funds available to Wisconsin for health care (Wisconsin taxpayers' money being returned to Wisconsin) became very clear in late 2012 and 2013.

One hundred percent of the federal poverty level was at that time $11,490 per year or less for a single person. Walker extended Medicaid coverage to some 60,000 childless adults who met this level. So far, so good. The governor deserves credit for this action. But again, "the rest of the story..."

Governor Walker changed the Medicaid eligibility requirement in Wisconsin. Before his change, adults and families living on wages up to 133 percent of the federal poverty level (FPL) were eligible for Medicaid. Governor Walker dropped eligibility to those at or below 100 percent FPL, thus establishing his definition of at what income levels people lived in poverty: $11,490 for one person, $15,510 for a family of two, $19,530 for a family of three, $23,550 for a family of four, and so on. Any household income above these amounts for these family sizes are not living in poverty according to Walker and therefore should not be eligible for Medicaid health insurance.

So while Walker added 60,000 childless adults to the Wisconsin Medicaid program, he knocked thousands of families off of Medicaid because their household incomes exceeded the above numbers. He explained that they could get their health insurance from the Obamacare insurance exchanges that he consistently criticizes. Thousands of low income families have not all gotten their insurance from the exchange. A major challenge for these families is that while the premiums are subsidized, the co-pays and deductibles are not.

Walker's other large decision regarding Medicaid has been to refuse to accept 100% of federal funding for the expansion of Medicaid coverage. He has refused to accept a projected $4.38 billion from the federal government to provide health insurance for these Wisconsin families through 2020. Why? Because he says the federal government might not keep their word in the future and stop or reduce these payments. This is so transparently foolish. He accepts federal money for education and highways to the tune of hundreds of millions of dollars every year without worrying about the federal government reneging on those programs. This seems to only be a problem for Walker when it affects poor people.

And oh, by the way, Walker and his family have had excellent health insurance paid for by the taxpayers since 1993. I'm glad his family has that taxpayer-paid health insurance. But what about the families with less household income than his that he knocked off of Medicaid?

"UNINTIMIDATED" — REALLY?

Governor Walker wrote his book and titled it "Unintimidated." The image he portrays in this title and in his stump speeches is that he is not afraid to be "bold" and does not back down.

But someone who is unintimidated does not:

1. Keep his plan to destroy public unions a secret during his 2010 campaign.

2. Keep his "divide and conquer" plans a secret during his 2010 campaign. He said this in January 2011, and it turned out to not only affect public vs. private unions, but led to angrily dividing the whole state.

3. He only took on groups who never were his supporters and never would be after Act 10: public employee unions including teachers.

4. He personally, as Wisconsin's governor, has largely hidden from the general public for over four years (no such thing as public meetings, often called town hall meetings). He never walks in the front doors of the State Capitol on his way to his office, even now, over three years after the turmoil. All of his predecessors in the past sixty years have done this. He blames death threats, but I had those too. I recall three occasions when my office was directed to turn the threats over to the authorities, but the one I remember best was someone who said, "Cullen, you better keep looking over your shoulder because unlike Governor Walker you don't have security." That was true, but I did not hide from the people I was elected to represent. He does, which seems awfully intimidated. Walker usually appears at private businesses where the situation and the audience can be controlled.

5. I don't believe anyone can point out any significant issue or legislation where Walker has opposed the position of his major financial supporters. None. I believe that an "unintimidated" governor would do this once in awhile.

6. The same goes for interest groups whose endorsements and campaign help he needs. Tell me one time where he told them they were wrong.

Walker brags that he is "bold" and "unintimidated" everywhere he goes. "Bold" is defined as "readiness to take risk," "daring," "fearless." Pretty flattering so far, right? Further definition is not so flattering: "too free in behavior or manner," "taking liberties," "impudent," "shameless."

I believe these latter definitions better fit the "bold" bombs he dropped on Wisconsin citizens; especially "impudent." "Impudent" is defined as "immodest" and "shamelessly bold and disrespectful." I wonder if Walker would refer to himself as a "bold" synonym, "impudent?"

GOVERNOR WALKER'S MOST FAMOUS PROMISE

Governor Walker's most famous promise was when he said over and over during his 2010 campaign for governor that if he was elected governor his policies would lead to the creation of 250,000 new jobs during his first term. This promise helped him win the election. Most people are now aware that he fell 100,000 jobs short during those four years.

Where did this 250,000 number come from? From some economic analysis? From some consensus from a jobs think tank? From some other type of credible source? None of the above. Walker picked this number because 250,000 was the number of jobs created during the first term of Republican Governor Tommy Thompson in 1987-1991! They picked it out of the history books!

WHY DID WALKER WIN THE 2012 RECALL?

Governor Walker's answer to this question is that the election was a referendum on his policies and the direction he had taken Wisconsin. His primary success was Act 10, destroying the power of public employee unions, as well as other issues. Governor Walker won the recall election by just over 52% of the vote, almost exactly the same as the margin of victory in both the 2010 and 2014 gubernatorial elections.

I believe a variety of other factors beyond his record played a huge if not decisive role in his winning the recall election. Following, in no particular order, are several large advantages he enjoyed:

1. Wisconsin recall election law allows the target of a political recall election to raise unlimited sums of money from individuals and organizations from the time the recall petitions begin to circulate (November 2011) until the election date is actually set (April 2012). This does not apply to candidates who oppose him. This gave Walker a huge fundraising advantage. Political opponents were limited to the usual state limits for gubernatorial elections ($10,000 maximum from individuals and about $43,000 from PACs) while Walker could take $200,000, $500,000, $1 million or more from anyone or any organization... and that is exactly what he did. He crisscrossed America for five months gaining a huge money advantage in the election.

   No previous governor of Wisconsin has ever pursued across the country a small number of very rich people and sought unheard of large sums of money for his campaign while making sure these people would know where else they could contribute to sources that would benefit him. We are talking about millions and millions of dollars poured into Wisconsin politics by people from somewhere else. He raised raised over

$1.5 million from Wisconsin residents and over $3.7 million from out of state donors.

Walker had a window where literally any amount of money was legal to raise, and many big donors took the opportunity to crawl in through that window (Appendix E).

2. Democratic candidates for governor in Wisconsin have historically enjoyed labor support, that is no secret, but they always ran as the "Democratic" candidate for governor. A combination of factors led the Democratic candidate, Milwaukee Mayor Tom Barrett, to look like the "public employee" candidate for governor... not a winning image when 90% of the voters are NOT public employees. I place no blame for this on Mayor Barrett, a dedicated public servant. The blame lies rather on the dominance of Act 10 as an issue (and Walker's non-stop efforts to make it the issue), the very public role that the public employee union leaders played in trying to dictate to the Democratic candidate, and the union-sponsored ads that continued to show footage from 2011 of the demonstrating crowds (they should have known they already had the voters who would appreciate those scenes). Hence, Barrett only won counties with large urban pockets, strong pro-labor histories, and large Democratic voting populations—and Walker won all the other counties.

3. The citizens of Wisconsin clearly felt "recall fatigue" between August 2011 and June of 2012. There were 11 state Senate recall elections. These recalls spent historically unheard of amounts of money, much of it on negative ads. Even though those districts amount to only about 30% of the state, the ads were aired in every television market in the state. For several months, 100% of Wisconsin citizens who watched TV saw this avalanche of negative ads. These recall elections spent from the low millions to $10 million in one Milwaukee area Senate

district. And these elections occurred over short periods of time, which added to a high number of ads per day compared to regular elections. By contrast, ordinary state Senate campaigns in Wisconsin seldom reached $500,000. So after millions of dollars in these negative ads for five months, the "big one" was now about to begin with tens of millions of dollars in more negative ads during the first six months of 2012. Over the election, Walker outspent Barrett by more than 2 1/2 to 1. Walker and groups supporting him spent $58.7 million and Barrett and groups supporting him spent $22 million.

Most people will tell you they hate negative ads, but of course the only reason they are used is because they work with the slice of the electorate they are aimed at.

How tired do you think voters were of recall elections that were the sole cause of all this negativity they had absorbed almost uninterrupted for one year (all during a time in which there were no regularly scheduled state elections). And which party was seen by many as the cause of all of this? The Democrats (or in this season, the "public employee union party"). The election "campaign" was really limited to Act 10 and the negative personal attacks. In a negative TV ad war, the most money usually wins.

4. The public opposes recalls in general—at least recalls for this purpose (voting records and positions on issues rather than criminal charges or scandal, etc.). Exit polls on Election Day confirmed this. Seventy percent of voters said they opposed recall elections in general or for policy reasons. With Walker getting 52%, this means that even if all of Walkers voters opposed the recall, even 18% of those who voted for Barrett also opposed this recall.

5. Possible winning issues for a Democratic candidate largely never got broad public attention. Enough attention was not

brought to a law Walker signed that reduced legal rights and access to important records for nursing home residents, the shamefully blatant reapportionment/gerrymandering of the state Legislature in 2011, and a Republican bill that decimated environmental protection regarding the negative impacts of mining in Wisconsin.

The governor's recall election plus the 11 state Senate recall elections, all held between the summer of 2011 and June of 2012, cost taxpayers $14 million. This did not please many "recall-weary" voters either.

Walker had all of these advantages, and still only received 52% of the vote. That, I believe, is the real conclusion to be drawn from this election.

RECALL ELECTIONS... GOOD OR BAD?

Wisconsin recall election laws date back to the Progressive Movement which began in the early 1900s. They are very open-ended and, put simply, allow for recall votes after gathering a defined number of signatures. These signatures can force a recall election of any elected official in the state if they have served at least one year of their term in office. The reasons for the recall can be almost anything. The purpose at the beginning was so the people could retain their power over the elected officials not only at election time, but also during the official's term.

There are those who support our law the way it is. Others say officeholders should face a recall election only if they've engaged in corruption or committed serious personal indiscretions. Still others say let a felony conviction remove them (which it would) or throw them out at the next election.

The recall elections faced by both Republican and Democratic state senators and the governor in Wisconsin in 2011 and 2012 were not due to any personal indiscretion, but rather due to strong disagreement with the office-holders' positions and votes on issues.

My view of this starts with the extremely common notion that people want their elected officials to "go to Madison, forget about all the darn politics, and just vote for what you believe is right and best for Wisconsin." Then how do you recall someone who presumably went to Madison and did just that even if you strongly disagree with how they voted?

I agree with this "just do what is right" view, and it caused me real angst during the recall elections. I decided to help the Democrats who were facing recalls in the state Senate (especially Senator Jim Holperin and Senator Bob Wirch) and to do nothing to help the recalls of Republican state senators. I do not think this helped my popularity with some members of my caucus.

I did help Tom Barrett in the gubernatorial recall. I justified this in my own mind because I had just watched Governor Walker deliberately divide Wisconsin in an angry way that I had never experienced, and he did it without signaling his intention until after the election. Robert La Follette, when he pioneered the recall in Wisconsin, said it should be used when an elected official engages in "misrepresentation or betrayal." And that is what Scott Walker did, in my opinion.

I do believe (and polls bear this out) that by the end of all the state Senate and gubernatorial recalls there was real "recall fatigue" in Wisconsin. I suspect there will not be policy-related recalls for another decade or much longer... until another era and another set of circumstances are in play.

12 GOVERNORS WHO WERE "UNITERS" AND WALKER THE "DIVIDER"

Elected officials in partisan offices are classified as Republicans or Democrats (and an occasional independent). Those party labels generally tell voters a lot about the official's views on issues.

But I believe that there are two other words that categorize elected officials—"uniters" and "dividers."

I have known personally the record of the ten governors who immediately preceded Governor Walker. I definitely believe they were all "uniters." They wanted to unite our state. They did not govern in a way that played groups of people against each other or organizations of people against each other as a means to give themselves some political gain. I believe that Governor Walker's approach to being governor, his actions and words, make him a clear divider of Wisconsin, and he takes this approach in order to suit his own political career.

Governor Walker's "divide and conquer" and "always have an enemy" strategy reminds me of a story about two farmers who lived next to each other. One had a cow which provided wonderful milk for his family, but the other farmer had no cow and resented that his neighbor did. So his solution was to go over and shoot the cow. Now they were both equal... neither one of them had a cow. A lot of people in Wisconsin today do not have a cow.

Governor Walker has used terms such as "divide and conquer" as a political strategy. He has said that he would be "dropping the bomb" when describing the plan to decimate public employee unions when the people had no idea it was coming. Dropping a "bomb" on Wisconsin that would clearly be enormously divisive just five days after the Packers won the Super Bowl!

I have had a front row seat as a state senator to Walker's style of leadership. He always seems to need an enemy, not just an opponent. He needs some group to "conquer" to enhance, in his view, the macho "I don't negotiate" image he is trying to sell across the nation. He apparently does not believe that his job is to get groups of people together to work out their differences. He shows no appreciation of the belief that problems can be addressed and solved without destroying individuals or groups.

The governor singled out public employees in 2011 as the problem. He played on non-public employees' feelings about how they did not have the health insurance, pensions, and "summers off" of public school teachers. Never mind that teachers spend more waking hours with our children than even the best of parents. What parent is able to spend six hours a day working with, playing with, teaching their child? That would mean 4pm to 10pm nonstop five days a week. And yes, those people who help our children learn were part of the middle class. So the farmer and Governor Walker had the same solution. The farmer shot the cow so no one had milk. Governor Walker has decimated public school teachers. He reduced their take home pay by several thousand dollars, drastically limited their chances to get pay raises (no more than the Consumer Price Index, which was 1.46% in 2014), and he eliminated their ability to collectively bargain anything else such as working conditions, pensions, and health insurance.

Now, did any of this raise anyone else into the middle class? The answer is no. The Governor used the same strategy as the farmer, and the results are the same... no milk for anyone in the low and middle classes. This governor may be remembered as the governor who shot a cow and dropped a bomb—more than one, actually.

CHAPTER 10
More Bombs

Act 10 was not the only unannounced "bomb" that Walker dropped on the citizens of Wisconsin. It has just received the most attention. Other "bombs" have been dropped, and I shall mention a few.

THE DESTROYING THE UW MERGER "BOMB"

Governor Walker, in the spring of 2011 and in the middle of the Act 10 events, proposed in the state budget to separate the UW-Madison campus from the rest of the University System. He wanted to create a separate authority to oversee Madison and appoint regents from select categories of Wisconsin citizens and not require state Senate confirmation.

A little history: All of the state university campuses were merged into one system with the flagship Madison campus in 1971. The campuses became known as "UW-Madison," "UW-Green Bay," "UW-Oshkosh," etc., and all would be governed by one board of regents rather than two. Opposition at the time centered on the belief that the worldwide status of the Madison campus (the largest by far and most prestigious) as a top level teaching institution and research center would be diminished if all campuses shared "equal" names. The name would switch from "The University of Wisconsin" to "UW-Madison" just like the other university campuses.

Since the change forty years ago, the system merger has been widely supported and accepted. Time has proved that "UW-Madison" has lost none of its prestige. Research dollars still pour in, and, if anything, the importance and quality of a degree from that institution has been enhanced since the change. The success of Badger athletics has helped, too. At the same time, the other institutions have benefited from having "UW" in front of their names and from having one strong board of regents looking out for all institutions rather than two boards of regents pursuing their own agendas with the Legislature and governor.

Now fast forward to 2011. Walker and then-Chancellor of UW Madison Biddy Martin announced that the budget would de-merge the system and create an "authority" to oversee the Madison campus. It amounted to a "quasi-privatization" of the Madison campus. This was a huge change with many unknown ramifications. So again, with no warning, no broad taxpayer, student, or faculty input, no study committee or Blue Ribbon Commission to review, investigate, and make recommendations about the implementation of the change and the impact it might have on all the campuses (funding, tuition, etc.), Walker drops this headline-grabbing "bomb." This is leadership?

I could say much more about this incident, but the good news is that the idea was rejected.

THE "ATTACK ACADEMIC FREEDOM" BOMB

During March of 2011 in the middle of the Act 10 turmoil and at the same time Walker proposed splitting UW Madison away from the system, another attack on the university was launched. The Walker Administration announced that emails of faculty were open and could be searched. They specifically asked for the emails of Professor William Cronon, one of the most distinguished history professors at Madison.

Cronon had written an op-ed in the *New York Times* on March 21, 2011 very critical of Governor Walker and his radical departure from Wisconsin's political culture. The request for faculty emails was a direct attack on academic freedom as enshrined in the statutes and policies of the regents. The legal counsel for UW Madison fought back and stated "faculty members must be afforded privacy in these exchanges in order to pursue knowledge... without fear of reprisal for controversial findings and without the premature disclosure of those ideas." Chancellor Martin stood firm and the regents promptly added the reaffirmation of academic freedom to the agenda of their next meeting on April 11.

At the request of Regent Loftus, a history of regent actions on establishing and defending academic freedom was written, and Professor Cronon was invited to address the board. The board reaffirmed once again the special role of academic freedom starting with the regent statement in 1894 in defense of a faculty member under attack then that guides the UW to this day: "Whatever be the limitations which trammel inquiry elsewhere, we believe that the great state University of Wisconsin should ever encourage that continual and fearless sifting and winnowing by which alone the truth can be found."

I urge you to take a moment to read Professor Cronon's column (Appendix F). He so concisely points out the major changes in the direction Walker is moving Wisconsin compared to the previous over 100 years. I have only been able to go back 65 years to make some of the same points, although I can certainly not match his eloquence.

I have also included in the a compilation of the "History of Academic Freedom in the UW System (Appendix G)." I thank Tom Loftus for gathering this information.

TENURE AND SHARED GOVERNANCE

The Walker administration backed off and the emails were not released. However the issue did not die. In the budget bill of 2015-17 Governor Walker proposed that tenure protection and the shared governance role of faculty, the pillars of academic freedom, be removed from state law. That passed. Now there is only regent policy, something much easier to tinker with than trying to change something that is the law of the state.

These two proposals will send shock waves across America and the world regarding how professors will look at Wisconsin as a place to stay teaching or a place to come to teach, and will cost Wisconsin untold hundreds of millions of research dollars and untold numbers of top teaching and research faculty.

THE "WISCONSIN IDEA" "BOMB"

Another huge unannounced "bomb" was the language change proposal in his 2015-2017 budget to the "Wisconsin Idea" that has been part of the UW Mission Statement for a hundred years (Appendix H).

I urge you to read what was and (thank goodness) still is the Mission Statement and look at the changes. Are you as astounded as I and so many other citizens of Wisconsin were? There was such a statewide uproar that Walker backed off on these changes and at first said they were simply "drafting errors." Subsequent information made clear that these were not drafting errors. Walker has refused to release documents and emails concerning how these changes were developed. He is being sued to force him to release those documents.

What jumps out in particular are the following:

- He no longer wants the "purpose of the system" to be the "search for the truth." Does this mean he wants the mission to be to the search for "untruths?"... or the search for what?... or stop searching?

- He wants to eliminate the "Wisconsin Idea"... the more than a century old view that the boundaries of the university are the boundaries of Wisconsin... that our universities should seek input and wisdom from all Wisconsin citizens and share the knowledge gained on the campuses with the people of Wisconsin.

- He no longer wants the universities to "serve and stimulate society."

- He no longer wants part of the mission statement to be to "improve the human condition."

- Adding "to meet the state's workforce needs" seems to be an effort to add more technical colleges.

You can find more in these changes to ponder. I will acknowledge that these proposed changes were "bold." They were boldly out of touch with the long-held values of the great majority of people in Wisconsin who had elected him to lead this state forward.

Governor Walker's bomb that was dropped on the "Wisconsin Idea" in early 2013 was addressed by Tom Loftus, a former Assembly Speaker, Ambassador to Norway, and former member of the UW Board of Regents in an eloquent response to the Governor's latest "bomb." I sincerely wonder if Governor Walker had any knowledge of the historical context that Loftus explains in a piece he wrote for the *Cap Times*:

"Chapter 36 of the statutes, where the Wisconsin Idea is defined, is a poem of faith in mankind. Indeed, it was his Christian faith and embrace of the advances that scientific discovery could bring to man that inspired John Bascom to give new meaning to the purpose of a college education.

Bascom was a sociologist and a theologian. He became the fifth president of the University of Wisconsin in 1874. He saw Darwin's new theory of evolution as proof of God's powers at work. He was a champion of women's rights and the dignity of labor. His idea was that the new university would educate more and more students to improve American democracy and expect from them service to society throughout their lives. This became the Wisconsin Idea. Robert M. La Follette credited Bascom as the Wisconsin Idea's true founder.

Bascom was an evangelist and believed scientific discovery, specifically evolution, was linked to the progress toward the kingdom of heaven on earth. He went on to write the book 'Evolution and Religion' in an attempt to explain it all. J. David Hoeveler Jr.'s "The University and the Social Gospel: The Intellectual Origins of the Wisconsin Idea" in the Wisconsin Magazine of History from summer 1976 (sidebar) describes Bascom's Christian philosophy and the connection to the Wisconsin Idea."

THE NO PARDON "BOMB"

Governor Walker announced early in his first term that he would grant no pardons to any person in Wisconsin regardless of the circumstances... and he has kept his word. Another "bomb" that reversed the action of at least his 12 most immediate predecessors. He never announced this during his 2010 campaign. Pardons are for people who served their time and are living crime-free in our communities with the rest of us. They have paid their debt to society for their crime. A pardon allows them to vote and is a necessity to get certain jobs. It also allows them to hunt.

Previous to Walker, Wisconsin governors have granted pardons based on investigation of the merits of the pardon request and a staff recommendation. Martin Schreiber issued 12 pardons, Lee Dreyfus issued 127 pardons, Tony Earl issued 224 pardons, Tommy Thompson issued 225 pardons, Scott McCallum issued 11 pardons, and Jim Doyle issued 260 pardons. No governor in recent memory (60 years) has announced at the beginning of his term that he will pardon no one. No facts in individual cases will matter, no recommendations from community leaders will matter, no Wisconsin citizen who has paid their debt to society no matter how positively and constructively they are leading their lives can ever be pardoned by this governor. Walker will not consider any facts. This "tough" political position is only important to his career.

The most classic example of Walker being "bold" and "unintimidated" on this pardon issue involved a military veteran who had served in Iraq. He served time for his crime and now wanted to be a police officer in a Wisconsin community. The community wanted to hire him, but they couldn't until Walker granted the veteran a pardon. Walker said no pardon, and the community didn't get the police officer they wanted. Being stubbornly consistent is not the same as being fair and smart.

This was another "bomb" that he is so proud of. No warning to the people of Wisconsin that he would never pardon anyone. No study committee to look at the results of previous governor's pardons. No study committee to try to determine whether pardons are good for society in general.

IT NEVER ENDS: WALKER AND REPUBLICANS WANT TO DESTROY THE GOVERNMENT ACCOUNTABILITY BOARD

Since 2007, our state's elections and any violation of election laws and campaign financing has been overseen by the Government Accountability Board (GAB). The Legislature created the GAB with the state Senate voting 33-0 and the state Assembly voting 97-2. All Republicans in both houses voted for it, including 24 who are still in the Legislature.

The GAB is overseen by a board of 6 retired judges appointed by the governor and confirmed by the state Senate. It replaced two boards: the State Elections Board and the State Ethics Board. Both of these boards were controlled by partisan appointees and had a poor record of aggressively investigating alleged wrongdoing, including the so-called caucus scandal that began in 2002. That investigation eventually led to the resignation and conviction (including jail time) of the Democratic Senate Majority Leader. And the former Republican Speaker was banned from ever seeking public office again.

The GAB has been praised nationwide as the best non-partisan structured board in the country. It is indeed a model for the nation. Regarding the election oversight in the various state's, Ohio State University law professor, Daniel P. Tokaji, stated, "The best American model is Wisconsin Government Accountability Board, which consists of retired judges selected in a way that is designed to promote impartiality."

Professor Tokaji followed up with a paper in 2013 titled, "America's Top Model: The Wisconsin Government Accountability Board." The paper points out that the United States is an outlier compared to most democratic countries as we have partisan people overseeing elections, and those countries "have an independent election authority that enjoys some insulation from partisan politics in running elections."

Professor Tokaji goes on to say, "There is one conspicuous exception to the partisan character of election administration at the state level: Wisconsin Government Accountability Board. The GAB oversees election administration, as well as enforcement of campaign finance, ethics, and lobbying laws. Its members are former judges chosen in a manner designed to ensure that they will not favor either major political party. This makes the GAB unique."

So why in the world does Walker want to replace it with something else that almost certainly will return partisan control over election, campaign financing, and ethics laws?

The fairly clear answer, as of the writing of this book, is that with their enjoyment of power they don't like some of the decisions made by the GAB (even though all 6 retired judges on the Board were appointed or reappointed by Governor Walker).

Looks like they are drunk with power to me. They apparently see the destruction of the GAB as the third piece of a trifecta of abuse of Wisconsin's long-held expectation of fair elections. The other two pieces they have already accomplished: rigging legislative elections with their 2011 gerrymandering, and their voter suppression legislation sold as "voter ID."

Walker and the Republicans have the legislature locked in until 2020. They have their majority on the Supreme Court, but they can't make the GAB make all their decisions the way they want. So their obvious power-play answer is to destroy the GAB!

The decision on this issue may be made by the time this book is published.

The "trifecta" attack on our voting, elections, ethics laws, and campaign spending should deeply concern the people of Wisconsin.

Lord Acton was right, "Power corrupts, and absolute power corrupts absolutely."

THE BRAZEN ATTACK ON WISCONSIN'S OPEN RECORDS LAW

Wisconsin has a proud tradition of strong open records laws that apply to public officials. The laws have a simple goal: Force our public officials to do their business in public. This includes discussion of public policy, motions that they review and order prepared, analyses they look at, briefings, opinions, the role of lobbyists in the development of legislation, etc.

The Legislature's most powerful committee, the Joint Finance Committee, snuck language into the state budget bill on July 2, 2015 (ironically just before the 4th of July weekend when citizens are busy celebrating freedom and democracy and not likely to be watching state government). In alignment with their past actions of sneaking policy into the budget bill at the last minute, the Republican lawmakers passed it late in the evening, just two hours after it was first unveiled.

This language would have shielded most, if not all, legislative action and decisions on public matters from the citizens of Wisconsin.

The frosting on this disgusting cake is that they made the changes retroactive to the day before (July 1) so that the Joint Finance Committee and the authors of the language could shield themselves from public scrutiny. Republican lawmakers refused to say who authored this new legislative language, which is very telling if you ask me. Either they think most of the public can't understand what's best for them, or they are not proud of their actions and they know most of their constituents would not approve.

The language would have slowed or ended inquiries into several currently ongoing, embarrassing, controversies, including Walker's role in destroying the "Wisconsin Idea" and the "search for truth" language in the mission statement of the University of Wisconsin.

Attorney General Brad Schimel, a Republican, said, "Transparency is the cornerstone of democracy. The provisions in the Budget Bill limiting access to public records moves Wisconsin in the wrong direction."

The good news is that, 4th of July weekend notwithstanding, citizens and editorial boards across the state erupted in opposition. The twelve Republican members of the committee who all voted for this assault on our open records law had to be in 4th of July parades back home in their districts. By the end of the day on July 4th, Walker and the Republican leaders refused to acknowledge any leadership or responsibility for the language. The language apparently arrived from the clouds sent by aliens. However they gave in and announced that this language would be taken out of the budget. Subsequent documents reveal the clear role of Assembly Speaker Robin Vos and Walker's office in writing the provision. If you think his office would be involved with this major effort without the clear knowledge and approval of the governor, I have some of that proverbial waterfront property in Arizona to sell you!

And it doesn't end there. Add to this the rigging of elections through gerrymandering, voter suppression, plans to destroy the GAB, plans to destroy the University Mission Statement, attempts to gut the Legislative Audit Bureau, diminishing the role of the Wisconsin Center for Investigative Journalism, and their willingness to raise unlimited (millions) of campaign dollars from out of state sources. So many of the pillars of a clean, open government in Wisconsin are either damaged, destroyed, or in the process of facing one or the other. Sad, sad, sad.

THE LATEST BOMB: DISMANTLING THE CIVIL SERVICE SYSTEM

Within days of dropping his presidential campaign, Walker publicly endorsed a legislative proposal to eliminate the 100-year-old civil service system in Wisconsin.

It is worth noting that in 2011 when he was pushing through the "Act 10" legislation he tried to reassure state employees that they would still have the protections of our civil service law after Act 10 took away most of their collective bargaining rights.

At that time Walker said the civil service system is "the protection that workers have that's most important in the state of Wisconsin... it was there long before collective bargaining, it'll be there long after." So now we know that Walker's definition of "long after" is four years!

We have a civil service system because the Progressives pushed it through to stop unqualified political appointees from getting state jobs which led to corruption and incompetent public servants.

Wisconsin was the first state to adopt a civil service system.

Changes may be needed, but shouldn't we study the need for changes through a governor-appointed commission with broad representation of Wisconsin citizens, and then await their recommendations before taking legislative action? This seems so logical to me, but clearly not to this governor.

Again, we are experiencing "imposed" government and not the "participatory" government of his 12 predecessors.

I must mention again that he pushes a major change in Wisconsin without any public discussion, no study committee to examine the current status of our civil service system and the rationale for these wholesale changes. This makes me concerned that he has learned nothing from his low 37% approval rating in Wisconsin or that the positions he took in his presidential race do not reflect the view of the majority of Wisconsin citizens.

WHY NO COLLEGE DEGREE FOR WALKER?

Most people know that Governor Walker, unlike all of his twelve predecessors, does not have a college degree. Let me be very clear: Not having a college degree does not mean a person isn't bright, talented, eligible for or capable of doing extremely important jobs, including public office.

My question is: why has he never felt it important to finish his college courses to earn his degree? He completed at least three years at Marquette University. He has said publicly that he moved and had children and never got back to it.

How difficult would it have been for him to complete his degree? I think this is a fair question. The short answer is it would have been very doable for him to complete his degree, still do his public job and take care of his family responsibilities. For example, his Marquette grades would transfer to the UW system. He was in the Wisconsin Legislature for 8 or 10 years and could easily have finished his degree in Madison. The job of a Wisconsin legislator who is not in leadership (and he was not) is not a full-time job. Many have earned a degree while serving in the Legislature. For example: Becky Young, Marty Schreiber, Mary Lou Munts, Dave Travis, John Norquist, Tim Carpenter, Mary K. Wagner, Fred Kessler, and the list goes on.

The question to ask is why was it not important to him? The answer to that question may tell us more about his view of the UW system, his attempt to change the UW mission statement, his willingness to drop one of his "bombs" without public input by proposing to split UW-Madison away from the rest of the UW system, and his lack of support for UW institutions like tenure and shared governance.

My point is that Walker not having a degree is not a disqualifier to be governor of Wisconsin. My point is two-fold: one, what is it in his world view that he feels a college degree is not an achievement worth accomplishing when it has been so easily in his grasp? And two, has this view led to not understanding or wanting to learn to understand the importance of the structure of our higher education system in Wisconsin?

By comparison, of Walker's twelve predecessors, all had college degrees, and eleven earned either an undergraduate degree or law degree from a UW institution. Governor Earl grew up in Michigan and earned his degree at Michigan State.

CHAPTER 11

Republican Gerrymandering and Voter Suppression in Wisconsin

M y dismay at the state's direction during the Walker administration is not limited to the governor. Rigging voting districts and suppressing the vote came out of the Legislature.

HANDLING OR ABUSING POWER

I have observed and I have had political power. My conclusion is that it is difficult to handle, and most can't help but abuse it in a small or large way. Power is intoxicating: you have control over a person or a situation and you feel no need to compromise or listen to another point of view.

In the statehouse, many legislators with a lot of power have not had much experience handling it. This is a bad combination.

There is no better example of abuse of legislative and gubernatorial power that I know of than gerrymandering the legislative districts in order to greatly favor your party. They do it for the oldest reason of all... because they can.

The Republican-controlled Legislature, with Governor Walker's support, drew partisan legislative maps that likely guarantee they will retain majority control of both houses of the Legislature until the next census in 2020 requires a new redrawing of the map.

This abuse of power is occurring not just in Wisconsin, but across the nation, and it is not an issue where one party is guiltier than the other. If either party has control of the governorship and both houses of the Legislature, they find it irresistible to draw district lines that strongly favor them. They usually justify this by saying the voters put them in the majority in the previous election. That is total baloney. Just think about it: Of all the reasons that you voted for a Republican or Democratic candidate in the last election, was a major one "I want the (fill in party name) to win so they can draw legislative maps that allow legislators to pick their voters, rather than the other way around?" Voters pick their candidates based on the economy, social issues, candidates they know, performance of the incumbent, their position on the most important issue to them, the best campaign, etc.

There has been important research analyzing the extent of gerrymandering after the 2010 census in all the states where one party had total control of state government. This research has determined the two most gerrymandered Republican-controlled states are Wisconsin and Michigan. The two most gerrymandered Democrat-controlled states are Massachusetts and Rhode Island. Again, neither party has the high ground on this issue. It is simply about having the power and not being able to resist abusing it.

The Republican gerrymandering of the Wisconsin legislature districts was particularly insulting to our citizens because the maps were drawn in secret, outside the Capitol, in private law offices, and paid for with $2 million in taxpayer money.

Democrats never saw the maps before their disclosure in the legislation required for them to become law, but the Republicans did see them before that. The Republican legislators were shown their own new district, only after they signed a sworn statement that they would not share what they saw with the public.

WHAT IS GERRYMANDERING?

Reapportionment, the redrawing of the district lines for state legislative seats and the United States Congress, is passed as a law every ten years by state Legislatures. The fundamental goal is to assure that each district has as near as possible the same number of people to meet the one-person, one-vote goal. This is to adjust for population changes over the previous ten years. This requirement goes back to the 1962 United States Supreme Court decision in Baker vs. Carr.

Gerrymandering is named after Massachusetts Governor Elbridge Gerry, who is first credited with signing a highly partisan district map in the early 1800s. The simple explanation of how this is done is to stack most of the voters who vote for the party that is not in power in the fewest number of districts, leaving a majority of the districts tilted to the party in power. For example, you can create a small number of districts that favor the minority party- 60%/40%, 70%/30%, or even higher, and then you are able to create a majority of districts that are at least 55% for the majority party. Absent a US Supreme Court decision which has not occurred yet, these district lines remain in place for ten years.

The previous 50 years of redistricting in Wisconsin is informative in understanding citizen reaction (or lack thereof) to the 2011 Republican gerrymandering. In each of the years after the census (1961, 1971, 1981, 1991, 2001), neither party had complete control of state government. This led to a bipartisan agreement in 1971, which eliminated the possibility of one party gaining a significant advantage, and the other four times the courts (a federal judge) drew the maps and did no significant favors to either political party.

So coming into 2011, the people of Wisconsin had never known this to be a problem and, to the extent they thought much about it, probably figured it was something "those politicians do." Some just said, "Well if the Democrats had been in charge, they would have done the same thing." They are right about this, but that is not the point. The point is you can't trust either party. This is not a partisan issue. The point is to change to an "Iowa" system so neither party can ever gerrymander Wisconsin again.

IOWA'S SOLUTION

Iowa has been using an alternative method of redistricting since 1980 that does not put map-drawing in the hands of legislators. Our constitutions say that the reapportionment map must be passed by the legislature. It does not say that the Legislature must draw the map.

Iowa's method is to have the same nonpartisan state agency that drafts all of the rest of their bills also draft the reapportionment bill. This map must not consider political concerns nor consider the residence of the incumbent. The map is then taken around the state for public hearings to give the public (and incumbents) the information and get their input. Then the map becomes a bill for the Legislature to consider. This process keeps in place the requirement that the Legislature must vote for the map. But the obvious big difference is that the legislature votes for the map but they don't get to draw it. The Legislature can vote the map down but they cannot amend it. The process then repeats itself. The state employee can alter the map based on input from the public hearings or send it back again to the Legislature unchanged. Since 1980, the Iowa Legislature has always approved the map either the first or second time.

My conversations with the person who draws the map and with an Iowa legislator informed me that the Iowa system of reapportionment is extremely popular with the public and neither party has made any serious effort to change it.

I believe the people of Wisconsin would love it, too. So why hasn't the Legislature adopted it? Because the current gerrymandered maps give the majority the safe seats they have now. They are so opposed to any change they would not even hold a public hearing on a bill that Senator Schultz and I introduced that would put the Iowa plan in place in Wisconsin for the reapportionment that will occur after the 2020 census.

I make the point later that gerrymandering allows safe seat legislators to ignore editorial opinion. They did just that on this issue as a large number of major newspapers in Wisconsin editorialized frequently on this issue, including imploring that they at least hold a public hearing. They totally ignored it all.

Please compare the gerrymandered maps of Wisconsin and Illinois' Legislative Districts with the maps of Iowa's Legislative Districts not drawn by the politicians (Appendix I). Please guess the ones that were not drawn by the politicians. I know this is an unannounced pop quiz but I'm guessing you picked the Iowa map. You get an A+.

These maps also make my point that gerrymandering is not a partisan problem. The Illinois gerrymander was drawn by the Democrats, the Wisconsin gerrymander was drawn by the Republicans, and the Iowa map was drawn by a nonpartisan state employee.

I learned a shorthand way to look at the maps and instantly tell who drew them. Look for right angles. Yes, more right angles show that counties have been kept intact and a respect for a "community of interest" has been retained. They also show that the political leanings of communities are not considered.

Gerrymandering of state Legislatures is all about partisan advantage. Congressional reapportionment, at least in Wisconsin, is about protecting incumbents regardless of party. Over the past forty years (at least) the senior Democrat and senior Republican congressmen from Wisconsin get together in Washington and draw the map. They then come to Madison to lobby the legislators of their respective parties to pass legislation that is identical to their map.

So what has been significant about the maps they have drawn? Put simply, the significance is they draw maps that make them all safe. Some members are already safe due to the traditional voting pattern of their areas of the state: i.e., Milwaukee suburbs are Republican and urban Milwaukee is Democratic.

The maps the Congressional leaders from Wisconsin drew in 2001 blatantly make my point. Two bright young representatives, one from each party, were elected in 1998: Democrat Tammy Baldwin from the 2nd district and Republican Paul Ryan from the 1st district. They were both re-elected in 2000, but Baldwin won by less than 52%, not a safe enough margin, so what did their leaders agree to do? There were some other modest changes, but there was one huge change that made both of them far safer for reelection: Ryan represented the heavily Democratic City of Beloit in Rock County and Baldwin represented several rural counties outside of Democratic Madison where she did not do well. The deal was simple. Replace the Republican rural areas in Baldwin's district with Democratic Beloit, and get Ryan out of Beloit and replace it with heavily Republican southern Waukesha county. Baldwin never again faced a close race for reelection. Republicans were preparing for a year when Ryan might be seeking a higher office.

Most people familiar with this process, including me, will be absolutely shocked if any Wisconsin congressperson wins with less than 56% in 2016.

WHAT IS THE HARM IN GERRYMANDERING?

Wisconsin Republicans had total control in 2011 and did, by any rational interpretation, gerrymander the Wisconsin Senate and Assembly. No one can, with a straight face, deny that this occurred. The following 2014 voting results tell the story in numbers:

- Governor Walker is re-elected with 52% of the vote. This is certainly no landslide, and we see how politically divided Wisconsin is. Now one could expect that the legislative results would likely show a slight majority for the Republicans.

- Not so fast... enter gerrymandering: The Republican candidates won 63 seats in the Assembly to just 36 for the Democrats. I call this a "gerrymander landslide."

- The final frosting on the cake is that statewide 200,000 more votes were cast for the Democratic candidates than for the Republican candidates in the Assembly races, yet the Republicans won nearly two-thirds of the seats. Case closed (in my mind).

Gerrymandering results in a huge majority of members of the Legislature being a lock to win the election in November either with weak or no opposition. It is important to point out several consequences of Wisconsin's 2011 Republican gerrymandering that are not in the public interest. With a large majority of State Assembly and State Senate seats drawn to favor one party or the other, the general election in November becomes much less important, and the August primary becomes the "real" election. That winner is a huge favorite (mostly prohibitive favorite) to win the November election. So people's votes in November (which, judging by voter turnout, most people treat as the most important election) are largely irrelevant. Votes in November matter in statewide governor and US Senate races but not state legislative races in most districts across Wisconsin. The only election that they need to worry about is the August primary. Ironically, the result is that the more secure you are as a candidate in November, the more vulnerable you can become in August. A "safe district" is so heavily Republican or Democrat that you must vote in a way that pleases your base, or risk a primary opponent in August. So another large reason not to work with the other party is that you face the risk of being labeled a moderate and attracting a primary opponent.

Another result of gerrymandering is that legislative leaders of both parties and the governor in his party gain even more power (than described in early chapters). These leaders have major control over large donors and independent expenditure groups. The message to the members is clear... "vote the way we tell you 100% of the time and we will not find and fund a primary opponent and will get you whatever money you need to win." We had exhibit A in Wisconsin of this strategy. My good friend, Republican State Senator Dale Schultz, had opposed Walker and his party on Act 10 and on a controversial mining bill during the 2011/2012 session. Following the 2012 election, the Republicans controlled the state senate 18 to 15 and therefore did not need Schultz's vote to get the 17-majority votes needed to win on issues. But they still found a primary opponent for Schultz 21 months before the 2014 election and were clearly going to make sure that opponent had all the necessary funding. This was obviously intended as an in your face message to any Republican in the Legislature: Vote with us 100% of the time or we'll "Dale Schultz you." Dale Schultz is a lifelong Republican with a career-long, solid Republican voting record. But 98% is not good enough for those in power in Madison now.

Not often discussed is the impact safe, gerrymandered seats have on the way state legislators in those safe seats do their jobs. 1. The vast majority of legislators in safe seats from both parties do not have to care about newspaper editorial opinions that disagree with their views. 2. They do not need to worry about general public opinion. 3. They do not have to meet with groups that might not agree with them. 4. They do not have to issue press releases on their views. 5. It is completely optional for them to attend summer parades, festivals, and other types of events where there would be people with a wide range of political views including those who disagree with them and where they would have to listen to them. They have their primary voters on email lists and other mechanisms to frequently communicate the views those folks (on left for Democrats and right for Republicans) want to hear.

All of the above describe the sad state of communication between elected officials and the people they are sworn to represent in a gerrymandered state Legislature. At the end of the day this system allows the elected officials to pick their voters rather than the other way around. But there are even more bad consequences for democracy.

Another frequent consequence of a huge majority of the legislators in the majority party having safe districts means that taking votes that would be in the best interests of the state or nation aren't made, because it could irritate their base. A legislator willing to irritate their base in a safe district has great political courage, as even one vote like that could lead to a primary challenger and losing that election. I deeply wish getting reelected wasn't such a high priority for so many.

There is one other result from gerrymandering that ought to irritate every citizen. Gerrymandering allows the majority party to guarantee themselves jobs for ten years by drawing district lines that make it almost impossible to lose their reelection. This also guarantees the jobs of the minority party legislators who are also given safe districts. In what other jobs in America can the workers, by their own action, guarantee themselves their jobs for the next ten years? Does it work that way in your workplace?

Attempts to stop gerrymandering in Wisconsin and other states by trying to get the Legislature and governor to accept and embrace reform clearly have not worked. Many people, including myself, have concluded that only the United States Supreme Court can stop gerrymandering. Federal lawsuits have been filed in Wisconsin. I hope this effort succeeds for the sake of democracy in Wisconsin and America.

I have tried to emphasize in this chapter that we need to stop "gerrymandering" period, because neither party can be trusted not to abuse the reapportionment process if they have total control. I therefore need to tell you that after the 1982 election had been conducted using state legislative maps drawn by a federal judge, the Democrats, including me, had complete control of state government. The Democrats in the Assembly changed the map in the state budget bill.

Democratic Governor Tony Earl vetoed these changes, saying they should not be in the budget, so a separate bill was subsequently passed and signed by the Governor.

The bill made some changes to the federal-court-drawn map, which had no particular partisan advantage. A big one was the court had split the cities of Oshkosh, Janesville, and Beloit in two. All these cities were very unhappy and two were in my state Senate district. There was no advantage to Democrats to put the cities back into one assembly seat. The bill did not do anything viciously partisan.

No matter how little gerrymandering occurred in this bill, it is something that (looking back after 32 more years of "life experience") I wish I would have opposed. But I did not.

I was the Senate Majority Leader, and I voted for it. I proposed no changes, and I certainly believed in reuniting Janesville and Beloit in my district. It's worth pointing out that with Beloit made whole in that Assembly seat, a Republican, Tim Weeden, won in 1984 after it had been held by a Democrat since 1970. This seems to show pretty clearly that the change was not intended to help Democrats.

Some changes and advantages the new map allowed:

- Helped Democratic State Senators Lynn Adelman and Russ Feingold.

- The map drawn by the federal judge drew several incumbent Democrats' homes outside their districts. This bill put their homes back in their districts.

- This new map did not put any Republican legislator's home outside their district.

The best proof that this new map was not terribly partisan is that in the very next election, 1984, the Democrats lost seven seats in the state Assembly.

VOTER SUPPRESSION

We live in this age of sharp political partisanship. Numbers do not lie: Wisconsin (and many other states) have higher turnout in the presidential election year and lower in the gubernatorial election year. The total turnout in the 2012 presidential year in Wisconsin was about 70%, or 3.2 million voters. The total turnout in the gubernatorial year of 2014 was 56.5%, or about 2.5 million voters.

Which political party does better with larger turnouts? Absolutely clearly, it is the Democrats. The Democratic candidate for president has carried Wisconsin every year since 1988. Yet in the gubernatorial elections starting in 1986, the Republican candidate has won 6 out of 8 times, and that's not counting the 2012 recall election.

I think you may know where this is going: Republicans do much better in Wisconsin elections when the turnout is lower. So what did Walker and the Republican majority do? They passed a broad piece of legislation camouflaged as the "Voter ID" law. They sold it to the people of Wisconsin as a needed measure to stop "voter fraud" despite the reality that there has never been an election fraud problem in Wisconsin. That little truth didn't stop them. They said, "You have to have an ID to check a book out of the library, so why not require one to vote?" This simple line, plus the "stop voter fraud" argument, helped (according to polls) to convince a majority of Wisconsin citizens to support the legislation. But checking out a book at the library is not a right guaranteed by the Constitution. The right to vote is!

Again, "the rest of the story..."

Similar to the gerrymandered redistricting maps that were made law, Walker and the Republicans pushed through this voter ID law for one simple yet crass reason: to reduce voter turnout, and to use the law to benefit their political party. The lower the turnout, the better for the Republicans, including Walker and the legislators who voted for it.

"The arc of history," to use Martin Luther King's phrase, on voting rights since the 1788 election of George Washington, is an arc toward expanding the right to vote and adopting election law that makes it easier to vote. For example:

- In the 1788 election, women, African-Americans, renters, and those not belonging to the "preferred church" could not vote. Over time, laws have been changed to allow all of those groups their voting rights.

- The voting age was lowered from 21 to 18.

- Early voting at the local clerk's office was created.

- Voting by absentee ballot was created.

- Election Day registration at the polls was allowed.

All of the following changes to Wisconsin election law that are included in the voter ID law, have one thing in common: Every item will suppress (reduce) voting and voter turnout. This is a blatant and intentional reversal of 227 years of progress toward expanding voting rights to all Wisconsin citizens by Walker and the Republican legislators.

Changes include:

- The legislation reduced the time period for people to vote by absentee ballot.

- The legislation stopped early voting with the election clerks on the Friday before the election, wiping out the previous right to vote up until the day before the Tuesday election. This will clearly reduce the number of people who are able to vote.

- Under prior law, a voter who registered before the close of registration (third Wednesday preceding an election) generally was not required to provide proof of residence when registering to vote. Now all voters, except a military or overseas voter, must provide proof of residence when registering. Under the Act, the requirement to provide proof of residence no longer depends upon the date an individual registers to vote.

- The legislation eliminated the ability to vote a straight-party ticket. This therefore requires every voter to go down the ballot and choose a candidate for each office on the ballot, and voters are not required to vote in every race in order for their ballot to count. This provision has nothing to do with "voter fraud" or a "voter ID" requirement. The voter already has the ballot in hand (or handle in front of them to pull). Some people (of any party) simply believe strongly in their party and prefer all of their party's candidates. Why take away their long-held right to vote a straight-party ticket? The explanation is a disturbing one, but everyone needs to know it:

Walker and the Republicans wanted to take away the straight-ticket voting option because they believe that their supporters are more informed and "civically conscious" and will take the time to vote all the way down the ballot, accepting the inconvenience that they had been able to avoid when straight-party voting was allowed.

Also, the Republicans believed from their ivory towers that Democratic voters, especially young, low income, 2012 Obama voters, cared most about voting for him (or other similar future top-of-the-ticket candidates) and would not take the time to vote in the rest of the races.

The law created what I call "down-the-ballot-voter-suppression." The goal was to turn the big-turnout-presidential-election year into a lower turnout election in other races appearing on the ballot that day.

Many other restrictive changes were made, including expanding the amount of time a voter must reside within their district, the requirement to sign a poll list when voting in person, stricter proof of residence and prior residence, and on the types of identification issued by colleges and universities that can be used by students.

The voter ID law affects an estimated 10-20% of the people of Wisconsin. The political cleverness of the law is that the actual requirements technically affect all voters so a claim can be made that this is not a partisan issue. If you have a driver's license, passport, military ID, or other acceptable form of identification, you have no problem. Most would agree that Walker's Republican base, therefore, would have no problem complying with the new requirements.

Wisconsin citizens who would have a problem complying with the requirements of the voter ID law are:

- Young people and students who change their address often or do not have a valid form of student ID.

- Those for whom transportation is difficult.

- People who do not own or have need for a vehicle (due to low income or because they live in an urban area).

- Those who do not travel outside the country and those who do not have a passport, including many older folks.

- Those who count on convenient early-voting and absentee-voting methods because of transportation/child care/work issues.

These citizens would likely be part of the Democratic base.

For low-income citizens with 2 (often minimum wage) jobs—especially those who are responsible for children—getting to the polls is difficult and sometimes means arriving near 8:00 p.m. and waiting in line for up to 2 hours. Hence reducing timeframes for other methods of voting hurts.

Voting should not be made a hassle for any American, and the Republicans seem to be intentionally making it more difficult. No reason for the changes made to voting rights in the Republicans' voter ID law justifies making it harder (or sometimes impossible) for even one person to vote.

Every citizen would agree that the right to vote is the greatest and most important right we have in the United States of America. Against the arc of history, which has always expanded the right to vote and created methods that make it easier to vote, Walker and the Republican legislators want to stifle that right in Wisconsin. These ugly truths were somehow never used in the Walker talking points on the need for voter ID legislation.

CHAPTER 12

Several Observations from 45 Years in the Public and Private Sectors

Spend nearly a half century working in government and private industry, and you learn a few things about how each operates. Here are a few of my takeaways:

LONGEVITY

I have noticed that there is an inclination in America toward being too impressed with longevity in office. A news story on the death of a long-serving legislator will frequently highlight their number of terms in office more than their accomplishments.

"SHIP OF STATE"

I believe in the "ship of state" theory of governing. A ship captain will steer away from the rocks regardless of whether that means turning the ship to the left or to the right. That is how I believe we should govern. Let the most practical route be the one taken at any given time rather than always trying to move the government to the political left or the political right. Continuing to steer into the rocks so that you are philosophically "pure" is, to put it bluntly, stupid. It reminds me of another great saying: "When you are in a hole, stop digging!"

A classic example of Governor Walker rejecting this "ship of state" view of governing is his position on Wisconsin's transportation funding.

Like all other states, Wisconsin's revenue from the gas tax (the major source of funding our transportation infrastructure) is shrinking because more fuel efficient vehicles require less gasoline and hence less revenue from the per gallon gas tax.

This reduction is not Walker's fault. However our roads and bridges need to be upgraded or replaced. But unlike the ship captain, he sticks to his philosophy of no tax increases for any reason and is steering our "ship" in the transportation area toward the rocks. His insistence on governing by philosophy and not common sense has led to delaying much needed road and bridge improvements that people of all political persuasions realize are needed. He asked his own Secretary of Transportation to prepare a list of funding recommendations. He prepared one and the governor rejected all of them

GOVERNMENT HAS NO DISCIPLINE, CAPITALISM HAS NO HEART

I came to this conclusion after spending about half my working years in each sector. This conclusion also has been made by Chandler McKelvey, a cabinet member in the Governor Lee Dreyfus Administration and a longtime executive in the private sector.

I believe this statement. I must make clear that I am talking about the nature of government and the private sector as institutions, not about any or all individuals who work in either sector.

Elected officials face a time frame reality... they are called elections. This most important part of our system of government, the free election, also often leads to a lack of discipline by elected officials who overwhelmingly want to get reelected. A tax cut that isn't funded is often irresistible before an election. Not making a very needed decision before an election is often what is done. Starting new programs, and increasing spending that is not funded is often done before elections. Not telling voters what you intend to do after the election because it may be unpopular occurs. The lack of discipline tilts the elected official to mislead voters before the election. This misleading can occur through words spoken or words unspoken.

Another reality of government is that officials do not receive much credit for avoiding a problem before it occurs. So making possibly unpopular changes to avoid a problem that the general public does not yet see is often not done. Discipline would call for action right away.

Capitalism has no heart because its purpose is to make money, not to solve human problems or emphasize kindness over success. There are many people in the private sector who have a kind and generous heart. They just do those good things as private citizens. A company might do things that show a heart, but that almost always is because it's good for the company and its bottom line, or because of a personal interest of the CEO.

PUBLIC/PRIVATE SECTOR DIFFERENCES: THE ROLE OF THE MEDIA

A major difference between the public and private sector is their respective relationship with the media. Put simply, the public sector should and mostly does do its work with the media looking over its shoulder. Media can demand emails that may have been sent yesterday or four years ago. Wisconsin's Open Meetings Law (from which the Legislature partially exempted itself) requires public business to be conducted in public. I have found that public officials at all levels overwhelmingly prefer to decide public issues in private.

The private sector does face some public scrutiny, especially if it is a publicly traded company, but nothing like the public sector. This difference has led, I believe, to the inability of some business people to understand the way the public sector acts, thinks, and decides issues. The best way for the private sector to understand the public sector is to imagine if the press had the right to attend and report on all of their board meetings and pre-board meetings.

A frequent public sector misunderstanding of the private sector is to expect businesses to address social issues like they have that responsibility. They don't.

PUBLIC/PRIVATE SECTOR DIFFERENCES: IMPORTANCE OF LOYALTY

I am talking here about loyalty between leaders and their staffs. I have found that loyalty is absolutely essential in politics, but not as essential in the private sector. Why do I say this? Because in politics the people around you need to be loyal to you because disloyalty can ruin your career. This can happen because of the ever-present need for scrutiny in the public sector. Loyalty in the private sector matters, but there is another tool available: more money and perks. In other words, you can "buy" loyalty in the private sector, while you can't in government.

I believe all of this drives hiring decisions. In politics the order of importance when hiring is loyalty first and competence second. In the private sector it is competence first, loyalty second.

One can make a case that CEOs and other top executives live

more today in the fishbowl of media scrutiny and thus are more susceptible to disloyal leaks to the media than in years past. Nevertheless, I believe that the public officials' "board of directors," the voters, can make some very "final" decisions on a public official on Election Day, whereas executives in the private sector can survive if their boards of directors want to stick with them.

PUBLIC/PRIVATE SECTOR DIFFERENCES: BUDGETING

A huge fundamental difference between the public and private sectors involves their basic approach to budgeting.

Leaders in the private sector begin putting together a budget by determining their expected revenues, and then they decide on expenditures based on those projections and profit-margin goals.

The public sector largely does it just the opposite way. They decide what they want to spend and then try to figure out where to get the revenue to pay for those expenditures.

The simple way to describe this approach to governing is "let's decide how much we want to spend and then we will hope and pray we can find a way to pay for it." What too often happens is that the "way to pay for it" part is often fiscally irresponsible... for instance delaying repayment dates and excessive bonding. We should ban the use of the word "bonding" for the public sector and instead require the use of the word "borrowing." Borrowing is what it is, and I believe voters would be less supportive of it if the legislators and governors had to keep talking about "borrowing" instead of "bonding."

STOCK OPTIONS

A key form of compensation for executives at publicly traded companies is stock options: options to sell shares of the company's stock at a price higher than the price the options are granted at. The employee then earns the difference. The stated purpose is to provide incentive for the executive to work hard to improve the company's performance and have that lead to a high stock price, making the stock option worth money if sold. Of course, if the stock price goes down, the options are worth nothing. I think stock options are fine. I benefited from them when I worked for publicly traded companies.

However, here is my question: If options do indeed motivate employees, why not grant them to more employees than just the top executives? Start with stock options for employees in customer service. This seems like a no-brainer, but I am not aware of many companies doing it. These people are the voice and face of the company. They answer the emails and calls. Customers seldom talk to CEOs and vice presidents. Executives get thousands or even millions of stock options. Why not give most employees 10, some 25, and some 50? One million stock options spread out over employees at these levels would motivate a lot of employees, and would verify that the official reason given for stock options (employees will work harder) is indeed the real reason for them.

SCHOOL BOARD TO STATE LEGISLATURE 2007-2011

I had a remarkable opportunity to serve on a non-partisan elected body, the Janesville School Board (2007-2010), and then immediately go to the highly partisan structure of the state Senate (2011). Put simply, my experience was much more pleasant and productive on the school board.

Candidates are elected to the school board in the spring non-partisan elections. Members do not come to the school board meetings wearing either a Democrat or Republican hat. This helps cooperation immensely. Take Dwayne Severson and me. When considering our personal political persuasions, Dwayne would proudly describe himself as a conservative Republican. On most issues I'm a liberal Democrat. Probably to the initial amazement of both of us we worked extremely well together on the school board. We agreed with each other on nearly every major issue that came before the board over the three years we served together.

Most of the issues faced by a school board are not overtly partisan or partisan at all and, most importantly, the vast majority of local government leaders don't try to make them partisan. We added Chinese as a foreign language offering. We ordered seat belts in all new school buses (still the only school district in Wisconsin to have done this). We started four-year-old preschool for every child. We hired a new superintendent. Dwayne and I agreed on all four of these.

I left the school board in 2010 and went back to the state Senate in 2011. It was as different as night and day. Each person in the Legislature is either a Democrat or a Republican. Every big issue is totally partisan whether it needs to be or not, and working with the other party can get you in trouble with your own party. I wasn't naive about this, but the difference from the school board was so stark.

We need to find a way to make the Legislature less partisan and work more like a school board. Maybe the answer is to adopt a legislative system like Nebraska. Nebraska has a unicameral Legislature with a total of 49 legislators (they are called state senators). They still run as Democrats or Republicans, but the Legislature is not organized in a partisan way. The speaker rather than a majority leader decides the legislative agenda.

STAYING TOO LONG

Appointed and elected executives of public bodies should stay no longer than a decade. I am talking largely about local governments with an elected board that appoints the top executive, the superintendent, city manager, county administrators, etc., but also governors and mayors.

In its simplest form, the school district's structure is supposed to work this way: The voters elect the board members and the board sets the policies of the district, including approving the budget. The board hires a Superintendent to oversee the day to day operations and carry out the policy decisions of the board. What I have just stated is about what a local government political science textbook would state. If it were only so clear and simple.

The following is what I have seen happen, and I firmly believe it occurs across many, many school districts and other governments:

- A school board in a given year chooses a new superintendent, who starts with the best of intentions to help educate children and follow the board's policy directives.

- Over time, the board members who chose the superintendent leave the board and are replaced by new members who did not choose the superintendent.

- The superintendent over time becomes far more "knowledge-able" than new board members, and the gradual shift of policy-making from the board to the superintendent takes place.

- Sometime after 5 or so years on the job the unelected superintendent gradually becomes the chief policy-maker and budget-maker, and each wave of new board members feel "less qualified" to challenge the direction of the long-serving superintendent.

- The longer the superintendent stays, the more the school district is personified in the superintendent and it becomes "his" or "her" district rather than the community's school district. The district is being run the way the superintendent wants. Once this happens, only trouble ensues. Now when board members or the public question school district policies or spending, it is taken as a personal criticism of the superintendent by the superintendent because by this time the district is operating the way the superintendent wants. It is no longer simply the right of elected board members and citizens to question their government, in this case, a school district.

One solution would be to have a tradition that when one half or two thirds of the board that originally hired the superintendent has left the board, the current board re-interview the superintendent to make sure they are still aligned. If the superintendent fights this idea, or the board is reluctant to do it so as not to upset the superintendent, then these would be very serious signals that their respective roles are already a problem.

An executive deals with a wide range of issues such as budgets, union negotiations, building issues, personnel matters, the media, technology issues, etc. However the number-one purpose of a school district is educating students and helping them learn. In other words, what matters is what happens in the classroom between roughly 8:00 a.m. and 3:00 p.m. The only school district employee there when that classroom door closes at 8:00 a.m. is the teacher, so the most important employee is not the highest ranking nor the highest paid.

Every point I make on this subject applies to city managers, mayors, county executives and administrators, and governors (presidents of course are limited to 8 years). I'm in favor of term limits for executives... two four year terms for governor, mayor, county executive, and appointed administrators; superintendents and city managers could have an 8-to-10-year limit.

The downside of this solution is that there are some great executives who would have their job end before their positive contributions were exhausted.

THE POWER OF THE STATUS QUO

I am a Christian and a Catholic, therefore I believe in God Almighty, and that he/she is the most powerful force in the world.

Who or what, then, is in second place? It is of course a very distant second place, but I would have to say after 45 years of observation that it is the status quo. Whether it is government, business mores, habits in any facet of life—you pick the area—the status quo is enormously powerful.

This book is mostly about government and politics so I will stick to those areas.

Being for "change" is frequently a winning campaign slogan, but after the elections are over, changing literally anything means defeating the second most powerful force in the world... the status quo.

Things are the way they are now for a reason. Things are not the way they are now by accident. Some people or some groups want it the way it is.

Trying to change anything in government at all levels is usually way more difficult than it seems it ought to be. The status quo doesn't always fight out in the open, and it doesn't always fight fair. It usually has lobbyists and campaign contributors.

Pick your effort at change, large or small. From changing the name of a street to reforming the nation's health care system, the status quo will fight you.

This combination of "change" being a winning campaign (and I believe generally sincere on the candidates part) and then the difficulty of getting that change made when in office is the source of much voter frustration with officeholders, i.e., "they get elected and then nothing gets done." Lots of people see the sharp partisan divide in our nation and in states with divided government as the reason "nothing gets done." I do not deny this is clearly a factor. But behind the position of one or both political parties is the power of the status quo. When nothing happens and there is "gridlock," the status quo wins. That is why both parties can get credit with the status quo lobbyists and campaign contributors if nothing happens.

MODERATES, BIPARTISANSHIP, COMPROMISE... GOOD OR BAD?

These three words have taken a beating in the public square by a lot of people on the political right and some on the political left. Let's take a look at them.

"Moderates." Some people believe moderates are people who don't stand for anything. But just because they have not spent their life as a left wing or right wing advocate doesn't mean moderates don't stand for anything. And there is nothing wrong with taking issues one at a time without regard to a set ideology. In fact, it's refreshing and makes for good government. The problem for moderates today is the true believers on the left and right risk alienating their base by associating with moderates or, God forbid, being called a moderate. And if you are a moderate, you quickly are called a RINO (Republicans in Name Only) or DINO (Democrats in Name Only).

"Bipartisanship." This is another word that has taken a beating in 21st century politics. People who are willing to work in a bipartisan way are accused of not having strong convictions and being willing to sell out just to get a deal. I believe the fundamental objection to bipartisanship is rooted in the belief by people on the extremes that "the other side" can never have a good idea.

Split government forces bipartisanship if anything is going to get done. The sad thing to me is that many people on the extremes (and remember that is where most of the money is) want no legislation to pass if it means a bipartisan bill. If one party has total control, then it is entirely up to them if bipartisanship is to occur at all.

"Compromise." Legislators willing to compromise are often considered weak. My philosophy on compromise comes from one of President Lyndon Johnson's favorite lines. He said, "Anyone not willing to settle for half a loaf has never been hungry." Amen.

I believe many people are frustrated by the unwillingness of more elected officials to compromise. Citizens understand that compromise is how we lead our lives outside our state and national capitols. Any couple married for more than five days (let alone 30 to 50 years) knows that compromise is essential in a marriage. It is essential in a long-term friendship. It is necessary from time to time in finding solutions in workplace issues all the way to the corporate boardroom. It is how people lead pleasant, sensible, happy lives. This disconnect is what I believe disappoints Americans so much.

There is one disconnect that has run consistently through these pages, and that is the one between Scott Walker and the long-standing ideals of the state of Wisconsin. It is what took 14 Democratic senators, including me, to Illinois in late winter 2011.

Eventually, we had to come home.

CHAPTER 13

Home from Illinois

On February 22, 2011—five days after the 14 Senate Democrats left Wisconsin for Illinois, to avoid providing a quorum for the controversial Act 10 legislation—one of the most amazing phone calls in Wisconsin political history took place.

A blogger located in upstate New York named Ian Murphy called Scott Walker's office identifying himself as David Koch, the billionaire Walker supporter. He actually got through to the governor by calling the phone number on the website and telling the person who answered that he was Koch. Here is a transcript of the conversation:

Walker: Hi; this is Scott Walker.

Murphy: Scott! David Koch. How are you?

Walker: Hey, David! I'm good. And yourself?

Murphy: I'm very well. I'm a little disheartened by the situation there, but, uh, what's the latest?

Walker: Well, we're actually hanging pretty tough. I mean-you know, amazingly there's a much smaller group of protesters-al-

most all of whom are in from other states today. The state As-
sembly is taking the bill up-getting it all the way to the last point
it can be at where it's unamendable. But they're waiting to pass it
until the Senate's in-the Senate Democrats, excuse me, the Assem-
bly Democrats have about a hundred amendments they're going
through. The state Senate still has the 14 members missing but
what they're doing today is bringing up all sorts of other non-fiscal
items, many of which are things that members in the Democratic
side care about. And each day we're going to ratchet it up a little
bit. The Senate majority leader had a great plan he told about this
morning-he told the Senate Democrats about — and he's going to
announce it later today, and that is: The Senate organization com-
mittee is going to meet and pass a rule that says if you don't show
up for two consecutive days on a session day, in the state Senate,
the Senate chief clerk-it's a little procedural thing here, but-can
actually have your payroll stopped from being automatically de-
ducted-

Murphy: Beautiful.

Walker: -into your checking account and instead-you still get
a check, but the check has to be personally picked up and he's in-
structing them-which we just loved-to lock them in their desk on
the floor of the state Senate.

Murphy: Now you're not talking to any of these Democrat bas-
tards, are you?

Walker: Ah, I-there's one guy that's actually voted with me on
a bunch of things I called on Saturday for about 45 minutes, uh,
mainly to tell him that while I appreciate his friendship and he's
worked with us on other things, to tell him, well, I wasn't going to
budge.

Murphy: Goddamn right!

Walker: Mainly, because I thought he's about the only reason-
able one over there and I figured if I talked to him, he'd go back to

the rest of the gang and say, you know, 'I've known Walker for 20 years, he's not budging.'

Murphy: Now, what's his name again?

Walker: His name is Tim Cullen.

Murphy: All right, I'll have to give that man a call.

Walker: Well, actually, in his case I wouldn't call him and I'll tell you why: He's pretty reasonable but he's not one of us, um, so I would let him be. I think he is in a position where he can maybe motivate that caucus, but he's not a, he's not an ally, he's just a, he's just a guy. He was in the Senate years ago. He was actually the Senate (word missing) here back in the '80s and Tommy Thompson hired him to be the head of Health and Human Services. He went into the private sector, made real money and, uh, became a little more more open-minded.

Murphy: Ha!

Walker: And last fall, he got elected to the Senate seat he was in 25 years ago. He's kind of one of these guys who, he really doesn't care, he's not there for political reasons, he's just trying to get something done. So he's good to reach out to for me, but he's not a, he's not a conservative. He's just a pragmatist.

Murphy: Now who could we get to budge on this, uh, collective bargaining?

Walker: Well, I think in the end, a couple of things are one, if the, uh, if the — I think the paycheck will have an impact. Secondly, one of the things we're looking at next, we'll probably announce in the next day or two, we've been working with our Republican leaders in the Legislature is, we may, we're still waiting on an opinion to see if the unions have been paying to put these guys up out of state, we think there's at minimum an ethics violation if not an outright felony.

Murphy: Well, they're probably putting hobos in suits.

Walker: Yeah.

Murphy: That's what we do. Sometimes.

Walker: Well, I mean paying for the senators to be put up. I know they're paying for these guy to be-I mean, people can pay for protesters to come in and that's not an ethics code, but, I mean, literally if the unions are paying the 14 senators-if they're paying for their food, their lodging, anything like that, uh, we believe at minimum it's an ethics code violation and it may very well be a felony misconduct in office because, see, technically, it's not just a political contribution it is, if they're being paid to keep them from doing their job, we think that's an, uh, legally an obstruction, not an obstruction of justice, but an obstruction of their ability to do their job. And we still've got, the attorney general's office is looking into it for us. So we're trying about four or five different angles, so each day we crank up a little bit more pressure. The other thing is I've got layoff notices ready. We put out the at-risk notices. We'll announce Thursday, and they'll go out early next week. And we'll probably get 5 to 6,000 state workers will get at-risk notices for layoffs. We might ratchet that up a little bit, you know.

Murphy: Beautiful, beautiful. Gotta crush that union.

Walker: Well it's one of those where, in the end, you know, the, the uh, and I've had not only Cullen, and I've talked to him my-self, I've had three or four of my other business-leader friends who know him over the years, and just kind of pass the message on to these guys, if they think I'm caving, they've been asleep for the last eight years 'cause I've taken on every major battle in Milwau-kee County and won, even in a county where I'm overwhelmingly overpowered politically, and, 'cause I don't budge.

Murphy: Goddamn right!

Walker: If you're doing the right thing, you stay firm and, in this case, you know, we say we'll wait it out. If they want to start sacrificing thousands of public workers who'll be laid off, sooner or later there's gonna be pressure on these senators to come back. We're not compromising, we're not gonna —

Murphy: Beautiful.

Walker: The other thing we may do, 'cause the senator I mentioned thinks that these guys — you've got a few of the radical ones, who, unfortunately, one of them is the minority leader, but most of the rest of them are just looking for a way to get out of this. They're scared out of their mind, they don't know what it means. There's a bunch of recalls up against them. They'd really like to just get back here and get it over with. So the paycheck thing, some of the other things threaten them. I think, collectively, there's enough going on and as long as they don't think I'm gonna cave — which, again, we have no interest in — an interesting idea that was brought up to me this morning by my chief of staff, we won't do it until tomorrow, is putting out an appeal to the Democrat leader that I would be willing to sit down and talk to him, the assembly Democrat leader, plus the other two Republican leaders — talk, not negotiate — and listen to what they have to say if they will in turn — but I'll only do it if all 14 of them come back and sit down in the state Assembly. They can recess it, to come back if we're talking, but they all have to be back there. The reason for that is, we're verifying it this afternoon, but legally, we believe, once they've gone into session, they don't physically have to be there. If they're actually in session for that day and they take a recess, the 19 Senate Republicans could then go into action and they'd have a quorum because they started out that way. Um, so we're double checking that. But that would be the only, if you heard that I was going to talk to them, that would be the only reason why. We'd only do it if they came back to the capital with all 14 of them. And my sense is, hell, I'll talk to them. If they want to yell at me for an hour, you know, I'm used to that, I can deal with that. But I'm not negotiating.

Murphy: Bring a baseball bat. That's what I'd do.

Walker: I have one in my office; you'd be happy with that. I got a Slugger with my name on it.

Murphy: Beautiful.

Walker: But in the end, this is, and this is, I even pointed it out last night 'cause I'm trying to keep out the, as many of the private unions as possible, I said this is about the budget, this is about public-sector unions. Hell, even FDR got it. Um, there's no place for the kind of, uh, I mean, essentially you're having taxpayer money be used to pay to lobby for spending more taxpayers' money. It's absolutely ridiculous.

Murphy: Beautiful.

Walker: So it's, uh, this is ground zero, there's no doubt about it. But, uh, I think, you know, for us, I just keep telling, I call, I tell the speaker, the senate majority leader every night, give me a list of the people I need to call at home, to shore 'em up. The New York Times, of all things, I don't normally tell people to read the New York Times, but the front page of the New York Times has got a great story, one of these unbelievable moments of true journalism, what is supposed to be objective journalism. They got out of the capital and went down one county south of the capital to Janesville, to Rock County, that's where the General Motors plant once was.

Murphy: Right, right.

Walker: They moved out two years ago. The lead on this story is about a guy who was laid off two years ago, uh, he's been laid off twice by GM, who points out that, uh, everybody else in his town has had to sacrifice except for all these public employees and it's about damn time they do, and he supports me. Um, and they had a bartender, they had, I mean, every stereotypical blue-collar worker type they interviewed, and the only ones that weren't with us were people who were either a public employee or married to a public employee. It's an unbelievable story. So I went through and called all these uh, a handful, a dozen or so lawmakers I worry about each day and said, "Everyone, we should get that story printed out and send it to anyone giving you grief."

Murphy: Goddamn right! We, uh, we sent, uh, Andrew Breitbart down there.

Walker: Yeah.

Murphy: Yeah.

Walker: Good stuff.

Murphy: He's our man, you know.

Walker: Well, it has been amazing to me the massive amount of attention I, I've don all, I want to stay ahead of this every day, tonight I'm actually doing a fireside chat, which the state TV stations are picking up and I guess a bunch of the national ones are, too, and, uh, in the last couple of days when I do the TV shows, I've been going after Obama because he stuck — although he's backed off now — but he stuck his nose in here. And I said, you know, he asked me what I thought about it and I said the last time I checked this guy's got a much bigger budget deficit than we do, maybe he should worry about that [Murphy laughs] and not stick his nose in Wisconsin's business. But you know, we've had, uh, you know, all the national shows, we were on [Sean] Hannity last night, I did "Good Morning America," the "Today" show and all that sorta stuff. I was on "Morning Joe" this morning. We've done Greta [van Susteren]. We're gonna, you know, keep getting our message out. Mark Levin last night. And I've gotta tell you the response from around the country has been phenomenal. I had Brian [Sadoval], the new governor of Nevada, called me the last night he said-he was out in the Lincoln Day Circuit in the last two weekends and he was kidding me, he's new as well as me, he said, "Scott, don't come to Nevada because I'd be afraid you beat me running for governor." That's all they want to talk about is what are you doing to help the governor of Wisconsin. The next question, you know, I talk to Kasich every day-John's gotta stand firm in Ohio. I think we could do the same thing with Vic Scott in Florida. I think, uh, [Rick] Snyder-if he got a little more support-probably could do that in Michigan. You start going down the list there's a lot of us new governors that got elected to do something big.

Murphy: You're the first domino.

Walker: Yep. This is our moment.

Murphy: Yeah. Now what else could we do for you down there?

Walker: Well the biggest thing would be-and your guy on the ground [Americans for Prosperity president Tim Phillips] is probably seeing this is the, well, two things: One, our members originally got freaked out by all the bodies here, although, I told them an interesting story when I was first elected county executive in Milwaukee of all places, the first budget I put through was pretty bold, aggressive, the union went nuts on me and I got all sorts of grief. But a couple of weeks later I'm in a Veterans Day parade and I'm going down the line and usually unless you're a veteran or, you know, marching with a veterans group, politicians all get polite applause but nobody gets up. I come down the line, 40-50 people in a row, hands up, thumbs up, you know, cheering, screaming, yelling, 'Way to go, hang in there, Walker!' And then after about 40-50 people like that, there's a guy flipping me off [Murphy laughs]. This goes on, you know, 40-50 [recording cuts out].

Walker: [recording resumes] right thing. The people who know it's right will cheer you, will applaud you, they'll run through a wall for you. And the people who don't like it, they're gonna flip you off. But stop worrying about, you know, them because — the other day, there were 70,000, probably two-thirds were against the bill, one-third were for, 70,000 people at the Capitol. All week there's been, you know, 15-30,000 a day. But I remind all our lawmakers, that there's five and a half million people in this state. And just because a bunch of guys who can jump off of work 'cause of their union rules, doesn't mean the rest of the people in your district aren't with them. So one thing, per your question is, the more groups that are encouraging people not just to show up but to call lawmakers and tell them to hang firm with the governor, the better. Because the more they get that reassurance, the easier it is for them to vote yes.

Murphy: Right, right.

Walker: The other thing is more long-term, and that is, after this, um, you know the coming days and weeks and months ahead, particularly in some of these, uh, more swing areas, a lot of these guys are gonna need, they don't necessarily need ads for them, but they're gonna need a message out reinforcing why this was a good thing to do for the economy and a good thing to do for the state. So to the extent that that message is out over and over again, that's obviously a good thing.

Murphy: Right, right. Well, we'll back you any way we can. But, uh, what we were thinking about the crowds was, uh, was planting some troublemakers.

Walker: You know, the, well, the only problem with that — because we thought about that. The problem — the, my only gut reaction to that is right now the lawmakers I've talked to have just completely had it with them, the public is not really fond of this. The teachers union did some polling of focus groups, I think, and found out that the public turned on 'em the minute they closed school down for a couple days. The guys we've got left are largely from out of state, and I keep dismissing it in all my press conferences saying, 'Eh, they're mostly from out of state.' My only fear would be is if there was a ruckus caused is that that would scare the public into thinking maybe the governor has gotta settle to avoid all these problems. You know, whereas, I've said, 'Hey, you know, we can handle this, people can protest. This is Madison, you know, full of the '60s liberals. Let 'em protest.' It's not gonna affect us. And as long as we go back to our homes and the majority of the people are telling us we're doing the right thing, let 'em protest all they want. Um, so that's my gut reaction, is that I think it's actually good if they're constant, they're noisy, but they're quiet, nothing happens, 'cause sooner or later the media stops finding 'em interesting.

Murphy: Well, not the liberal bastards on MSNBC.

Walker: Oh, yeah, but who watches that? I went on "Morning

Joe" this morning. I like it 'cause I just like being combative with those guys, but, uh. You know they're off the deep end.

Murphy: Joe-Joe's a good guy. He's one of us.

Walker: Yeah, he's all right. He was fair to me, I mean, the rest of them were out there. Although I had fun. They had [senator Chuck] Schumer over from New York on, ripping me, and then they had a little clip of a state senator hiding out ripping me, and it was almost too easy. I walked in and Joe asked me a question and I say, well, before I answer that, let me just point out the amazing irony, the fact that you've got a United States senator from New York, a senator, who, by the way, is part of a team that can't seem to balance the federal budget, talking about my budget. At least he's coming into work to talk about something, although it's mine. And you got one of these 14 state senate Democrats, uh, who can't even bother to show up and deal with the budget he's elected to do something about. And, uh, I said that kind of tells you the whole story right there.

Murphy: Beautiful, beautiful. But you gotta love that Mika Brzezinski.

Walker: Oh, yeah.

Murphy: She's a piece of ass.

Walker: You know, a couple of weeks ago [unclear], I was having dinner with Jim Sensenbrenner when I came in to D.C. for a day to do an event, and we were going over to do the Greta show. I had dinner with congressman Sensenbrenner, and right next to us was the two of them and then their guest was [Obama advisor David] Axelrod. I came over [Murphy laughs], I introduced myself.

Murphy: That son of a bitch!

Walker: Yeah, no kidding, huh? I introduced myself. I said, I figured you probably knew who I was since your boss was in campaigning against me. But, uh, it's always good to let 'em know you know what's going on.

Murphy: Well, good, good. Good catching up with ya'.

*Walker: Yeah, well, thanks. This is an exciting time. This is —
you know, I told my cabinet, I had a dinner the Sunday, or excuse
me, the Monday right after the 6th. Came home from the Super
Bowl where the Packers won, and that Monday night I had all of
my cabinet over to the residence for dinner. Talked about what we
were gonna do, how we were gonna do it. We'd already kinda built
plans up, but it was kind of the last hurrah before we dropped the
bomb. And I stood up and I pulled out a picture of Ronald Reagan,
and I said, you know, this may seem a little melodramatic, but
30 years ago, Ronald Reagan, whose 100th birthday we just celebrated the day before, had one of the most defining moments of his
political career, not just his presidency, when he fired the air-traffic
controllers. And, uh, I said, to me that moment was more important than just for labor relations or even the federal budget, that
was the first crack in the Berlin Wall and the fall of Communism
because from that point forward, the Soviets and the Communists
knew that Ronald Reagan wasn't a pushover. And, uh, I said this
may not have as broad of world implications, but in Wisconsin's
history — little did I know how big it would be nationally — in
Wisconsin's history, I said this is our moment, this is our time to
change the course of history. And this is why it's so important that
they were all there. I had a cabinet meeting this morning and I
reminded them of that and I said for those of you who thought I
was being melodramatic you now know it was purely putting it in
the right context.*

*Murphy: [Laughs] Well, I tell you what, Scott: once you crush
these bastards I'll fly you out to Cali and really show you a good
time.*

*Walker: All right, that would be outstanding. Thanks, thanks
for all the support and helping us move the cause forward, and we
appreciate it. We're, uh, we're doing the just and right thing for the
right reasons, and it's all about getting our freedoms back.*

Murphy: Absolutely. And, you know, we have a little bit of a vested interest as well. [Laughs]

Walker: Well, that's just it. The bottom line is we're gonna get the world moving here because it's the right thing to do.

Murphy: All right then.

Walker: Thanks a million!

Murphy: Bye-bye!

Walker: Bye.

Wow! We seldom hear any governor's comments recorded when they think they are not being recorded. I think his comments about me are pretty accurate, and I appreciate his endorsement. I find his comments, however, to be a very important insight into his mindset, his view of government, and his view of how a legislator should perform. Especially insightful is his comment about me, "he's not one of us—he's not there for political reasons, he's just trying to get something done." Since Walker and Koch (and the rest of "them") are not like me, in state government "to get something done" and they are not like me who is "not there for political reasons," I guess that means they are there for political reasons: not to get something done?

I also found it beneath the dignity of a governor of Wisconsin to be borderline giddy over a plan to lock state senators' checks in their Senate floor desks so they would give up on the issue and the cause and return to Wisconsin—tails between their legs—to get a $2900 check (and behave like that in front of the whole world). This reminds me of a favorite saying of a friend of mine... "Don't judge others by your own behavior or you won't think much of people." Are we to think then that the Governor and Senator Fitzgerald would have given up on a cause and humiliated themselves in order to get a $2900 check? They never implemented this plan. My guess would be because there were still some adults in the Senate Republican Caucus who talked them out of it.

Another insight into Walker's mindset occurs when the Koch

impersonator suggests to Walker the idea of "planting some troublemakers" in the crowds (presumably to create turmoil and violence that would be blamed on the otherwise peaceful protesters). Walker does not reject the idea because it is wrong, not the way he believes public officials should act, etc. This son of a pastor, this Eagle Scout, rejects it because he had concluded it would not work to their advantage. So much for the moral high ground from the self-described highly religious governor of Wisconsin.

This transcript provides great insight into character. For any candidate, it is almost impossible to get past their canned response messages and poll-tested talking points. There is much more that can be analyzed in the call. I printed the entire transcript so you can read it and draw your own conclusions.

I also observed somewhat humorously, somewhat seriously, Walker's farewell words to the person he thinks is David Koch. He says, "Thanks a million." If this was a Freudian slip regarding a campaign contribution, I believe he was greatly understating the dollar amount.

Fair questions for people to ask after reading this entire Koch impersonator call tricking Governor Walker into talking with him: Is this tactic fair? Do I agree with doing it? Would I do it?

I do not think it is fair and I would not do it. I do not agree it should be done. But it was. I have put it in this book because of what Walker said. He said what he said. No one made him make those comments. No one, including Walker, has tried to say he didn't mean what he said. So we have an honest series of comments from the governor of Wisconsin elicited in a manner I disagree with. He wasn't forced to say anything. I used it as an indication of Walker's thought process and views that he was completely willing to share with David Koch, although I presume he did not wish to share with the general public. There also has been no claim by Walker or his team that his answers were altered or "doctored" by Murphy or anyone else.

NEGOTIATIONS?

When that infamous phone call occurred, February 22, my Senate colleagues and I had been in Illinois for five days. As I noted, we moved around quite a bit, first Rockford, then Freeport, Woodstock, and finally Gurnee.

We were still in Gurnee near the end of February. It was not a particularly pretty time of year, and we were definitely not on vacation. I don't remember whether I talked to Jerry Whitburn, someone I had known since our days in Governor Thompson's cabinet in the 1980s, before this point, but late in February I received a phone call from him. We were political friends. We didn't lunch together or go out on double dates with our wives. I had been to his home once many years ago when I was in the Cabinet. We had a mutual respect for each other. He knew I was a Democrat, I knew he was a Republican, but we agreed on the issue of making government work.

He is a loyal Republican and it was clear he was talking to Walker and Republican Senate Majority Leader Scott Fitzgerald. Perhaps there would be some negotiation. I got the call from Whitburn at La Quinta. He said that Scott Fitzgerald was going to call me in 15 minutes, which happened. Fitz wanted to get together to talk. I asked where and when, and he asked where I wanted to meet. We decided to meet at a McDonald's outside Kenosha on the following Monday morning, and Bob Jauch was going to come with me. The three of us spoke for a couple of hours. It was cordial but we were far apart from any kind of agreement to modify the Act 10 bill.

I think, but don't know, that Senator Fitzgerald wanted to meet to gauge whether or not we had interest in coming back and what the conditions might be. We went there with a list of about 8 things we wanted to change in the bill. He dismissed several of them and always made clear that he had to clear things with his brother, Jeff, who was the Speaker of the Assembly, and the Governor. Senator Jauch and I had prepared the list. I don't think anyone in the caucus knew we had this meeting until after it happened. We told Senator Miller when we came back from the meeting. The meeting with Senator Fitzgerald didn't go well, there was some general interest in some topics but not enough to really amount to a hill of beans. I think he was there not to work out a deal, but to gauge our temperature. I think he wanted to see if we were anxious to get back, how it was going in Illinois. Only Senator Fitzgerald can answer these matters.

I remember we ended things with Senator Fitzgerald with him saying he would communicate our message to his colleagues and let us know how it went the next day. Senator Jauch and I went back to the hotel and we weren't particularly hopeful that things had gone well. Senator Fitzgerald wasn't in a position to make changes to the bill. The next night we had a caucus in a different location for some reason, a different hotel, different community, and the caucus knew we had the meeting the day before. I told them it didn't go well, but Senator Fitzgerald was going to get back to me with a counter offer.

I called my office and tried to reach Senator Fitzgerald. He faxed me a response at the hotel. It wasn't much, minimal. I brought it back to the caucus and the consensus was that they were not serious, just playing games. That looked like the end of any compromise that would lead us to come back. I can't remember if Senator Fitzgerald said it there or if it was said at the second meeting with the governor's staff which we were about to have, that if we agreed on changes they wouldn't put them in this budget bill. They would put them in the big budget bill months later as Amendment One to the budget bill. That would have required a lot of trust on our part. The caucus thought that was baloney. It looked like that was the end of negotiation. A few days later Jerry Whitburn called me again. He said I was going to get a call from the governor's chief of staff in 15 minutes. The call came, again just as Whitburn said. I talked to Governor Walker's chief of staff, Keith Gilkes, and he wanted to bring the deputy chief of staff to meet with Senator Jauch and me. I told them I'd be happy to meet with them and they wanted to meet that night. It was 6:00 p.m. and they wanted to drive two hours to meet that night. I believed this to mean they were serious.

We guessed that Fitzgerald was the wrong guy to be negotiating with. He and his brother all along had been telling their caucuses "no changes to the bill," so for one of them to negotiate changes with us was not going to happen. It made sense that the governor's people were the right ones to talk to. It's his bill. Bob and I decided to tell Miller and take him with us to the meeting. If we were going to affect the caucus it was essential that he be involved and informed. The three of us talked over dinner and met the Governor's people at the same McDonald's at 9 p.m. on Sunday night, February 27, in Kenosha.

There was interest in trying to negotiate something and I thought the meeting went pretty well. They got away from the idea of putting changes in a future bill and said they were willing to put changes in this bill. That told me their polling wasn't going well. The governor of the state gets credit for what goes well and what doesn't go well in the state, whether he deserves it or not. That's the way it's always been. I concluded that having a Legislature that was unable to meet was not reflecting well on the governor and they were interested in getting us to come back from Illinois. The second possibility was that the Senate caucus was cracking and they needed to get us back and get this done or they would lose Republican senators. They may well have had other motives.

They wanted to try to work out a deal. It went until about 11:00 that night, and as we were driving back to Gurnee, Senator Jauch and I felt pretty good about getting some movement on the issues and the idea of getting changes in the bill now. Senator Miller didn't say much, he was on the phone most of the way. We had a caucus the next morning and as it started, I heard Senator Miller say that their proposals were minimal. Senator Jauch and I thought there was a seriousness about the chief of staff. They said that they felt good about the meeting and felt good about some progress. They even called the governor after the meeting that night and woke him up to tell him how well the meeting went and that possibilities were open. Nothing was agreed upon, but there was a start. The majority of our caucus was not interested.

I mean by a "deal" on these items that there would have needed to be a press conference including myself and any other Democratic senators who came back with me and the governor and Senator Fitzgerald and Speaker Fitzgerald. They would need to say publicly that they could and would pass this through their respective houses of the Legislature. The governor would need to agree with the changes and publicly state that he would not tamper with this agreement with his veto pen.

It is worth asking at this point what did Republican state Senators in Madison know about this Jauch/Cullen negotiation effort, and what did they think about it?

I have been told by more than one of those senators that they were all aware of the negotiations and that several, as many as six, wanted the negotiations to be successful. These senators would have much preferred something of a compromise that they could vote for. This would mean they would get a little less criticism from the public employees in their district, yet they would not have been the ones to demand these changes; and they would always be able to say to Governor Walker and his strong supporters that they had stuck with the governor all the way and then voted for the modified bill because the governor supported it.

It also must be clearly stated that a compromise like this would be swimming against the strong currents on both sides that had already decided to have the political war, including several recall elections.

Public employee labor leaders would need to get in front of the large crowds in Madison and try to slow this movement down... not an easy task after they had revved the crowds up in the first place. They also were not getting the right to have automatic payroll deduction of union dues.

It was now the first week in March. There was an impasse and no contact by either side. Then Jauch called Walker's chief of staff and asked whether there was a desire on their part to meet and try again. The answer was yes. They suggested we meet on Sunday, March 6, in South Beloit, Illinois, at Jauch's hotel. I thought this willingness to drive to South Beloit on a Sunday afternoon showed they were serious at some level again.

We talked for about two hours. We had at least a tentative list (that they needed to take back to Governor Walker and the Fitzgeralds for sign off). So, it is an exaggeration to say we had a tentative deal. But I would have returned to Madison for that list of changes. I know I could have defended it. I do not know who else if anyone would have come back with me.

The changes in the discussion were as follows:

1. Allow collective bargaining on "workplace safety" issues for teachers, nurses, and prison guards (I felt this kept collective bargaining alive as clever negotiators could describe a lot of issues as workplace safety).

2. The bill limited public employee pay raises to the CPI. Any higher amount would have to be approved by a local referendum, hence no real collective bargaining on wages. They were willing to take the CPI cap off and not require a local referendum. This restored collective bargaining on wages.

3. The bill would require each public employee labor union to hold a re-certification vote every year, and require that it

pass with a majority of the whole membership- not simply a majority of those voting. This was expensive and time consuming for unions. They were willing to move this to once every four years—better but not great.

4. The bill also completely eliminated the nurses' union at the UW Hospital. The rest of the unions were decimated by the bill, this union was eliminated. These were the same nurses who took care of me when I had cancer in 2002, so it was personal to me. I thought, "What did they do so wrong that their union had to be eliminated? They helped save my life." They were willing to restore that union and take that language out of the bill.

5. Regarding the part of the bill where the Legislature would have lost all oversight of our state health programs—BadgerCare, Medicaid, and SeniorCare—we negotiated that any changes to those would have to come to the Joint Finance Committee in order to have a public hearing and vote. With Republican control, the governor would still get what he wants, but he would have to show it in public and go through the hearing process and give those who want a chance to oppose the changes to have their say in public in the Capitol. In future years, with split control of state government, this would restore legislative oversight of these programs making the legislative branch of government equal again with the governor.

Governor Walker would have had to agree that peace and calm in Wisconsin was important enough to him to agree with this compromise, which may have hurt the national image he had quickly built that "he doesn't negotiate," he is "bold" and "unintimidated." This right wing base he was trying to appeal to is not known for its love of political compromise.

I would have faced certain criticism for not getting "enough," for not staying in Illinois with all of the other Democratic Senators, that I left them "high and dry," that I didn't stick with the team, that I cut a deal "too soon," and could have gotten more if I had been more patient, etc.

I realized the "politically safe" thing to do was just stay in Illinois and let the issue play out. I was 67 years old. I didn't need the job. I came back to solve problems. This was a bigger problem than I could have ever imagined just a month earlier.

But the deal was never reached and the political war commenced.

Walker's staff had said from the beginning that restoring the provision that allowed for automatic labor union dues as a payroll deduction for public union employees was not on the table; it was a nonstarter. That tells you what Governor Walker was really about... busting unions, not balancing the budget. That was their one non-starter and could not be negotiated.

Something that was completely understood by both sides from the beginning was that we were not negotiating changes to the bill in order to come back and vote for it. The complete understanding on both sides was that we were negotiating changes to the bill in exchange for just coming back. We were going to oppose it when we came back, we were going to talk against it, vote against it. It was just about coming back. I think there was some misunderstanding or confusion about that in our caucus. When you look at it in the context of were these changes going to make the bill better, absolutely yes. But it would still be a terrible bill. And we wouldn't be voting for it. But it was 100% clear to me by this time: A) we were in Illinois, B) we were in the minority, and C) the only way to kill this bill was to stay in Illinois the whole two year session. Whenever we came back they would have a quorum and pass the bill. Anybody who thought we could stay in Illinois for two years and not be recalled was nuts. So to me the course was clear; get the most changes, agree to it, and get back to Madison.

Some talked a bit about the fear of being recalled, but the great majority of the caucus was comfortable politically being there. The majority of their districts were heavily Democratic and the constituents were happy they were there. I remember Fred Risser said only half jokingly, "I'm more popular the longer I stay here." He has a huge number of public employees in Madison. That wasn't true for all of us. There was some concern for Holperin. There were at least 8 or 10 out of the 14 who were not worried about themselves politically. Regardless of how much politicians talk about doing things for the good of the "team," no elected official ever forgets about the consequences in their own district. It was now early March and there was some talk that maybe we ought to stay through the Supreme Court election on April 5th to help defeat Justice Prosser. That meant another month! There was some small chatter about maybe we just stay through the budget, which would have meant staying until July. I thought this was beginning to be lunacy.

The caucus dismissed the efforts we made the night before with Walker's staff. Our meeting with the governor's staff ended about 3 o'clock on Sunday, March 6, and Bob and I felt really good about being close. At the end of our stay in Illinois, if we didn't do this, we were going to go home with nothing. I thought, "Let's get what we can." Being in Illinois and in the minority, I thought we had a lot accomplished regarding concessions.

We assumed they (chief of staff and deputy chief of staff) were coming with orders from the Fitzgeralds and governor about how far to go and what not to do. The money was never negotiated. In other words, we never tried to say the employees had to pay less in pensions or health insurance than what the Republicans wanted. That was this governor's and this majority's way of balancing the budget and they were in power. We didn't believe we could change that. We were primarily interested in saving collective bargaining for public employees. With our negotiations they would be able to negotiate for pay raises and this broad category called "workplace safety."

I have always tried to be a problem solver, and not much of an ideologue. Les Aspin was a problem solver rather than an ideologue. The reality is, when I think about myself, I am pretty liberal on just about every issue. The difference between me and some other people who are liberal is that I'm willing to negotiate something less than what I'd really like to have, and give the other side something. I believe it's better to get some of what you want and reach an agreement.

IT'S OVER

Whitburn called me that night of March 6, after we had negotiated that Sunday afternoon, and said, "You know that governors and majority leaders have a lot of power if they want to exercise it." I agreed. He said people were getting restless and I had two days to negotiate a settlement or agreement, or they were going to exercise their power. He didn't say what they were going to do. I don't know if he even knew what they were going to do in two days, but I thought they might split the bill up and jam it through. Whitburn had been right every time before, so I thought we had until Tuesday night to reach an agreement. Jauch and I drove back to Gurnee Monday afternoon. We reported to the caucus about this list of changes we had presented; knowing it was not to be voted for, but just for us to return. It wasn't received well by the caucus. It wasn't enough.

I believe at that point that the caucus understood that the negotiations were just to get us back to Wisconsin. There were certain themes running through the mindset of the caucus that are worth talking about. One of them was that this had become a political war that the governor had started, and there was a great desire to carry on the war and see who wins the hearts and minds of the people of Wisconsin through recalls or whatever.

I can't emphasize enough that at this point, March 7th, 2011, both "sides" had decided to have the war. No compromises, no deals... let the war happen. I really was in no man's land. I have found that the problem with wars is that one side loses. The stakes are high.

So the phrase that started getting used was, "If we're going to lose this bill, we should lose with clarity." It was a phrase that I found astounding. To me that was like saying it's better to get nothing than to get something. That view was held by at least a majority of our caucus. The labor leaders were told what we were negotiating and when they saw that the dues checkoff was not on the list, they didn't see much value in the other items.

The other thing that I think was rather amazing and pretty much unknown is that another phrase started being used in the caucus. That was that when we go back we need to go back to a "soft landing." What they meant by a soft landing was that we would come back as highly appreciated and receive a warm welcome. They didn't want the labor union supporters to say we hadn't been gone long enough or tried hard enough. So "lose with clarity" and "soft landing" were the mantra of a lot of people in the caucus.

What that meant to me was that the people who could deliver a soft landing were the labor leaders. Once you go to them and say, "Give us a soft landing when we come back," you have turned the decision on when to come back over to them (the union leaders). They would be able to decide when to provide the soft landing. I thought that was lunacy, too. We've abdicated control over when we come back to people who are not elected officials.

We were aware of the crowds and protests in Madison. Of course the left wing news shows were on every night and senators were on those shows a lot. One of the things that never endeared me to my colleagues on the left was that I wouldn't go on the Rachel Maddow show or Ed Schultz show. I had nothing against those shows. I didn't like the set-up. Senators would drive to a location a ways away from where we were actually staying. Senator Jon Erpenbach, who was not with us in caucus a lot and was in Chicago, was on Rachel Maddow often. I thought he did a great job; he was articulate and I thought he served us well by being there rather than by being with the caucus. But most of those who went to be on the show were props. Rachel or Ed would talk to Miller or a couple other people and once in awhile ask a question to everyone, but most of the time the caucus was just sitting there helping keep the audience until the end of the show. The "Fab 14 from Wisconsin" was the lead story and they would tease the headline until the end of the show. Now everyone has given up 3 or 4 hours of their time to be a prop for a ten-minute segment. I was not going to do that, it didn't make sense to me. That made me a little more suspicious in our caucus, too.

Jauch and I reported to the caucus on Monday afternoon, March 7, regarding our Sunday afternoon meeting with Walker's staff and it seemed pretty clear to everyone, I think, that we were getting somewhere. Some substantive stuff was going to be in the bill and the agreement was we were only coming back, not voting for the bill.

I remember I was in Janesville, buying a newspaper, on that Monday morning. My cell phone rang and it was Governor Walker. He asked about my health, I had had a cough, but there was no discussion of the issues or the details of any agreement. It was a five-minute phone call. I thought the call was odd, but it was like our previous conversations; pleasant but no substance.

Miller sent a letter to the governor that day, which had the effect of giving the governor a reason to end the Jauch/Cullen negotiations. I was not aware of the letter until I heard about it through the media. The governor had a press conference and was waving it around. The letter said two main things to the governor. One was that Senator Miller was prepared to begin negotiations with a mediator present. You can imagine how that would go over on the governor's side. He knows that we've already been negotiating. The second was that Miller was prepared to meet the governor at the state line to begin negotiations. Well, no governor in their right mind, Republican or Democrat, would ever agree to that... to trot himself down to the state line to accommodate some senators who were out of state!

Governor Walker waved the letter around at a press conference. He said it showed that the Democrats were not interested in negotiating in good faith, etc. He then said that he knew there were some Democratic senators interested in negotiating and that he just talked to Senator Tim Cullen that morning.

I now realized how Governor Walker uses people. That phone call was made so he could say he talked to me that morning even though we discussed nothing about the issues, nothing of substance. That told me a lot more about the guy. That letter gave them an excuse to blow up the negotiations, and the call to me made him look like he was reaching out to try to reach some common ground.

But my sense now is that they were going to blow up negotiations anyway. They didn't believe that we were going to get a deal, or maybe the things they brought back from Jauch and I that Sunday were unacceptable to one or both Fitz's or the governor. Wednesday came and Senator Fitzgerald quickly assembled a conference committee and took up a bill.

One tentative change, as I mentioned, was to keep the nurses' union at the UW Hospitals and Clinics in existence. Walker's Act 10 legislation eliminated it entirely. So that is what Walker did to the nurses who helped save my life in 2002. What did they ever do to him to have deserved this fate?

This bill had only the collective bargaining changes in it, not the bonding, which was the bill's original purpose, to balance the current budget. By taking all the money out of the bill, a quorum of 20 was no longer needed, only a majority of 17, which they had. The bill passed 18 to 1 with Senator Dale Schultz being the only Republican senator to vote "no." It was over. Any reason for us to stay in Illinois was actually ended by Scott Fitzgerald, which leaves open the question that will never be answered. When were we going to come back if Fitz hadn't passed the bill?

Collective bargaining was gone and so was our reason to stay in Illinois. The decision was made to quickly get back to Madison and get on the floor to debate this thing, talk for a long time, and fight it to the end. I was called to get to Madison right away and I had to pick up Jauch because he didn't have a car. I was on my way to pick up Jauch in South Beloit when I got another call letting me know that Fitz jammed it through and to forget it. Fitz played fast and loose with the open meetings law, time frames, and everything else. I've never asked him about this, but I suspect that he learned we were coming back and the last thing he wanted was an all-night session. He wanted to get it done and out of there and so he rushed it without giving proper notification.

The decision was made to come back on March 12th. Labor provided the "soft landing," which was a huge rally at the Capitol on that Saturday. There were over 100,000 people there that day. We walked around the Square and were welcomed as heroes. It was an amazing experience having all those people cheering for us, but I couldn't help thinking to myself how close we had come to saving collective bargaining. If we had been able to have the changes, or at least some, and been able to save collective bargaining, we might have tamped down the recall elections. We will never know. Maybe it would not have made a difference. I do know that we had a chance to modify the bill in some significant ways just in exchange for coming back, and it didn't work out.

LONG-RANGE FALLOUT FROM ACT 10

There has been an enormous amount of coverage in the media about the details of Act 10. People are generally familiar with the fact that almost all collective bargaining for public employees has been taken away, and also that public employees are paying more of the cost of their health insurance and pensions. I think fewer people know that going forward pay raises are limited to the increase in the consumer price index (CPI). It was a 1.46% maximum in 2014. The teachers of our children and grandchildren only deserve a maximum 1.46% raise? Really.

I want to mention here the long-range damage Act 10 does and will keep doing to K-12 public education in Wisconsin:

1. Teacher morale is low in most school districts.

2. Teachers are moving to the school districts where they believe they will be appreciated and respected. I do not blame them at all. I blame the school boards that do not want to understand that we are now in the "post" Act 10 era. Each teacher is a "union of one" and can go where they can use their skills at helping kids learn and enjoy their workplace.

3. The big-time losers are the kids who lose the great teachers to another school district.

4. Students studying to get their education degree at our universities are telling their professors that they want to be teachers... but not in Wisconsin. They can go to Minnesota and earn more and be appreciated.

5. It will take a long time to stop and reverse these trends. Many, many students will suffer from this in many, many school districts for a decade or more. You can't restock a school district with great teachers in just a few years after all this damage.

6. College students in Wisconsin are more skeptical about choosing a career in education than at any time I can remember. What a sad legacy from this political war started by our "bold" leader.

The people of Wisconsin will catch on to this and rise up and it will get better. But for those who think that just getting rid of Governor Walker will fix things, I am afraid they're in for a rude awakening. It will take a long time.

FINAL THOUGHTS

The main criticism of the Democratic Senators who went to Illinois was that we were not in Madison "doing our job"—voting on bills—and our absence prevented the Republicans from passing legislation. Well, we certainly went there to slow down (if not stop) the legislation now known as Act 10. What other legislation was being held up? The answer is close to nothing. What is the proof of this? Well, we just need to look at how soon the Senate met and how often it met after we returned.

We came back to Madison on March 12. When did Senator Fitzgerald schedule the next session day? The next week? No. Try April 5th. The agenda for that day was almost nothing (Appendix J) except for the bonding authority for the then-budget deficit ($137 million).

So when did we meet in session again? With all of this supposed backlog we were accused of creating it must have been April 6th and April 7th, right? Wrong. We were not called back into session again until May 10th. And that was largely a day dedicated to honoring Wisconsin soldiers who had lost their lives in Iraq or Afghanistan. Their families were present in the Senate Chamber to receive citations and the thundering applause of all the state Senators.

The bottom line: The Republican majority had no urgent or major legislation that needed Senate attention. It was all about politics and not about the people's business.

The rules of the Wisconsin State Senate do not provide protection for the right to filibuster. The United States Senate rules do allow for a filibuster. The state Senate rules say, "A motion to adjourn is in order at any time." This means that the majority leader can adjourn the Senate for the day whenever he wants to. So no filibuster unless the majority leader wants one. Do you think Senator Fitzgerald would have allowed the 14 Democratic Senators to filibuster the Act 10 legislation?

Therefore our only filibuster was to do what Abraham Lincoln did... get out of the building and avoid a quorum. Going to Illinois was the only filibuster available to us.

ABRAHAM LINCOLN AVOIDS A QUORUM

The future President Lincoln was serving in the Illinois State Assembly in 1840. He was opposing a banking bill and wanted to slow the bill down or kill it by keeping the State Assembly from having a quorum (sound familiar?). What did the future first Republican President of the United States do to avoid a quorum? He climbed out of a window of the building the state Assembly was meeting in and therefore avoided a quorum. When I left the Capitol to go to Illinois, I walked out a front door.

I have often wondered why Governor Walker and the Fitzgeralds have never criticized Lincoln.

WAS COLLECTIVE BARGAINING THE PROBLEM?

The political lines used by Governor Walker in 2011 to justify taking collective bargaining rights away from public employees and to pursue public funding of private schools through a statewide voucher program are well known. Walker said the public union support of politicians led to those politicians rewarding public employees with higher wages and higher benefits, which the taxpayer could no longer afford, etc.

Walker said the problem was collective bargaining and it needed to be eliminated. He said money for public education needed to be diverted to private schools. He said we had "failing" public schools. Really?

I want to focus on public education in Wisconsin and specifically K-12 public education. What was the condition of public education in Wisconsin at the beginning of 2011? Did Walker's solutions fit the challenge, problems, and needs that existed?

Test scores such as the ACT put Wisconsin at or near the top in the nation. Teachers wanted to teach in Wisconsin. Polls showed broad public support for public education.

LET'S LOOK AT THE REAL PROBLEMS IN PUBLIC SCHOOLS. DID HIS SOLUTIONS ADDRESS THEM?

Problem 1: Deteriorated family structure: More homes with only one parent, more homes with alcohol and drug problems, more homes where parents are not married, more urban and rural poverty (a contributor to poor student performance but in my view not an excuse), more homes with no role models to emphasize the importance of education. For far too many students the safest and most nurturing place is school as opposed to home. These conditions varied in severity depending on the school district, but existed all across Wisconsin.

Problem 2: These conditions led me to coin a term while I was on the Janesville School Board in 2008: the "un-child." I did not and do not mean by using this term that a kid is not a child. Rather that the un-child is faced with so many "uns." The "un-child" is unread to at home, unfed at home, un-hugged at home, undisciplined at home, unencouraged at home. No one makes sure the child gets to bed at night or up in the morning, no one makes sure the homework is done. In a word, the child is often unloved. The frequent result of these problems is that the student arrives at school (if at all) unready to learn. Simple and sad! Less likely to graduate, less likely to be attentive in class, and more likely to be disruptive. This all leads to lower grades, lower test scores, and lower graduation rates.

What are teachers doing in today's world that was unheard of thirty or more years ago? The problems students bring to school have become the problems teachers and teacher's aides try to alleviate every day. Teachers often must bring clothes to school for students and have washing machines at school to wash the dirty clothes some students arrive wearing. Teachers are now also social workers and police officers dealing with family matters and violence against them and other students.

The following are two stories that I was told that describe the real world for many in public schools:

An elementary school teacher sent home a permission slip for a parent to sign to allow their child to go on a school field trip. The student came back the next day with the permission slip unsigned. When the teacher asked why he didn't get it signed, the student said his dad was in jail and his mom was passed out on the couch! The teacher told me that beyond the tragedy of this child's home life was the fact that the child told her this information in such a casual and unembarrassed way; this was apparently normal to the child.

The other story involved a school bus stopping to pick up a six-year-old. One day the child did not come out to the bus so an aide went to the door. The six-year-old answered the door dressed, but said he could not come to school because he had to stay home to take care of his one-year-old brother. A six-year-old missing school to be responsible for a one-year-old!

These are the real conditions for many teachers and students in many places in Wisconsin and America. Please tell me how taking away collective bargaining rights or sending these students to private schools with public money will have any effect on any of these problems and challenges.

Problems brought into the school have become the teachers' problems if learning is to be a possibility for these children and the rest of the class. And the more attention these students receive the less the other students receive. These are problems in our society that are brought into the schools.

Are there problems in our schools that do need addressing? Yes. A better system to allow school boards to remove poor performing teachers was needed. We have 60,000 teachers in Wisconsin. Some are not good teachers. This is the case in every profession.

Some changes to the management structure of the Milwaukee Public School system were needed.

Teachers needed to pay some more for their health insurance and pensions. Our citizen support for our public institutions and public employees is best continued if things like benefits are not significantly different in the private and public sectors. Of course, it would be best if benefits in the private sector would stop disappearing. And if Walker was dead-set on reducing public sector benefits, at least he could have said he intended to do this before the election, and could have phased it in over four or five years.

My point is not that I want or get any pleasure out of teachers and other public employees paying more. I just believe that we are all in the same world, and public- and private-sector employees need to be on the same team.

Destroying collective bargaining was not needed to fix any of the challenges public education faced in 2011. Destroying it decimated a political opponent and therefore served the personal political goals of Scott Walker.

Were excessive teacher pay raises a problem in Wisconsin in 2011? The short answer is no. Wisconsin had in place, since 1993, a law called the Qualified Economic Offer or QEO. This basically limited teacher pay raises to a maximum of 3.8%. Negotiations between a teachers union and a school board often led to lower raises. Some may think those types of raises are excessive. I don't.

Act 10 was unnecessary and divisive. It was a state-splitting action that fit Walker's personal political career and did not address or solve the actual problems in K-12 education in Wisconsin.

WALKER'S PRIORITIES: NOT PUBLIC EDUCATION

A general criticism of Walker is that he balanced his budget on the back of public education. Well, it's true... and here are the numbers:

State School Aid (pre-K- 12 public education)	
2009-2011 Budget (pre-Walker)	2015-2017 Budget (current)
$10,640,400,000.00	$10,689,400,000.00

That is about as flat as you can get. A $49 million increase on a $10 billion budget over six years!

Costs do go up. Maintenance, 1.4% pay increases, utilities, etc., etc. Just a 2% annual increase would have added an additional $1,276,848,000 in state aid to public education over these six years.

It is also necessary to point out that the state law prohibits the school district from making up for state aid shortfalls from the property tax (the other major source of school funding) without a local referendum.

The public also deserves to know that while Walker was treating public education this way, he made two other expenditure changes that reduced the money available for public schools:

- Walker transferred hundreds of millions of dollars from the general fund (where above expenditures come from) to the Department of Transportation (which of course has its own funding sources such as the gas tax and licensing fees).

- Walker increased tax dollars going to private schools through private school program and independent charter school programming by $261 million during the same six years. This is money that would otherwise likely have gone to public schools.

My source for these numbers is the Wisconsin Legislative Fiscal Bureau—the nonpartisan state agency that oversees the state budget process.

How has Governor Walker shown his commitment to the University of Wisconsin System of the two-year and four-year universities in our state? He has treated them worse than K-12 education. The UW System receives less state aid in real dollars in the 2015-2017 budget than it received in 2009- 2011 before Walker took office:

UW System State Aid	
2009-2011 Budget (pre-Walker)	2015-2017 Budget (current)
$2,228,900,000	$2,053,400,000

This is an actual decrease of $155 million over six years.

CHAPTER 14

Examples of Politics Today

The enactment of Act 10 is a clear example of what has happened to politics in Wisconsin. There wasn't anything isolated about this. There are now people in both parties—I'm talking about legislators, legislative staff, interest groups, the whole entourage of people and groups that surround government—who wake up in the morning to fight the "war." This was very different from the first time I was there, and it made me feel really disappointed. My plans for what I wanted to do had blown up, my caucus was not happy with me, Republicans weren't interested in negotiating with me, and I was not going to get much done for Rock County. The "middle" is a pretty lonely place in today's politics.

Right after we came back from Illinois I still hadn't given up. I had lunch with Eric Schutt, then deputy chief of staff for the governor, to talk about ideas I had to put in the state budget in exchange for me voting for it. This was in April and Eric, who I have always gotten along with very well, to his credit, said this budget bill is going to be so bad for a Democrat that he doesn't see any way in the world that I would ever vote for it. There is no reason for the governor's office to negotiate with me about my issues for Rock County. We ended the conversation in a gentlemanly fashion. They weren't even slightly interested in getting votes from the Democrats and knew they were putting together a budget that no Democrat could vote for anyway. I actually thought it was an honorable, direct thing for him to say.

This was probably when I started thinking that I might not run for reelection. There is a very important role for the minority party, and that is to call out the majority party when you disagree with it and try to persuade public opinion against the majority party's decision. You have to know, as a member of the minority party that you have to make the speech and then lose, make the speech and then lose, make the speech and then lose. That's just not me. It became increasingly clear to me as time went on that the 15th District, if I didn't run again, would replace me with a Democrat who could vote and lose. I thought there were other things that I could do as a private citizen.

Republicans have a big problem, only worse now because they are in the majority. Their interest groups know they have the votes to deliver whatever the interest group wants. Republican leaders can't walk away from WMC, the Koch brothers, mining companies, the NRA, school vouchers supporters, on any issue those groups want. It's interesting that the legislative leaders have centralized the power in themselves in regard to running campaigns and fundraising, but then have lost control of the process to those that have all the money. Their power over their colleagues then comes by appeasing those who give the big money to the campaign. Here's the irony. Those who wanted to centralize power wound up losing it. Power now is in the hands of a relatively small number of groups with huge chunks of money. The legislative leaders took the power from their members but then lost it to the money!

These kinds of changes occur gradually, to the extent that people can realize what is going on. When I was there before, we had staff who worked on campaigns on weekends, off the public clock. Near the end of my time in the Capitol, people had their staffers start to take vacation time during the week to work on campaigns. That was legal. This is the old slippery slope... first just a Friday, then maybe a Monday, then a whole week. And soon that wasn't enough, so people started looking the other way as staff worked on campaigns on the public clock.

No staffer when I was at the Capitol in the 1970s and 1980s raised money. It was unheard of. When that changed, it led to the centralization of power. The more staff the leadership would send out there, the more money needed to be raised, and the more money that could be raised, the more beholden the leadership is to the contributor. You start having elected officials going to Madison who were beholden to their leadership on their first day in the Legislature. The leadership had their claws in them on day one.

CHAPTER 15

Wisdom from the Past and Hope for the Future

The events of the first few months of Scott Walker's governorship showed me that the way the state government ought to operate is gone for now. I don't know how to come back from this. But here's a start: It's going to take a governor who is going to say I have the power to do what I want, but I'm not going to do it. Instead, I'm going to listen to all points of view and try to unite Wisconsin. But the thing is, by doing so, they would have to irritate their base. It will take a special person.

UNITY BEYOND POLITICS

Wisconsin is special. Historically, events and activities unite Wisconsin's citizens in ways that are unrelated to politics and make our state unique. Wisconsin Pride should be recognized and honored. The twelve governors that preceded Walker knew this, but Walker doesn't acknowledge this list's role in uniting us as a people. Almost every Wisconsinite will tell you their state is special because of (to name a few):

1. The Friday night fish fry: It is simply the most popular meal in Wisconsin.

2. The Green Bay Packers: The only professional team that is owned collectively by the fans rather than some billionaire. Wisconsin citizens love their Packers with an intensity that may be difficult for many people across the nation to understand.

3. Up North: Deer hunting, fishing, snowmobiling, atv trails, camping, summer vacations... the people of Wisconsin have a healthy respect and appreciation for the state's wildlife and wild places. As a practical matter, a clean and accessible environment "Up North" has the support of much of Wisconsin, not just those who live there year-round.

4. Wisconsin Dells: A tourist's paradise in the middle of the state. A huge majority of Wisconsin families have experienced the Dells' natural beauty and unique attractions.

5. The Wisconsin Badgers: They have the only division one football team in the state. And what Wisconsinite doesn't get behind Badger basketball led by Bo Ryan? (Maybe some Marquette Golden Eagle fans?)

6. Door County: A beautiful tourist destination north of Green Bay.

7. Summerfest: A weeklong festival of music, food, drink, and other entertainment along the lakefront in Milwaukee. It's total attendance in 2014 was 851,879.

This list and others that I didn't think to mention gives me great hope that all of these things in common will help lead us back to being much more united than we are today.

ARE WE STILL A MERITOCRACY
(IN WISCONSIN AND THE NATION)?

Thomas Jefferson wanted America to be a meritocracy. He wanted merit to determine who became our elected leaders. He did not want an aristocracy based on what family you are in. By and large that has not been a problem in America or Wisconsin state government. The only exception in Wisconsin is arguably the La Follettes and nationally the Kennedys and Bushes, and maybe the Clintons and Roosevelts. Meritocracy, however, is threatened today in a different way than what worried Jefferson.

The vast amount of unregulated, undisclosed campaign money is changing us toward a plutocracy. Governor Walker joined a number of Republican presidential hopefuls who seemed more than willing to travel anywhere that a billionaire resides to beg for their support. Of course it didn't work out for Walker. He dropped out of the presidential race early. But money remains key to campaigns. It does not take too many billionaires to finance an entire race. The $100 giver, the $1,000 giver, for that matter the $10,000 giver is appreciated but not like they were before. Today, the coveted action is with the billionaires who can spend hundreds of millions of dollars during campaigns. My concern is not partisan. Supporters of Hillary Clinton hope to raise $2.5 billion for her campaign, and billionaire Democrats will spend lavishly, just as the Koch Brothers do.

THOMAS JEFFERSON WAS RIGHT

I believe Thomas Jefferson was right when he said, "Great innovations should not be forced by a slender majority." Our third president said this in 1808. I have interpreted this to mean that fundamental changes enacted by narrow majorities can lead to turmoil and opposition from citizens, and that these changes should be passed with bipartisan support. I believe very strongly that Jefferson had this right over 200 years ago and yet today political leaders of both parties continue to ignore his wisdom.

Act 10 certainly helped put Scott Walker on the national stage. That was, to me, clearly on his mind in 2011. Act 10 passed with only Republican votes and there was no concern for getting Democratic votes or support. Deliberately dividing your state because in one election your party was given total control does not mean that your constituents expect you to ignore the opinions of a large minority. Whether you agree with or oppose Walker's Act 10, no one can deny that it angrily divided Wisconsin more than anytime in at least the last 65 years. And we are still divided today in what I believe is an unhealthy way.

The twelve governors that preceded Walker governed in a way which Wisconsin had come to expect. They gave the public broad knowledge on their ideas and received major input through study commissions or committees. These governors never surprised the people of Wisconsin on any of their big ideas that, if implemented, would lead to change that would greatly affect the people of Wisconsin. Contrast this approach to governing Wisconsin with Scott Walker's continuing approach of no warning on major changes... his self-described "dropping the bomb" style.

Which leadership style is better for the people of Wisconsin? For our nation? I am convinced it is the "containment" approach of Walker's 12 predecessors, and I believe we will return to the values of the pre-Walker Wisconsin and to the wisdom of Thomas Jefferson.

OPTIMISM, THE MOST TOLERANT AND OPEN-MINDED GENERATION, AND THE INTERNET

I believe the direction Governor Walker has taken Wisconsin is wrong. I am deeply concerned about the enormous influence of money on our government and politics. The major social divisions in America are still there and have been since the beginning of our nation.

Yet, I am optimistic. Tom Brokaw has referred to the World War II generation as the "Greatest Generation." I believe we have another generation that deserves a name. People in their 30s and younger are America's "Most Tolerant Generation." They are tolerant of people who are "different" from themselves. The difference could be skin color, sexual orientation, or opinions they disagree with (particularly if the people with different views respect their views, too.)

There always seems to be a desire to categorize groups. Is this generation "Democrat" or "Republican?" Are they "liberal" or "conservative?" My observation is that they are disenchanted with both major political parties. Many of their views are libertarian. They want people to respect their right to live their own lives as they see fit (peacefully, of course) and want that for others, too.

They are not big supporters of unions, but they do believe in fair treatment of people in the workplace. I believe their answer is to put them at the top of companies and they will treat employees well, pay them fairly, and workers won't need unions. This "Most Tolerant Generation" does not seem to be big on church-going like most of their parents and grandparents are or were, yet I find their value system and their concern for others, not just themselves, for example, are consistent with the teachings of all the great religions' leaders. They seem to me to believe in the teachings of Jesus Christ, Gandhi, Dr. Martin Luther King, Jr., etc.

Another reason for my optimism is the Internet. The ability to communicate and organize people with similar views to raise money for causes they believe in and do all of this more quickly and inexpensively cannot be overrated. The Internet is the "little person's" counter to billionaire money in politics. People across the nation and world who share the same views on issues can find each other and organize together with speed and efficiency.

Aberrations happen, and by definition are the exception. They don't last. I see a future where "people power" will be the power in Wisconsin and in America, and this people power, harnessed by the "Most Tolerant Generation," will lead us as we continue to strive to be "a more perfect union."

AND AT THE END OF THE DAY...

I believe that during the next decade Wisconsin will look back on the Walker years as an aberration, and that Wisconsin politics will return to the "containment" approach to governing that was the approach of Walker's 12 predecessors between 1950 and 2010.

I believe we will gradually stop being angry and divisive in our approach to politics. We Wisconsinites have far too much in common to not realize we need to get back together and move Wisconsin forward together.

I hope we never again have a governor who will surprise the state with policy changes by dropping "bombs" and have a strategy of "dividing and conquering" the very citizens of the state he governs; a governor who will never issue a pardon, but will diminish public education; or a governor who shows a serious misunderstanding of the role of the University of Wisconsin System, while turning down over half a billion dollars in federal money for Medicaid.

Times will get better.

APPENDIX A

Title	Governor	Date Created
Improved Expenditure Management	Knowles	2/26/1965
Resources Priorities Board	Knowles	11/1/1965
Gov's Marquette Tercentenary Committee	Knowles	4/13/1966
Gov's Task Force on the Outdoor Recreation Act Program	Knowles	9/28/1966
Task Force on Computer Services	Knowles	2/15/1967
Task Force on Medical Education	Knowles	2/22/1967
Adv. Com. on Securities	Knowles	5/13/1967
Employment Relations Com.	Knowles	2/12/1969
Special Task Force on Education	Knowles	2/19/1969
Gov's Comn. on Law Enforcement and Crime	Knowles	2/21/1969
Council on Criminal Justice	Knowles	2/21/1969
Urban Affairs Council	Knowles	5/6/1969
Gov's Comn. on Children and Youth	Knowles	5/13/1969
Adv. Com. on State Employment Relations	Knowles	5/13/1969
State Manpower Council	Knowles	10/26/1969
Interagency State Planning Council	Knowles	5/13/1970
Wis. Arts Foundation & Arts Council	Knowles	5/13/1970
Gov's Com. on Eminent Domain	Knowles	5/13/1970
Gov's Committee for the Employment of the Handicapped	Knowles	5/13/1970
Consulting Com. to the Federal Historic Sites Preservation Act of 1966	Knowles	5/13/1970
Wis. Development Authority	Knowles	5/13/1970
Gov's Committee on the United Nations	Knowles	5/13/1970
Adv. Comprehensive Health Planning Council	Knowles	5/13/1970
Gov's Study Committee on Migratory Labor	Knowles	5/13/1970
Gov's Council on Physical Activity and Sports for Fitness	Knowles	5/13/1970
Northern Great Lakes Area Council	Knowles	5/13/1970
Project Sanguine Study Committee	Knowles	5/13/1970
Advisory Council on Vocational Education	Knowles	5/13/1970
Comn. on Status of Women	Knowles	5/13/1970
Gov's Com. on Children and Youth	Knowles	5/13/1970
Mission 70 Steering Group and Advisory Council	Knowles	5/27/1970
Committee on Special Learning Needs	Knowles	6/3/1970
Committee on Special Learning	Knowles	9/24/1970
Task Force '71 on Agricultural and Rural Affairs	Lucey	2/12/1971
Task Force '71 on Commerce and Industry	Lucey	2/12/1971

Task Force '71 on Consumer Protection	Lucey	2/12/1971
Task Force '71 on Commerce and Industry	Lucey	2/12/1971
Task Force '71 on Environmental Protection and Natural Resources	Lucey	2/12/1971
Citizens Study Committee on Judicial Organization	Lucey	Apr-71
Citizens Study Committee on Metropolitan Troubles	Lucey	Apr-71
State Health Planning and Program Council	Lucey	4/2/1971
Wis. Environmental Council	Lucey	5/10/1971
Gov's Health Planning and Policy Task Force	Lucey	5/12/1971
Study Com. on Offender Rehabilitation	Lucey	5/21/1971
Gov's Task Force on Voter Registration and Elections	Lucey	7/15/1971
Gov's Recycling Task Force on Solid Waste	Lucey	7/15/1971
Wis. Land Resources Com.	Lucey	7/22/1971
Gov's Blue Ribbon Commission on Cable TV	**Lucey**	**11/5/1971**
Gov's Task Force on Educational Financing and Property Tax Reform	Lucey	1/28/1972
Study Com. on the Arts & Wis. Arts Council	Lucey	2/4/1972
Coun. On Consumer Affairs	Lucey	Mar-72
Com. to Review Timber Management on State-Owned Lands	Lucey	4/18/1972
Gov's Study Committee on Mass Transit	Lucey	4/28/1972
Spec. Comn. to Investigate State Real Estate Purchasing and Leasing Policies	Lucey	7/27/1972
No-Fault Legislative Advisory Com.	Lucey	11/6/1972
Kickapoo Area Advisory Committee	Lucey	2/5/1973
Gov's Task Force on Problems of People with Physical Handicaps	Lucey	3/16/1973
State Interagency Energy Committee	Lucey	11/2/1973
Adv. Com. on Income Maintenance	Lucey	7/3/1974
Advisory Committee on Mental Health, AODA and other Disabilities	Lucey	7/3/1974
Gov's Advisory Com. on Children and Youth	Lucey	1/27/1975
Adv. Com. on Income Maintenance	Lucey	1/27/1975
Adv. Com. on Mental Health, AODA, Alcoholism & other Disabilities	Lucey	1/27/1975
Historic Preservation Review Board	Lucey	1/27/1975
Affirmative Action Executive Commission	Lucey	4/23/1975
Gov's Commission on State-Local Relations and Financing Policy	Lucey	Oct-75
Gov's Committee for People with Disabilities	Lucey	10/17/1975
Gov's Council for Spanish-Speaking People	Lucey	12/30/1975
Employment Relations Study Comn.	Lucey	6/10/1976
Council on Rural Area and Community Development	Lucey	9/17/1976
Gov's Manpower Council	Lucey	2/16/1977

State Historical Records Advisory Board	Lucey	4/4/1977
Gov's Advisory Bicycle Coordinating Council	Lucey	6/29/1977
Wis. Coastal Management Council	Schreiber	10/7/1977
Gov's Manpower Planning Office	Schreiber	10/24/1977
Blue Ribbon Tax Reform Study Comn.	Schreiber	1/26/1978
Gov's Committee for Hispanic Affairs	Schreiber	8/25/1978
Task Force on Hazardous Materials Safety	Dreyfus	1/22/1979
Gov's Advisory Council for the Intergovernmental Personnel Act	Dreyfus	1/22/1979
Wis. Sentencing Study Committee	Dreyfus	1/22/1979
Gov's Youth Advisory Council	Dreyfus	1/22/1979
Citzens Council on AODA	Dreyfus	1/29/1979
Gov's Comn. on the Dept. of Natural Resources Evaluation	Dreyfus	4/5/1979
Gov's Employment and Training Office	Dreyfus	5/1/1979
Gov's Employe Safety Task Force	Dreyfus	8/2/1979
Gov's Advisory Council on Children and Families	Dreyfus	10/30/1979
Wis. Energy Poiicy Task Force	Dreyfus	1/31/1980
Task Force on County Government Organization & Adm.	Dreyfus	Feb-80
Gov's Conference on Aging for 1980	Dreyfus	2/18/1980
Gov's Pardon Advisory Board	Dreyfus	3/16/1980
Education Adv. Council	Dreyfus	4/11/1980
Gov's Advisory Council on Asians	Dreyfus	6/19/1980
Gov's Advisory Council on Blacks	Dreyfus	6/19/1980
Gov's Advisory Council on Hispanics	Dreyfus	6/19/1980
Gov's Special Com. on State Mandates	Dreyfus	8/29/1980
Gov's Cuban Resettlement Fact Finding Comn.	Dreyfus	8/29/1980
Ad Hoc Radiation Disposal Committee	Dreyfus	11/22/1980
Displaced Homemaker Task Force	Dreyfus	12/18/1980
Homemaker Task Force	Dreyfus	12/18/1980
Marital Economic Task Force	Dreyfus	12/18/1980
Single Parent/Single Woman Task Force	Dreyfus	12/18/1980
Violence Against Women Task Force	Dreyfus	12/18/1980
Gov's Council on Forest Productivity	Dreyfus	3/23/1981
Arbor Month Committee	Dreyfus	3/25/1981
Spec. Com. on Forest Fire Management	Dreyfus	5/9/1981
Com. on International Trade	Dreyfus	6/24/1981
Gov's Special Com. on Transportation Aids	Dreyfus	10/18/1981

Ad Hoc Technical Advisory Com. on Low-Level Radioactive Waste	Dreyfus	10/26/1981
Task Force on Tourism	**Dreyfus**	**3/19/1982**
Gov's Special Com. on Transporation Revenue	Dreyfus	4/7/1982
Fox River Locks Task Force	Dreyfus	6/16/1982
Civil Rights Compliance Task Force	Dreyfus	7/24/1982
Wis. Women's Council	Earl	2/1/1983
Gov's Council on Lesbian and Gay issues	Earl	3/29/1983
Gov's Council on Physical Fitness and Health	Earl	4/19/1983
Council on Economic Affairs	Earl	5/16/1983
Gov's Task Force on Solid Waste Recycling	Earl	8/4/1983
Faculty Compensation Study Commission	Earl	9/22/1983
Interagency Wis. Environmental Policy Act Coordinating Comn.	Earl	9/25/1983
Gov's School Finance Task Force	Earl	10/20/1983
Gov's Task Force on Nursing Homes	Earl	12/29/1983
Wis. Strategic Development Comn.	Earl	3/12/1984
Wis. - Heilongjiang Coordinating Committee	Earl	3/19/1984
Wis. State Senior Managers Council	Earl	3/20/1984
Comn. on the Quality of Education in Metropolitan Milwaukee Public Educatio	Earl	6/8/1984
Statewide Occupational and Information Coordinating Council	Earl	5/15/1985
Wis. Land Records Com.	Earl	8/7/1985
Task Force on Professional and Occupational Discipline	Earl	11/5/1985
Wis. Expenditure Comn.	Earl	11/26/1985
Farm Mediation Board	Earl	3/21/1986
Alcohol Fuels Study Com.	Earl	3/21/1986
Commission for Indian and Non-Indian Cooperation	Earl	6/20/1986
Strategic Planning Council	Earl	9/4/1986
Wis. Bicentennial Committee on the Constitution	Earl	10/31/1986
Gov's Council on Asian Affairs	Thompson	1/21/1987
Local Property Tax Relief Comn.	Thompson	2/6/1987
VTAE Study Commission	Thompson	2/25/1987
State Job Training Coordinating Council	Thompson	3/4/1987
State Emergency Response Comn.	Thompson	4/15/1987
Gov's Nursing Education Coordinating Council	Thompson	4/21/1987
State Interagency Coordinating Council re handicapped children	Thompson	6/16/1987
Gov's Council on Biotechnology	Thompson	6/23/1987
Gov's Clean Water Fund Task Force	Thompson	9/22/1987

Gov's Nursing Study Com.	Thompson	10/8/1987
Gov's Comn. on Law Enforcement and Crime	Thompson	11/25/1987
AIDS Advisory Council	Thompson	12/23/1987
Gov's State Housing Task Force	Thompson	1/6/1988
Gov's Rural Development Coordinating Council	Thompson	5/16/1988
Wis. Retirement System Study Committee	Thompson	5/19/1988
Gov's Comn. on Taliesin	Thompson	6/27/1988
Gov's Council on Economic Issues	Thompson	7/25/1988
Gov's Committee for Minority Affairs	Thompson	7/25/1988
Task Force on Family and Chidren's Issues	Thompson	1/2/1989
Gov's Committee on Long-Term Care of Solid and Hazardous Waste Facilities	Thompson	11/24/1989
Comn. on Schools for the 21st Century	Thompson	12/14/1989
Gov's Advisory Com. on Recreational Business Development	Thompson	1/11/1990
Com. on Minority Participation in Post-Secondary Vocational and Technical Ed	Thompson	1/22/1990
Gov's Science and Technology Council	Thompson	1/24/1990
Comn. for a Qualtiy Workforce	Thompson	1/31/1990
Housing Policy Task Force	Thompson	3/9/1990
Gov's Council on Urban Indian Affairs	Thompson	6/15/1990
Telecommunications Relay Service Council	Thompson	6/19/1990
Gov's Special Task Force on Fort McCoy	Thompson	6/27/1990
Gov's Committees on Area Promotion in Northern Wis.	Thompson	7/2/1990
Gov's Council on Natural Resources in Northern Wis.	Thompson	7/2/1990
Gov's Comn. on Children and Families	Thompson	8/1/1990
Gov's Council on Forestry	Thompson	1/25/1991
Commission for a Quality Workforce	Thompson	1/25/1991
Gov's Council on African American Affairs	Thompson	2/21/1991
Gov's Blue Ribbon Commission on Lottery Advertising	Thompson	3/11/1991
Blue Ribbon Task Force on Gambling	Thompson	10/20/1991
Comn. on UW System Compensation	Thompson	12/4/1991
Gov's Advisory Council on Mandates	Thompson	3/19/1992
Gov's Comn. on Dental Care	Thompson	6/18/1992
Task Force on Regulatory Barriers to Affordable Housing	Thompson	8/25/1992
Council on Youth Village - Milwaukee	Thompson	2/25/1993
Task Force on UW Accountability Measures	Thompson	3/17/1993
Blue Ribbon Telecommunications Infrastructure Task Force	Thompson	3/29/1993
State Rehabilitation Advisory Council	Thompson	7/1/1993

Governor's Clean Air Act Amdts. Implementation Task Force	Thompson	8/3/1993
Statewide independent Living Council	Thompson	1/10/1994
Gov's Milwaukee Stadium Commission	Thompson	3/1/1994
Glass Ceiling Comn.	Thompson	6/23/1994
Task Force on Creation of a Wis. Business Court	Thompson	7/3/1994
Comn. on School Violence	Thompson	7/28/1994
Gov's Export Strategy Comn.	Thompson	9/7/1994
Wis. Resource Investment Council	Thompson	9/9/1994
State Interagency Land Use Council	Thompson	9/15/1994
Wis. Strategic Growth Task Force	Thompson	9/15/1994
Wis. Humanities Council	Thompson	1/20/1995
Gov's Law Enforcement and Crime Comn.	Thompson	1/20/1995
Education Block Grant Advisory Com.	Thompson	1/20/1995
Comn. on Human Resources Reform	Thompson	10/10/1995
Commission on Human Resource Reform	Thompson	10/10/1995
Gov's Advisory Task Force on Edcuation and Learning	Thompson	1/24/1996
Blue Ribbon Commission on Mental Health Care	Thompson	5/13/1996
Gov's Blue Ribbon Commission on 21st Century Jobs	Thompson	7/1/1996
Gov's Task Force on the Compulsory School Attendance Age	Thompson	7/18/1996
Blue Ribbon Commission on Campaign Finance Reform	Thompson	11/19/1996
Wis. International Trade Council	Thompson	11/19/1996
Gov's Council on Model Academic Standards	Thompson	1/24/1997
Comn. on Teaching in the 21st Century	Thompson	2/17/1997
Gov's Comn. on Teaching in the 21st Century	Thompson	2/17/1997
Gov's Blue Ribbon Task force on the Stewardship Program	Thompson	3/14/1997
Wis. Science Advisory Council on Metallic Mining	Thompson	4/7/1997
Blue Ribbon Task Force on Acquaculture	Thompson	5/21/1998
Gov's Blue Ribbon Commission on Year 2000 Preparedness	Thompson	7/27/1998
Wis. Land Council	Thompson	7/29/1998
Gov's Task Force on Building Tomorrow's Workforce	Thompson	1/30/1999
State Rehabilitation Council	Thompson	2/10/1999
Gov's W2 and AODA Task Force	Thompson	2/19/1999
Gov's Blue Ribbon Task Force on Passenger Rail Service	Thompson	3/29/1999
Gov's Task Force on Privacy	Thompson	7/16/1999
Menomonee River Council	Thompson	9/14/1999
Gov's Blue Ribbon Task Force on Manufactured Housing	Thompson	11/10/1999

Gov's Council on Workforce Investment	Thompson	11/17/1999
Gov's Task Force on Racial Profiling	Thompson	12/27/1999
Task Force on Growing Wisconsin Agriculture	Thompson	3/15/2000
Commission on State/Local Partnerships for the 21st Century	Thompson	4/5/2000
Poet Laureate Nomination Council	Thompson	7/31/2000
Gov's Advisory Task Force on the Proposed Federal Roadless Initiative	Thompson	10/30/2000
Gov's Task Force on Invasive Species	McCallum	5/23/2001
Wis. Commemorative Quarter Coucil	McCallum	9/20/2001
Gov's Task Force on Terrorism Preparedness	McCallum	10/1/2001
Task Force on Financial Education	McCallum	11/15/2001
Gov's Comn. on Historic Sites	McCallum	11/15/2001
Gov's Year of the Trails Commission	McCallum	11/15/2001
Gov's Task Force on Financial Education	McCallum	11/15/2001
Gov's Task Force on Jails and Community Corrections	McCallum	1/16/2002
Task Force on State and Local Government	McCallum	3/5/2002
Gov's Task Force on Ethics Reform in Government	McCallum	5/15/2002
Wisconsin Encourages Healthy Lifestyles (WEHL) Council	McCallum	6/24/2002
Gov's Homeland Security Council	Doyle	3/18/2003
Gov's Task Force on Educational Excellence	Doyle	8/22/2003
Task Force on Energy Efficiency and Renewables	Doyle	9/30/2003
Gov's Interagency Council on Homelessness	Doyle	8/9/2004
Wis. Citizens Corp. Council	Doyle	9/7/2004
State Interoperability Executive Council (SIEC)	Doyle	2/2/2005
Gov's Council on Financial Literacy	Doyle	3/30/2005
Gov's Council on Financial Literacy	Doyle	3/30/2005
Autism Adv. Council	Doyle	4/5/2005
Consortium on Biobased Industry	Doyle	5/27/2005
Gov's Taks Force on Waste Materials Recovery and Disposal	Doyle	6/14/2005
Board for eHealth Care Quality and Patient Safety	Doyle	11/2/2005
Healthy Wis. Council	Doyle	7/5/2006
Comn. on Reducing Racial Disparities in the Wis. Justice System	Doyle	3/21/2007
Gov's Task Force on Global Warming	Doyle	4/5/2007
Gov's Business Council	Doyle	4/17/2007
Task Force on Campus Safety	Doyle	5/2/2007
Wisconsin Lincoln Bicentennial Commission	Doyle	4/7/2008
Racial Disparities Oversight Comn.	Doyle	5/13/2008

Gov's State Advisory Council on Early Childhood Education and Care	Doyle	10/30/2008
Reentry Task Force	Doyle	4/17/2009
WIRED for Health Board	Doyle	12/1/2009
Board for the Wisconsin Relay of Electroinc Data for Health (WIRED)	Doyle	12/1/2009
Gov's Comn. on Waste, Fraud and Abuse	Walker	1/3/2011
Birth to Three Interagency Coordinating Council	Walker	1/21/2011
Independent Living Council	Walker	1/21/2011
Historical Records Advisory Board	Walker	1/21/2011
State Interoperability Council	Walker	1/21/2011
Early Childhood Advisory Council	Walker	1/21/2011
Gov's Read to Lead Task Force	Walker	3/31/2011
Gov's Council on Financial Literacy	Walker	4/6/2011
Wis. Next Generation Reserve Fund Board	Walker	9/28/2011
Wis. Technology Com.	Walker	11/4/2011
College and Workforce Readiness Council	Walker	1/13/2012
Information Technology Steering Committee	Walker	4/26/2013
Council on Veterans Employment	Walker	6/13/2014

Appendix B

The text is below. I've crossed out the vetoed part and what remains is in bold. This is on pages 373-374 of the 2005-07 budget, 2005 WI Act 25.

Chopped up, it reads:

(4f) The department of transportation shall transfer to the general fund from the transportation fund in the 2005-07 fiscal biennium, $427,000,000.

(4f) ~~AGENCY REQUEST RELATING TO MARQUETTE INTERCHANGE RECONSTRUCTION PROJECT BONDING. Notwithstanding section 16.42 (1) of the statutes, in submitting information under section 16.42 of the statutes for purposes of the 2007–09 biennial budget act,~~ **the department of transportation shall** ~~include recommended reductions to the appropriation under section 20.395 (3) (cr) of the statutes for each fiscal year of the 2007–09 fiscal biennium reflecting the~~ **transfer** ~~from this appropriation account~~ **to the** ~~appropriation account under section 20.395 (6) (au) of the statutes, as created by this act, of amounts for anticipated debt service payments, in each fiscal year of the 2007–09 fiscal biennium, on~~ **general** ~~obligation bonds issued under section 20.866 (2) (uup) of the statutes, as created by this act.~~

~~(4w) PASSENGER RAIL SERVICE.~~

~~(a) The department of transportation may submit, in each fiscal year of the 2005–07 biennium, a request to the joint committee on finance to supplement the appropriation under section 20.395 (2) (cr) of the statutes by up to $572,700 in fiscal year 2005–06 and up to $629,900 in fiscal year 2006–07 from the appropriation account under section 20.865 (4) (u) of the statutes for passenger rail service. Any request submitted under this paragraph shall be submitted by the due date for agency requests for the joint committee on finance's second quarterly meeting under section 13.10 of the statutes of the year in which the request is made. The committee may supplement the appropriation under section 20.395~~

(2) (er) of the statutes by up to $572,700 in fiscal year 2005–06 and up to $629,900 in fiscal year 2006–07 from the appropriation account under section 20.865 (4) (u) of the statutes for passenger rail service and, notwithstanding section 13.101 (3) of the statutes, the committee is not required to find that an emergency exists prior to making the supplementation.

(b) If the joint committee on finance determines that the moneys provided under section 20.395 (2) (er) and (ex) of the statutes are sufficient for passenger rail service in any fiscal year of the 2005–07 biennium, the committee may:

1. Supplement, by up to to $572,700 in fiscal year 2005–06 and up to $629,900 in fiscal year 2006–07 from the appropriation account under section 20.865 (4) (u) of the statutes, other department of transportation appropriations. Notwithstanding section 13.101 (3) of the statutes, the committee is not required to find that an emergency exists prior to making the supplementation.

2. Transfer moneys from the appropriation account under section 20.395 (2) (ex) of the statutes that are not needed for passenger rail services to other department of transportation appropriations. Notwithstanding section 13.101 (4) of the statutes, the committee is not required to find, prior to making the transfer, that unnecessary duplication of functions can be eliminated, more efficient and effective methods for performing programs will result, or legislative intent will be more effectively carried out because of such transfer.

(c) If the committee approves a supplement under paragraph (a), the committee may supplement, by the amount by which the supplement it approves under paragraph (a) is less than $572,700 in fiscal year 2005–06 or $629,900 in fiscal year 2006–07, other department of transportation appropriations. Notwithstanding section 13.101 (3) of the statutes, the committee is not required to find that an emergency exists prior to making the supplementation.

(d) If, in considering a request made under paragraph (a), the joint committee on finance determines that $572,700 in fiscal year 2005–06 or $629,900 in fiscal year 2006–07 is not sufficient to **fund** passenger rail service, the committee may supplement the appropriation account under section 20.395 (2) (cr) of the statutes, **from** the appropriation under section 20.865 (4) (u) of the statutes, by an amount that would not cause **the transportation fund** to have a negative balance. Notwithstanding section 13.101 (3) of the statutes, the Vetoed In Part Vetoed In Part Vetoed In Part Vetoed In Part Vetoed In Part Vetoed In Part Vetoed In Part Vetoed In Part Vetoed In Part Vetoed In Part Vetoed In Part Vetoed In Part 2005 Wisconsin Act 25 — 374 — 2005 Assembly Bill 100 committee is not required to find that an emergency exists prior to making the supplementation.

(5f) VILLAGE OF OREGON STREETSCAPING PROJECT. **In the 2005−07 fiscal biennium,** from the appropriation under section 20.395 (2) (nx) of the statutes, the department of transportation shall award a grant under section 85.026 (2) of the statutes of **$4**84,000 to the village of Oregon in Dane County for a streetscaping project on Main Street and Janesville Street in the village of Oregon if the village of Oregon contributes funds for the project that at least equal 20 percent of the costs of the project.

(5g) CHIPPEWA COUNTY CROSSING AND RAMP. In the 2005−07 fiscal biennium, from the appropriation under section 20.395 (2) (nx) of the statutes, the department of transportation shall award a grant under section 85.026 (2) of the statutes of $8**0,000** to Chippewa County for the construction of a pedestrian−railroad crossing and handicap−accessible ramp related to the Ray's Beach revitalization project on Lake Wissota in Chippewa County if Chippewa County contributes funds for the project that at least equal 20 percent of the costs of the project .

Source: https://docs.legis.wisconsin.gov/2005/related/acts/25.pdf

APPENDIX C

July 19, 2012

Mr. Kennan R. Wood
Wood Communications Group, Inc.
4801 S Biltmore Ln
Madison, WI 53718

Dear Kennan:

Thank you for taking the time to meet with Kurt, Scott and me on the mining issue. As a follow-up, I would like to reiterate some of our observations about recent WMA activities surrounding the proposed mining legislation.

First, we view the purpose of mining law reform to be the establishment of a reasonable regulatory structure that is acceptable to Gogebic Taconite. Therefore we need to take our cues from the company on the substance of any legislation and the strategy to get it enacted. At the end of the day the only logical goal of mining reform legislation is to get the Gogebic Taconite Company to build a mine in Wisconsin. Pursuing legislation that does not work for them is a waste of time.

It is also important to note that there will be no substantive action on any legislation for the remainder of 2012 and the make-up of the legislature that reconvenes in January 2013 is unknown at this time. The November elections will tell the story. A change of two members in the Senate – which is very likely- would pave the way for passage of Honadel's mining bill. We know that his bill would create a regulatory environment that is acceptable to at least one mining company. That scenario represents our best shot at creating mining jobs in Wisconsin in the foreseeable future.

However, if the majority does not shift with a two vote margin it is unlikely we will be able to secure passage of a mining bill that is acceptable to any company that might be interested in the Gogebic deposit.

Given these realities, I think it is premature, at best, to be discussing alternative mining legislation with George Meyer, Bob Jauch or anybody else. What can pass hinges on the make-up of the 2013 legislature and we won't know that until November. Compromise may be necessary at some point, but, as you know, timing is everything when it comes to striking a deal in the legislature. Premature discussions will only make it more difficult to get an acceptable bill passed latter if we find we have the votes.

We are also concerned that the proposed study comparing Wisconsin's regulatory environment to other states could be a potential quagmire. The complexity of the regulatory framework both here and in other states makes it difficult to make an "apples to apples" comparison. As a result there will always be room for mining opponents to use the study to argue for more regulation, or different regulation based on the laws and regulations in other states. This could further confuse legislators and opinion leaders and make it more difficult to pass a bill that is acceptable to the mining industry. In the end, I believe that such a study is likely to raise additional questions, rather than provide answers.

Lastly, I was wondering when we might see a financial statement for the association. As a board we have a fiduciary responsibility to members/contributors and should therefore be apprised of the association's financial position.

---

501 East Washington Avenue, Madison, WI 53703-2914 • P.O. Box 352, Madison, WI 53701-0352
Phone (608) 258-3400 • Fax (608) 258-3413 • www.wmc.org

WMC is a business association dedicated to making Wisconsin the most competitive state in the nation.

In summary we do feel we need to wait until after the November elections, when the make-up of the legislature is settled, before we develop appropriate legislation and a strategy to get it enacted.

Thanks again for taking time to meet with us and consider our perspective.

Sincerely,

James A. Buchen
Senior Vice President

CC: Wisconsin Mining Association Board of Directors

STATE RANKINGS: 1ST QUARTER JOB GROWTH

Over the past decade, Wisconsin has mostly ranked in the middle of all states for employment growth. Among Midwestern states, Wisconsin was once among the leaders, but in recent years others states have gained. How states rank in year-over-year percent change of private-sector employees for the first quarter ending in March each year:

| | GOV. JIM DOYLE | | | | | | | | GOV. SCOTT WALKER | | | | |
Rank	2003	2004	2005	2006	2007	2008	2009	2010	2011	2012	2013	2014	2015
1													
2									MICH				
3													
4										MICH			
5									IND				
6													
7													
8							IOWA	IND					
9											MICH		
10								IOWA	MINN				
11													
12													
13										IND			
14										OHIO			
15				MINN									
16										MINN			
17	WIS					IOWA							
18									WIS				IND
19									OHIO				MICH
20			IOWA					MINN			MINN	MICH	MINN
21									ILL				
22		IOWA								IOWA			
23	IND		WIS			MINN						IOWA	
24													
25							MINN						
26				ILL			WIS	WIS					
27						WIS	ILL	MICH			OHIO		
28			MINN	IOWA			MICH						
29											IOWA	IND	
30					ILL								WIS
31						ILL							
32		WIS		ILL			OHIO			ILL	WIS		OHIO
33	IOWA										IND	ILL	
34												WIS	
35													
36			IND	IND				OHIO		WIS		MINN	IOWA
37	OHIO				IOWA			ILL					
38		IND			WIS				IOWA		ILL		
39	ILL						IND						
40													ILL
41													
42													
43				WIS									
44					IND	OHIO							
45	MICH					IND							
46		MINN	ILL	OHIO		MICH							
47		OHIO	OHIO		MINN								
48		ILL											
49			MICH	MICH	OHIO		MICH						
50		MICH			MICH								

SOURCE: U.S. Bureau of Labor Statistics, Quarterly Census of Employment and Wages

To view chart in color: http://host.madison.com/business/wisconsin-lags-midwest-job-growth-state-rankings/html_94b31476-74a1-11e3-9597-0019bb2963f4.html#.VbFUDSAhbAY.email

APPENDIX E

Date	ContributedTo	ContributorName	City, StateZip	Employer	InterestCategory	Amount
4/13/12	Walker, Scott	Hendricks, Diane M	Beloit, WI 53511	ABC Supply Co	Construction	$500,000
3/30/12	Walker, Scott	Adelson, Sheldon	Las Vegas, NV 89109	Las Vegas Sands	Tourism/ Leisure/ Entertainment	$250,000
3/16/12	Walker, Scott	Devos, Richard M	Lantana, FL 33462	Alticor	Health Services/ Institutions	$250,000
1/17/12	Walker, Scott	Perry, Bob J	Houston, TX 77234	Perry Homes	Construction	$250,000
1/14/12	Walker, Scott	Humphreys, David C	Joplin, MO 64803	TAMKO Building Products	Construction	$250,000
1/13/12	Walker, Scott	Atkins, Sarah	Joplin, MO 64802	TAMKO Building Products	Construction	$250,000
1/17/12	Walker, Scott	Herzog, Stanley M	St Joseph, MO 64502	Herzog Contracting Corp	Road Construction	$240,000
11/16/11	Walker, Scott	Perry, Bob J	Houston, TX 77234	Perry Homes	Construction	$230,000
5/27/12	Walker, Scott	Pieper, Richard R	Mequon, WI 53092	Pieper Electric	Construction	$100,000
4/23/12	Walker, Scott	Childs, John W	Waltham, MA 02451	JW Childs Associates	Banking & Finance	$100,000
4/23/12	Walker, Scott	Kern, Patricia E	Waukesha, WI 53189	Generac Corp	Manufacturing & Distributing	$100,000
4/23/12	Walker, Scott	Kern, Robert D	Waukesha, WI 53189	Generac Corp	Manufacturing & Distributing	$100,000
3/22/12	Walker, Scott	Stephens, Warren A	Little Rock, AR 72207	Stephens Inc	Banking & Finance	$100,000
1/14/12	Walker, Scott	Rees-Jones, Trevor D	Dallas, TX 75225	Chief Oil & Gas LLC	Natural Resources	$100,000
11/16/11	Walker, Scott	Friess, Foster	Jackson, WY 83001	Friess Associates Inc	Banking & Finance	$100,000
11/16/11	Walker, Scott	Uihlein, Elizabeth A	Lake Forest, IL 60045	U-Line Corp	Construction	$100,000
11/16/11	Walker, Scott	Uihlein, Richard E	Lake Forest, IL 60045	U-Line Corp	Construction	$100,000
4/23/12	Walker, Scott	Kellner, Ted D	Milwaukee, WI 53202	Fiduciary Management	Banking & Finance	$90,000
2/01/12	Walker, Scott	Ryan, Patrick G	Winnetka, IL 60093	Ryan Specialty Group	Insurance	$90,000
1/24/12	Walker, Scott	Ricketts, J Joe	Bondurant, WY 82922	Ameritrade	Banking & Finance	$90,000
1/12/12	Walker, Scott	Kovner, Bruce	New York, NY 10022	Caxton Alternative Management...	Banking & Finance	$90,000
1/10/12	Walker, Scott	Shannon, Mary Sue	Milwaukee, WI 53226	Homemaker	Retired/ Homemakers/Non-income...	$90,000

Source: www.wisdc.org and http://www.gab.wi.gov

Senator Tim Cullen

6/02/12	Walker, Scott	Nau, John L	Houston, TX 77219	Silver Eagle Distributors LP	Manufacturing & Distributing	$50,000
6/01/12	Walker, Scott	Roberts, Richard H	Lakewood, NJ 08701	URL Pharma	Health Services/ Institutions	$50,000
5/22/12	Walker, Scott	Roberts, Richard H	Lakewood, NJ 08701	URL Pharma	Health Services/ Institutions	$50,000
4/16/12	Walker, Scott	Bacon, Louis M	New York, NY 10020	Moore Capital Management	Banking & Finance	$50,000
3/15/12	Walker, Scott	Hertog, Roger	New York, NY 10151	Retired	Retired/ Homemakers/Non-income...	$50,000
1/04/12	Walker, Scott	Fabick, Jere C	Oconomowoc WI 53066	Fabco Equipment Inc	Road Construction	$50,000
12/20/11	Walker, Scott	Kerbell, Robert A	Eau Claire, WI 54702	Lorman Education Services	Education	$50,000
12/09/11	Walker, Scott	Kuester, Dennis J	Milwaukee, WI 53202	Retired	Retired/ Homemakers/Non-income...	$50,000
12/05/11	Walker, Scott	Schuette, Ruth J	Wausau, WI 54401	Wausau Homes	Construction	$50,000
12/05/11	Walker, Scott	Schuette, Thomas J	Wausau, WI 54401	Wausau Homes	Construction	$50,000
11/29/11	Walker, Scott	Schuette, Gretchen	Sugar Grove, IL 60554	Wausau Homes	Construction	$50,000
12/15/11	Walker, Scott	Hiles, Marcus	Grand Prairie, TX 75050	WRPS LP	Real Estate	$41,000
5/1012	Walker, Scott	Walton, Christy	Jackson, WY 83001	Walmart Stores	Business	$40,000
4/03/12	Walker, Scott	Bacon, Louis M	New York, NY 10020	Moore Capital Management	Banking & Finance	$40,000
2/13/12	Walker, Scott	Luddy, Robert L	Raleigh, NC 27616	CaptiveAire	Construction	$40,000
12/23/11	Walker, Scott	Sinquefield, Rex A	Westphalia, MO 65085	Show-Me Institute	Political/ Ideological	$40,000
11/30/11	Walker, Scott	Hanley, William L	Palm Beach, FL 33480	Lexington Management Group	Tourism/ Leisure/ Entertainment	$40,000
11/29/11	Walker, Scott	Hertog, Roger	New York, NY 10151	Retired	Retired/ Homemakers/Non-income...	$40,000
12/21/11	Walker, Scott	Willer, Todd	Freedom, WI 54130	Milksource	Agriculture	$34,000
1/05/12	Walker, Scott	Templeton, John M	Bryn Mawr, PA 19010	Physician	Health Professionals	$30,000

Date	Candidate	Donor	City	Employer	Industry	Amount
11/28/11	Walker, Scott	Shiely, John S	Elm Grove, WI 53122	Attorney	Lawyers/ Law Firms/ Lobbyists	$30,000
5/31/12	Walker, Scott	Ricketts, Todd M	Wilmette, IL 60091	Chicago Cubs	Tourism/ Leisure/ Entertainme nt	$25,000
5/17/12	Walker, Scott	McNair, Robert C	Houston, TX 77019	Houston Texans	Tourism/ Leisure/ Entertainme nt	$25,000
5/15/12	Walker, Scott	Fehsenfeld, Fred	Indianapolis , IN 46260	Heritage Group (Indianapoli s)	Road Constructio n	$25,000
5/07/12	Walker, Scott	Uihlein, Richard E	Lake Forest, IL 60045	U-Line Corp	Constructio n	$25,000
5/01/12	Walker, Scott	Nelson, Grant E	Prescott, WI 54021	Retired	Retired/ Homemaker s/Non- income...	$25,000
4/06/12	Walker, Scott	Druckenmill er, Stanley F	New York, NY 10019	Duquesne Family Office	Banking & Finance	$25,000
4/04/12	Walker, Scott	Burke, John J	Fox Point, WI 53217	Burke Properties	Real Estate	$25,000
4/03/12	Walker, Scott	Marcus, Bernard	Atlanta, GA 30327	Retired	Retired/ Homemaker s/Non- income...	$25,000
3/31/12	Walker, Scott	Dhein, Jere	Green Bay, WI 54304	Tosca Ltd	Manufacturi ng & Distributing	$25,000
3/26/12	Walker, Scott	Gallun, Edwin A	Hartland, WI 53029	Metalcraft of Mayville	Manufacturi ng & Distributing	$25,000
3/26/12	Walker, Scott	Shields, JV	New York, NY 10005	Wellington Shields & Co LLC	Banking & Finance	$25,000
3/26/12	Walker, Scott	Wendt, Gary C	Fort Lauderdale, FL 33316	Deerpath Capital Managemen t	Banking & Finance	$25,000
3/22/12	Walker, Scott	Uihlein, Richard E	Lake Forest, IL 60045	U-Line Corp	Constructio n	$25,000
3/15/12	Walker, Scott	Kuester, Jonathan	Watertown, WI 53098	Carpenter	Constructio n	$25,000
3/14/12	Walker, Scott	Callan, James J	Fox Point, WI 53217	James Callan Inc	Real Estate	$25,000
2/21/12	Walker, Scott	Goodnight, James H	Cary, NC 27513	SAS Institute Inc	Telecommu nications & Computers	$25,000
2/13/2012	Walker, Scott	Dennis, Richard J	Chicago, IL 60606	Commodity trader	Banking & Finance	$25,000
2/06/12	Walker, Scott	Fedler, Ronald G	Dodgeville, WI 53533	Gold Leaf Developme nt	Real Estate	$25,000
1/31/12	Walker, Scott	Crow, Margaret	Dallas, TX 75205	Crow Holdings	Real Estate	$25,000
1/14/12	Walker, Scott	Marcus, Bernard	Atlanta, GA 30327	Retired	Retired/ Homemaker s/Non- income...	$25,000

1/03/12	Walker, Scott	Gray, C Boyden	Washington, DC 20007	Boyden Gray & Associates	Lawyers/ Law Firms/ Lobbyists	$25,000
12/23/11	Walker, Scott	Bidwill, Michael J	Phoenix, AZ 85002	Arizona Cardinals	Tourism/ Leisure/ Entertainme nt	$25,000
12/16/11	Walker, Scott	Fisher, John	San Francisco, CA 94111	Pisces Inc	Banking & Finance	$25,000
12/16/11	Walker, Scott	Jenkins, Howard M	Tampa, FL 33661	Retired	Retired/ Homemaker s/Non-income...	$25,000
12/15/11	Walker, Scott	Carlton, Rick	Nashville, TN 37205	Real estate developer	Real Estate	$25,000
12/15/11	Walker, Scott	Couri, Gerald	Waukesha, WI 53186	Couri Insurance Agency	Insurance	$25,000
12/15/11	Walker, Scott	Cummins, Robert P	Wayzata, MN 55391	Primera Technology Inc	Business	$25,000
12/15/11	Walker, Scott	Hendry, Bruce	Minneapolis, MN 55401	Cable Publishing	Business	$25,000

The Opinion Pages | OP-ED CONTRIBUTOR

Wisconsin's Radical Break

By WILLIAM CRONON   MARCH 21, 2011

Madison, Wis.

NOW that a Wisconsin judge has temporarily blocked a state law that would strip public employee unions of most collective bargaining rights, it's worth stepping back to place these events in larger historical context.

Republicans in Wisconsin are seeking to reverse civic traditions that for more than a century have been among the most celebrated achievements not just of their state, but of their own party as well.

Wisconsin was at the forefront of the progressive reform movement in the early 20th century, when the policies of Gov. Robert M. La Follette prompted a fellow Republican, Theodore Roosevelt, to call the state a "laboratory of democracy." The state pioneered many social reforms: It was the first to introduce workers' compensation, in 1911; unemployment insurance, in 1932; and public employee bargaining, in 1959.

University of Wisconsin professors helped design Social Security and were responsible for founding the union that eventually became the American Federation of State, County and Municipal Employees. Wisconsin reformers were equally active in promoting workplace safety, and often led the nation in natural resource conservation and environmental protection.

But while Americans are aware of this progressive tradition, they probably don't know that many of the innovations on behalf of working people were at least as much the work of Republicans as of Democrats.

Although Wisconsin has a Democratic reputation these days — it backed the party's presidential candidates in 2000, 2004 and 2008 — the state was dominated by Republicans for a full century after the Civil War. The Democratic Party was so ineffective that Wisconsin

Source: http://nyti.ms/1O59aDz

politics were largely conducted as debates between the progressive and conservative wings of the Republican Party.

When the Wisconsin Democratic Party finally revived itself in the 1950s, it did so in a context where members of both parties were unusually open to bipartisan policy approaches. Many of the new Democrats had in fact been progressive Republicans just a few years earlier, having left the party in revulsion against the reactionary politics of their own senator, Joseph R. McCarthy, and in sympathy with postwar liberalizing forces like the growing civil rights movement.

The demonizing of government at all levels that has become such a reflexive impulse for conservatives in the early 21st century would have mystified most elected officials in Wisconsin just a few decades ago.

When Gov. Gaylord A. Nelson, a Democrat, sought to extend collective bargaining rights to municipal workers in 1959, he did so in partnership with a Legislature in which one house was controlled by the Republicans. Both sides believed the normalization of labor-management relations would increase efficiency and avoid crippling strikes like those of the Milwaukee garbage collectors during the 1950s. Later, in 1967, when collective bargaining was extended to state workers for the same reasons, the reform was promoted by a Republican governor, Warren P. Knowles, with a Republican Legislature.

The policies that the current governor, Scott Walker, has sought to overturn, in other words, are legacies of his own party.

But Mr. Walker's assault on collective bargaining rights breaks with Wisconsin history in two much deeper ways as well. Among the state's proudest traditions is a passion for transparent government that often strikes outsiders as extreme. Its open meetings law, open records law and public comment procedures are among the strongest in the nation. Indeed, the basis for the restraining order blocking the collective bargaining law is that Republicans may have violated open meetings rules in passing it. The legislation they have enacted turns out to be radical not just in its content, but in its blunt ends-justify-the-means disregard for openness and transparency.

This in turn points to what is perhaps Mr. Walker's greatest break from the political traditions of his state. Wisconsinites have long believed that common problems deserve common solutions, and that when something needs fixing, we should roll up our sleeves and work together — no matter what our politics — to achieve the common good.

Mr. Walker's conduct has provoked a level of divisiveness and bitter partisan hostility the likes of which have not been seen in this state since at least the Vietnam War. Many citizens are furious at their governor and his party, not only because of profound policy differences, but because these particular Republicans have exercised power in abusively nontransparent ways that represent such a radical break from the state's tradition of open government.

Perhaps that is why — as a centrist and a lifelong independent — I have found myself returning over the past few weeks to the question posed by the lawyer Joseph N. Welch during the hearings that finally helped bring down another Wisconsin Republican, Joe McCarthy, in 1954: "Have you no sense of decency, sir, at long last? Have you left no sense of decency?"

Scott Walker is not Joe McCarthy. Their political convictions and the two moments in history are quite different. But there is something about the style of the two men — their aggressiveness, their self-certainty, their seeming indifference to contrary views — that may help explain the extreme partisan reactions they triggered. McCarthy helped create the modern Democratic Party in Wisconsin by infuriating progressive Republicans, imagining that he could build a national platform by cultivating an image as a sternly uncompromising leader willing to attack anyone who stood in his way. Mr. Walker appears to be provoking some of the same ire from adversaries and from advocates of good government by acting with a similar contempt for those who disagree with him.

The turmoil in Wisconsin is not only about bargaining rights or the pension payments of public employees. It is about transparency and openness. It is about neighborliness, decency and mutual respect. Joe McCarthy forgot these lessons of good government, and so, I fear, has Mr. Walker. Wisconsin's citizens have not.

William Cronon is a professor of history, geography and environmental studies at the University of Wisconsin–Madison.

A version of this op-ed appears in print on March 22, 2011, on page A27 of the New York edition with the headline: Wisconsin's Radical Break

Senator Tim Cullen

APPENDIX G

HISTORY OF ACADEMIC FREEDOM IN THE UW SYSTEM

BACKGROUND

The concept of academic freedom has a long history in the University of Wisconsin System. According to one definition used by higher education institutions, academic freedom encompasses the right of faculty members to full freedom in research and in the publication of results, freedom in the classroom in discussing their subject, and the right to be free from institutional censorship or discipline when they speak or write as citizens[1]. In response to Regent interest, a listing of laws and policies related to academic freedom in the UW System has been compiled.

REQUESTED ACTION

For discussion.

DISCUSSION

Materials on academic freedom in the UW System can be categorized into: (1) laws; (2) UW and Board of Regents History; and (3) UW institutional rules or policies.

---

[1] American Association of University Professors (http://www.aaup.org/AAUP/about/mission/glossary.htm)

1

Laws on Academic Freedom

(1) Wisconsin Statutes: The Board of Regents' responsibility with respect to academic freedom is embodied in the UW System's statutory mission: "The mission of the system is to develop human resources, to discover and disseminate knowledge, to extend knowledge and its application beyond the boundaries of its campuses and to serve and stimulate society by developing in students heightened intellectual, cultural and humane sensitivities, scientific professional and technological expertise and a sense of purpose... Basic to every purpose of the system is the search for truth."[2]

(2) Wisconsin Administrative Code: In the procedures for faculty dismissal for cause, the regulations state: "A faculty member is entitled to enjoy and exercise all the rights and privileges of a United States citizen, and the rights and privileges of academic freedom as they are generally understood in the academic community."[3]

UW and Board of Regents History

The following table includes some of the key developments in the Board of Regents' actions related to academic freedom:

DATE	EVENT OR ACTION

---

[2] Section 36.01(2), Wis. Stats.
[3] Wis. Adm. Code § UWS 4.01(2).

2

DATE	EVENT OR ACTION
August-September 1894	The Board of Regents held a hearing in response to a Board member's allegation that Professor Richard Ely's "teaching and writings provided moral justification for attacks on life and property."[4] In exonerating Professor Ely, the Board affirmed its commitment to academic freedom: "...Whatever may be the limitations which trammel inquiry elsewhere, we believe that the great state University of Wisconsin should ever encourage that continual and fearless sifting and winnowing by which alone the truth can be found."[5]
July 1962	In a statement to the Board of Regents, University Vice President Fred Harrington explained why the University of Wisconsin is a great university: "...[W]e at Wisconsin have not been afraid to speak out. We of the faculty, and you of the Board of Regents, have been in favor of freedom of speech and academic freedom. In fact, Wisconsin has been one of the leaders of the country in this field. We are abused for this, sometimes, but we have persevered and we have made a national contribution. Other institutions often have been praised for doing things on occasion with reference to free speech that we do routinely. This is an important part of our greatness. I am pleased that members of this Board have felt so and insisted on retention of this tradition...."

---

[4] Miller, Harry, Sifting and Winnowing: Academic Freedom and Ely Trial, Wisconsin Stories: School Days, (http://www.wisconsinstories.org/2002season/school/closer_look.cfm)
[5] Report of the Board of Regents investigating committee, September 18, 1894.

3

	"… In speaking out, and saying different things, and insisting on democracy, we have made great national contributions, and in doing so, have developed a great University."[6]
January 1964	In approving faculty rules for appointment, tenure and dismissal procedures, the Board offered the following statement: "…In adopting this codification of the rules and regulations of the University of Wisconsin relating to academic tenure, the Regents reaffirm their historic commitment to security of professorial tenure and to the academic freedom it is designed to protect. These rules and regulations are promulgated in the conviction that in serving a free society the scholar must himself be free. Only thus can he seek the truth, develop wisdom and contribute to society those expressions of the intellect that ennoble mankind. The security of the scholar protects him not only against those who would enslave the mind but also against anxieties which divert him from his role as scholar and teacher. The concept of intellectual freedom is based upon confidence in man's capacity for growth in comprehending the universe and on faith in unshackled intelligence. The University is not partisan to any party or ideology, but it is devoted to the discovery of truth and to understanding the world in which we live. The Regents take this opportunity to rededicate themselves to maintaining in this University those conditions which are indispensable for the flowering of the human mind."[7]

[6] Statement by University Vice President Fred H. Harrington, Board of Regents minutes, Exhibit E, pp. 1-4, July 14, 1962, Board of Regents Collections, University of Wisconsin Digital Collections.
[7] Statement by Regent Jensen, Board of Regents minutes excerpt, pp. 3-4, January 10, 1964, Board of Regents Collections, University of Wisconsin Digital Collections.

4

December 1985	In preparing for the Regents' Study Group on the Future of the UW System, President Lyall read a 1955 report from a commission on the University of Wisconsin, chaired by then-Senator Warren Knowles. The report included a recommendation that no restrictions be placed on freedom of speech or assembly, beyond those established by state or federal laws. Reflecting on threats to academic freedom in 1955 posed by McCarthyism, and present-day threats posed by the activities of Accuracy in Academia, a national group whose purpose was to monitor universities for professors with Marxist or left-leaning views, in 1985 President Lyall offered the following statement, with which the Board of Regents concurred: "…Lest there be any doubt, I would like to reaffirm clearly that the University of Wisconsin System will continue in the future as it has in the past to insist on maintaining the academic freedom of students and faculty to speak, argue, debate, sift and winnow ideas and values openly and without fear of reprisal or intimidation. Disagreement and debate is the stuff of which learning is made. We do not fear it, but it should be done openly and without threat or coercion. Great universities share this common commitment to open expression."[8]
October 1994	The Board of Regents, commemorating the 100-year anniversary of the Board's exoneration of Professor Ely, passed resolution 6787 reaffirming its commitment to academic freedom: "…Now therefore, be it resolved that the Regents of the University of Wisconsin System, meeting one hundred years after our predecessors guaranteed Professor

[8] Statement by UW System President Lyall, Board of Regents minutes excerpt, pp. 13-14, December 6, 1985, Board of Regents Collections, University of Wisconsin Digital Collections.

5

Ely's academic freedom, reaffirm our commitment to the untrammeled search for truth.

We call upon all members of our several academic communities -- administrators, faculty, staff, and students alike -- to guard this precious legacy, to consider differing points of view, and always to engage in 'that continual and fearless sifting and winnowing by which alone the truth can be found'".[9]

---

[9] Excerpt of Resolution 6787, University of Wisconsin Board of Regents minutes, pp. 3-5, October 7, 1994. http://www.wisconsin.edu/bor/minutes/bor/1994/october.htm

6

UW System or Institutional Policies

The University of Wisconsin System Board of Regents and several of the individual campuses have adopted policies or other authority related to academic freedom:

(1) UW Board of Regents Policies

   a. The University of Wisconsin System Mission (RPD 1-1): The UWS Mission statement was adopted by the Board of Regents on June 10, 1988. It mirrors Chapter 36, Stats., and states:

   "Each institution of the University of Wisconsin System shares in the mission of the system. The mission of this system is to develop human resources; to discover and disseminate knowledge; to extend knowledge and its application beyond the boundaries of its campuses; and finally, to serve and stimulate society by developing in students heightened intellectual, cultural, and humane sensitivities, scientific, professional, and technological expertise, and a sense of value and purpose. Inherent in this mission are methods of instruction, research, extended education, and public service designed to educate people and improve the human condition. Basic to every purpose of the system is the search for truth."[10]

   b. Racist and Other Discriminatory Conduct Policy (RPD 14-6): In prohibiting discrimination, the policy also states that not every act which may be offensive to an individual or group will be considered to be racist and discriminatory conduct and a violation of system or institutional policy, and due consideration will be given to the

---

[10] http://www.uwsa.edu/bor/policies/rpd/rpd1-1.htm

7

Senator Tim Cullen

protection of individual First Amendment rights to freedom of expression and academic freedom.[11]

    c. Guidelines for Tenured Faculty Review and Development (RPD 20-9): Plans for tenured faculty review and development should include effective criteria to measure progress for accomplishments of faculty and a description of the methods for conducting the evaluation and any review methods should fully respect academic freedom.[12]

(2) UW Institutional Policies (The following is not intended to be a comprehensive list but, rather, provides examples from several UW institutions.):

    a. UW-Green Bay Faculty Academic Freedom Policy: The faculty adopted the American Association of University Professors (AAUP) policy and interpretive comments[13] as its academic freedom policy. (See UW-Milwaukee example, below, for excerpts from the policy.) The policy provided the following reasons for doing so: (1) the statement has significant legal standing in case law; (2) any other policy adopted by the faculty could conceivably require a test in court before it would have legal standing and the protection that such standing grants to faculty, and; (3) in the absence of an academic freedom policy, a court would likely assume that the AAUP statement provides the effective principle.[14]

    b. UW-Madison Faculty Policies and Procedures: The current policy on Faculty Rights (8.01) refers to "the principles of academic freedom as they are generally understood in

---

[11] http://www.uwsa.edu/bor/policies/rpd/rpd14-6.htm
[12] http://www.uwsa.edu/bor/policies/rpd/rpd20-9.htm
[13] http://www.aaup.org/AAUP/pubsres/policydocs/contents/1940statement.htm
[14] http://www.uwgb.edu/sofas/rules/facultyhandbook.pdf

8

higher education."[15] The policy also references the Regents' "commitment to security of professional tenure and the academic freedom it is designed to protect."[16]

    c. UW-Milwaukee Academic and Administrative Policies: The Public Expression of Opinion policy addresses the rights of faculty members to express opinions in both areas of professional competence and as individual citizens, and provides three principles from the American Association of University Professors' 1940 statement, which states that: "(1) teachers are entitled to full freedom in research and in the publication of the results, subject to the adequate performance of their other academic duties…; (2) teachers are entitled to freedom in the classroom in discussing their subject, but they should be careful not to introduce into their teaching controversial matter which has no relation to their subject…; (3) college and university teachers are citizens, members of a learned profession, and officers of an educational institution…"[17]

    d. UW-Oshkosh Faculty Constitution: The faculty constitution is prefaced with a statement on the preservation of academic freedom and provides several principles to support academic freedom, such as: (1) the dependence of the common good on the "free search for truth and its free exposition;" (2) the premise that "[a]cademic freedom in its teaching aspect is fundamental for the protection of the rights of the teacher in teaching and of the student to freedom in learning;" and (3) that while a faculty member "should be free from institutional censorship or discipline" he or she "should at all times be accurate, should exercise appropriate restraint, should show respect for the opinions of others, and should make every effort to indicate that he or she is not a spokes-person for the institution."[18]

---

[15] http://www.secfac.wisc.edu/governance/fpp/Chapter_8.htm#801
[16] Id.
[17] http://www4.uwm.edu/secu/acad+admin_policies/S44.htm; AAUP 1940 statement, supra note 8.
[18] http://www.uwosh.edu/faculty_senate/faculty-constitution

9

    e. UW-River Falls Faculty and Academic Staff Handbook: Faculty members are provided with full academic freedom in the classroom, in research, and elsewhere as outlined in the American Association of University Professors statements on academic freedom.[19] Members of the faculty are also free from institutional censorship or discipline when acting as citizens or in matters of academic freedom, but must acknowledge and accept their responsibilities as professional people, and any public statement must clearly state whether they speak as individuals or as representatives of the University.[20]

RELATED REGENT POLICIES

Regent Policy Documents 1-1, 14-6, and 20-9.

---

[19] http://www2.uwrf.edu/faculty_senate/handbook/chapter3-2.htm#C32III; AAUP 1940 statement, supra n.8.
[20] Id.

10

APPENDIX H

a. Text of the Wisconsin Idea:

The *Wisconsin Idea* is the mission statement of the University of Wisconsin System and as such is outlined in State Statute 36.01 (2).

State Statute 36.01: Statement of purpose and mission.

> **(2)** The mission of the system is to develop human resources, to discover and disseminate knowledge, to extend knowledge and its application beyond the boundaries of its campuses and to serve and stimulate society by developing in students heightened intellectual, cultural and humane sensitivities, scientific, professional and technological expertise and a sense of purpose. Inherent in this broad mission are methods of instruction, research, extended training and public service designed to educate people and improve the human condition. Basic to every purpose of the system is the search for truth.

Link to State Statute: *https://docs.legis.wisconsin.gov/statutes/statutes/36/01/2*

b. Governor Walker's proposed changes to the *Wisconsin Idea*:

Walker's suggested changes were reflected in Section 1111 of his proposed budget, Senate Bill 21.

Walker's proposed revised statute reads as follows: *(Taken from the Milwaukee Journal Sentinel-link below)*

State Statute 36.01: Statement of purpose and mission.

> **(2)** The mission of the system is to develop human resources <u>to meet the state's workforce needs</u>, to discover and disseminate knowledge, ~~to extend knowledge and its application beyond the boundaries of its campuses~~ and to ~~serve and stimulate society by developing~~ <u>develop</u> in students <u> </u> heightened intellectual, cultural, and humane sensitivities, scientific, professional and technological expertise, and a sense of purpose. ~~Inherent in this broad mission are methods of instruction, research, extended training and public service designed to educate people and improve the human condition. Basic to every purpose of the system is the search for truth.~~
>
> *(PLEASE NOTE: underlined portions are phrases that Governor Walker sought to add while portions struck through are phrases the Governor sought to remove.)*

Link to Milwaukee Journal-Sentinel (MJS) article: *http://www.jsonline.com/news/statepolitics/documents-show-walker-administration-seeking-removal-of-uws-wisconsin-idea-b99439710z1-290927651.html*

Source: https://docs.legis.wisconsin.gov/statutes/statutes/36/01/2
http://www.jsonline.com/news/statepolitics/documents-show-walker-administration-seeking-removal-of-uws-wisconsin-idea-b99439710z1-290927651.html

APPENDIX I

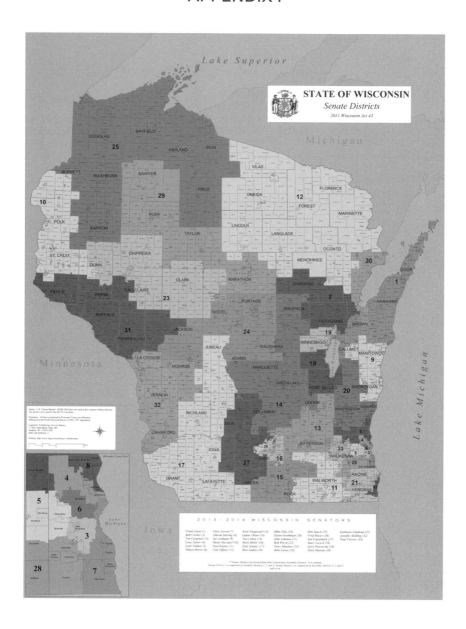

To view maps in color: http://legis.wisconsin.gov/ltsb/gis/maps/

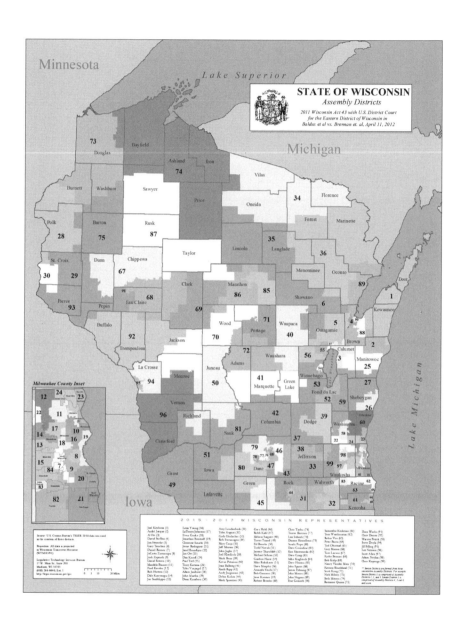

STATE OF WISCONSIN
Assembly Districts
2011 Wisconsin Act 43 with U.S. District Court
for the Eastern District of Wisconsin in
Baldus et al vs. Brennan et. al, April 11, 2012

Legislative Districts of Illinois

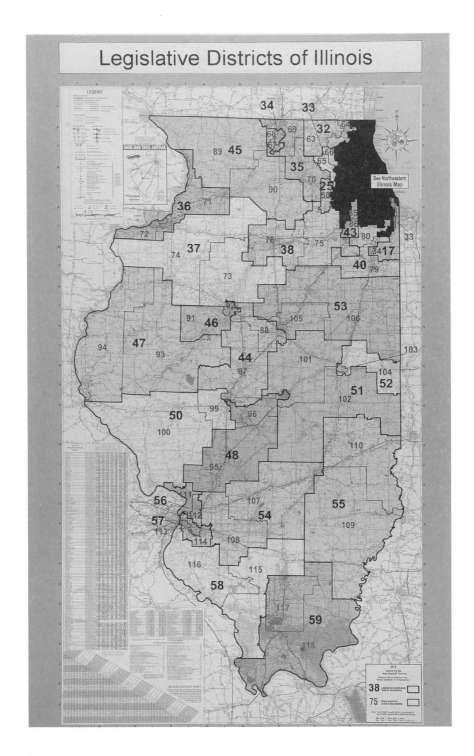

IOWA HOUSE DISTRICTS
Effective Beginning with the Elections in 2012 for the 85th General Assembly

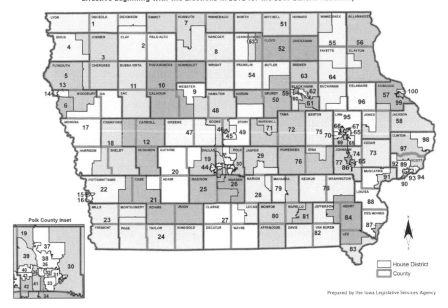

IOWA SENATE DISTRICTS
Effective Beginning with the Elections in 2012 for the 85th General Assembly

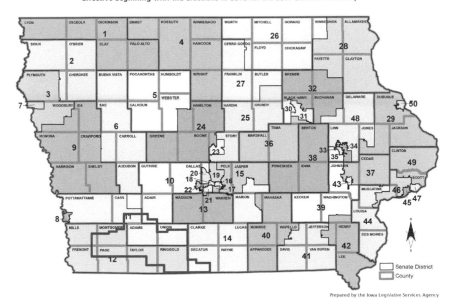

APPENDIX J

State of Wisconsin
SENATE CALENDAR
One-Hundredth Regular Session
Tuesday, April 5, 2011
11:00 A.M.

First Order.	Call of Roll.
Second Order.	Chief clerk's entries.
Third Order.	Introduction, first reading and reference of proposals.
Fourth Order.	Report of committees.
Fifth Order.	Petitions and communications.
Sixth Order.	Referrals and receipt of committee reports concerning proposed administrative rules.
Seventh Order.	Advice and consent of the Senate
Eighth Order.	Messages from the Assembly.
Ninth Order.	Special Orders.
Tenth Order.	Consideration of motions, resolutions, and joint resolutions not requiring a third reading.
QUESTION:	Shall the joint resolution be adopted?

Senate Joint Resolution 17. Relating to: the life and public service of David Kachel. By Senator Kedzie; cosponsored by Representatives Wynn, Nass, and August.

Senate Joint Resolution 18. Relating to: the life and public service of Carl Otte. By Senators Leibham, Holperin, Miller, Olsen, and Risser; cosponsored by Representatives Endsley, Barca, Kessler, LeMahieu, Loudenbeck, A. Ott, Sinicki, Spanbauer, Ziegelbauer, and E. Coggs.

Eleventh Order.	Second reading and amendments of senate joint resolutions and senate bills.
Twelfth Order.	Second reading and amendments of assembly joint resolutions and assembly bills.
QUESTION:	Shall the bill be ordered to a third reading?

Assembly Bill 4. Relating to: automobile insurance coverage limits, permissible policy provisions, and proof of financial responsibility. By Representatives Nygren,

Senator Tim Cullen

Petersen, Steineke, Klenke, Knilans, Krug, Petryk, Rivard, Endsley, Tranel, Marklein, Severson, Wynn, Bernier, Tiffany, Jacque, Weininger, Knudson, T. Larson, Kooyenga, Farrow, Kuglitsch, Litjens, August, Kapenga, Thiesfeldt, Williams, Honadel, Ripp, Nerison, J. Fitzgerald, Kramer, Suder, Vos, Knodl, Ballweg, Mursau, Murtha, Kestell, Meyer, Petrowski, Tauchen, Brooks, A. Ott, J. Ott, Bies, Van Roy, Kaufert, Stone, Kerkman, LeMahieu, Strachota, Kleefisch, Nass, Spanbauer, Pridemore, Ziegelbauer, and Fields; cosponsored by Senators Lasee, Lazich, Taylor, Darling, Hopper, Wanggaard, Galloway, Kapanke, Leibham, Harsdorf, Kedzie, and Vinehout.

Thirteenth Order.	**Third reading of joint resolutions and bills.**
Fourteenth Order.	**Motions may be offered.**
Fifteenth Order.	**Announcements, adjournment honors, and remarks under special privilege.**
Sixteenth Order.	**Adjournment.**

State of Wisconsin

SENATE CALENDAR

January 2011 Special Session
Tuesday, April 5, 2011
11:00 A.M.

First Order.	Call of Roll.
Second Order.	Chief clerk's entries.
Third Order.	Introduction, first reading and reference of proposals.
Fourth Order.	Report of committees.
Fifth Order.	Petitions and communications.
Sixth Order.	Referrals and receipt of committee reports concerning proposed administrative rules.
Seventh Order.	Advice and consent of the Senate
Eighth Order.	Messages from the Assembly.
Ninth Order.	Special Orders.
Tenth Order.	Consideration of motions, resolutions, and joint resolutions not requiring a third reading.
Eleventh Order.	Second reading and amendments of senate joint resolutions and senate bills.
QUESTION:	Shall the bill be ordered to a third reading?

January 2011 Special Session Senate Bill 12. Relating to: state finances, the Medical Assistance program, granting bonding authority, and making appropriations. (FE) By Committee on Senate Organization, by request of Governor Scott Walker.

Senate Amendment 1 pending

Twelfth Order.	Second reading and amendments of assembly joint resolutions and assembly bills.
Thirteenth Order.	Third reading of joint resolutions and bills.
Fourteenth Order.	Motions may be offered.
Fifteenth Order.	Announcements, adjournment honors, and remarks under special privilege.
Sixteenth Order.	Adjournment.

ABOUT THE AUTHOR

Tim Cullen was born and raised in Janesville, Wisconsin. Cullen graduated from UW-Whitewater with a Major in Political Science with a minor in History. The first election he won was to the Janesville City Council in 1970. Four years later Cullen was elected to the State Senate at the age of 30. He went on to become Senate Majority Leader and in 1987 he became Secretary of the Department of Health and Social Services under Governor Tommy Thompson. In 1988 Cullen took a job with Blue Cross and worked with them for the next 20 years. In 2010 he decided to run for his old Senate seat. He was elected and served until 2015. Today Cullen still lives in Janesville and spends his time working with the two foundations he started.

Cullen will donate all profits from this book to the Janesville Multicultural Teachers Opportunity Fund he started in 2008. The sole purpose of the Fund is to raise money for college scholarships for Janesville students of color. The goal is to support those students who wish to become teachers and are willing to return to Janesville to teach for at least three years.

PRAISE FOR "RINGSIDE SEAT"

❝ A candid and illuminating account of one of the most important periods in the history of Wisconsin by one of the state's most respected business and political leaders. His two stints in the state legislature give him a unique perspective of the recent dramatic changes in Wisconsin political fortunes." —**Dale Schultz, Republican State Legislator 1982-2014**

❝ I have served with many great lawmakers and Tim Cullen is one of the best. On vital issues Tim served the good of the whole rather than mere partisanship and his book reminds readers of a proud Wisconsin heritage where governing was based upon mutual trust and respect compared to politics today when conquering smothers cooperation, ideology trumps ideals, division replaces unity, and special interest dominates the public good. Anyone concerned about good government will appreciate this insightful memoir from a respected long term lawmaker who gave public service a good name." —**Bob Jauch, Democratic State Senator 1986-2015**

❝ Tim Cullen gives us a well-written memoir of his years in politics. It starts with optimism and enlightened public policy advances under six governors from each party. He then gives an insider's account of how, during his return to the State Senate after an absence of over two decades, the new world of big money, ideology, and a gerrymandered majority ruled and ruled absolutely. And, in stunning detail, this book gives an eyewitness account of the Jekyll and Hyde character of Scott Walker." —**Thomas Loftus, Assembly Speaker 1983-1990, US Ambassador to Norway 1993-1997, Member UW Board of Regents 2006-2013**

66 I enjoyed working closely with Tim Cullen while governor. Tim has an enduring love for the state of Wisconsin. That, combined with his engaging Irish humor, created an atmosphere of camaraderie and things got done. Our entire state has benefited from his many years of legislative leadership. This book is a great contribution to understanding an important era in Wisconsin's political history."
—Anthony Earl, Governor of Wisconsin 1982-1986

66 Tim Cullen has enjoyed great success over the past half a century trying to creatively solve public policy challenges and is fearless in confronting those in politics that embrace the status quo. He's a skilled problem-solver and someone I consider a friend."
—Tommy Thompson, Governor of Wisconsin 1987-2001, US Secretary of Health and Human Services 2001-2005

66 A sign on a stable says: 'I have fast horses for fast riders, slow horses for slow riders, and for those who have never ridden, we have horses that have never been ridden.' Tim's book tells what happens when those who have never ridden get on." —Bill Kraus, Chair of Common Cause in Wisconsin, former Republican who was an insider with Governor Warren Knowles and Governor Lee Dreyfus

66 Tim Cullen is well known to me from our common 'roots' in Janesville and our coinciding time in state government. He has always been an excellent judge about what is 'good' in 'good public policy.' From my time in Governor Dreyfus' office I have respected him for his courage, council, and continuous search for solutions."
—Mary Markham Williams, UW Board of Regents 1965-1976 and office manager for Governor Lee Dreyfus

A FEW FINAL THANK YOUS...

My grandchildren, ranging in age from 6 to 16, visit often, and here and there they would see me working on this book and ask what I was writing now, or how the book was going and offer encouragement. When the youngest ones, Tate and Sloan, asked me if their names—and the names of all of their and our pets (both current and those in Doggy and Kitty Heaven)—would be in the book, of course I could not say no.

So, to Brock and Connor MacKinnis; to Cooper and Tate Jacobson, their cats Malone and Fenster, fish Dorothy and Zoot, and dogs Piper and Kingston; to Sloan Fellows and her cats Silas and Clive and dogs Augie, Saul, Bromley, Balu, and Bronson; and to our children's Timmy and Katharine's dogs Bean, Pedro, and Beau-Beau and cat Freeway... thank you for all of your love and encouragement.